A Roomful
Of Elephants
& Other Essays

MICHAEL K. EIDMAN

EDITED BY HANNAH EIDMAN and DANIEL S. WOHLFARTH

LAYOUT AND EDITORIAL ASSISTANCE BY DAPHNE EIDMAN

ORIGINAL COVER ART & PHOTOGRAPH BY AARON EIDMAN

DEDICATION

This book is dedicated to three remarkable women. Fannie (née Bodian) Teller, of blessed memory, was my maternal grandmother; she watched over me when I was young and I have no doubt that she is still watching. My mom and school teacher par excellence, Florence (née Teller) Eidman, taught me her most important lessons through the exemplary way she has lived her life. Finally, during the past thirty (plus) years, my amazing wife, Daphne (née Fuhrer) Eidman, has never failed to go above and beyond, at home, at work and everywhere else, so that I could have a much better life.

My writing, for better or worse, has also been inspired, informed and influenced by two singular men. It was from watching my dad, Seymour Eidman, that I learned not to merely dabble; I learned from watching him that if something is worthy of your time, then it is worthy of your full attention. And it was Bob Dylan who taught me that while I might never figure out all the answers, the important thing is to keep asking questions.

IN APPRECIATION

The Eidman family is loaded with talent and I did not hesitate to enlist the aid of several family members to help me complete this project.

My very smart and sharp niece, (Visions of Jo) Hannah Eidman served bravely as my editor-in-chief. If these essays are comprehensible, it is mostly due to her fearless relegation of my run-on sentences to the cutting room floor. I am especially appreciative of her gentle advice regarding topics where my sensibilities were a bit outmoded and clueless, particularly in areas such as youth culture and current notions of political correctness.

My great friend and honorary member of the Eidman clan, Danny Wohlfarth, did some preliminary editing on about a dozen of these essays. During my 36 years in law practice, I have met many attorneys but have never encountered a more competent draftsman (draftsperson, Hannah?) than Danny.

It is a luxury to have an artist in the family and my brilliant nephew Aaron not only created the cover drawing for this book but contributed a couple of the of the original photographs. My only regret is that budgetary constraints forced me to reformat Aaron's gorgeous color photograph of Fiddle's Dari King (and many of the other photographs in this book) into black and white.   To check out Aaron's work, visit his website at www.aaroneidman.com.

Finally, I want to give a very loud shout-out to my wife Daphne who brought her usual array of "jane of all trades" skills to this project. Unfazed by her inexperience, Daphne handled the numerous and difficult technical aspects of formatting and laying out this book for publication, all of which were miles beyond my limited capabilities. She also offered sound advice whenever I asked for it (and sometimes when I didn't). Most of all, I appreciate her encouragement and support, even as this project occupied many more of her hours than I anticipated.

CONTENTS

MY FAVORITE STOP LIGHT 1

THROUGH THE PAST DARKLY: MTA HIGH SCHOOL 7

BY THE TIME I GOT TO WOODSTOCK 23

NOVEMBER 22, 1963 36

SUGAR BLUE PLAYS ROSA'S LOUNGE IN CHICAGO 44

ORLANDO'S RECORD SHOP 52

MEAN MIKE NATURE AND THE SUMMER OF 1975 58

THE WORLD'S GREATEST GAME 74

MY DAY JOB 84

FRANCIS DEWITT AND KINFOLK 92

MY GREAT GRANDMOTHER 101

SHABBOS WITH THE ALLMAN BROTHERS BAND 105

MUSKY FISHING ON THE ST. LAWRENCE RIVER 119

FM 125

FROM TURKA TO ENGLEWOOD 133

"ALVIN CHARLES DAVIDOFF" 140

THE DAY MY FATHER TURNED 33 153

BOB DYLAN's "ANOTHER SELF PORTRAIT" 162

A YANKEE HATER'S VIEW OF DEREK JETER 169

REFLECTIONS ON DEATH AND DYING 187

NOT YOUR AVERAGE SUMMER VACATION 193

MY FRIEND LARRY 200

ON LITTLE POND 208

THE BLIZZARD OF 1969 214

A MEMORABLE CLIENT 222

A BRIEF COMMENT ABOUT RAP MUSIC AND FOLK MUSIC... 241

"DOWN ON THE CORNER, OUT ON THE STREET": 248

SOME THOUGHTS ABOUT REPENTANCE,

   BEFORE THE HIGH HOLY DAYS 256

ON THE ROAD WITH THE GUYS 263

A ROOMFUL OF ELEPHANTS 276

   Part One: Elephants & Gorillas 276

   Part Two: Mom & Dad 284

   Part Three: On Getting Unmarried 286

   Part Four: My Three Sons (& A Daughter-In-Law) 287

   Part Five: Friends (not the overrated TV show) 289

   Part Six: A Criminally Brief Note Concerning Daphne 290

   Part Seven: A Quick Look in the Mirror 292

   Part Eight: Ecclesiastes, Bob Dylan and Modern Times

      (not the Dylan album) 295

ACKNOWLEDGEMENTS 305

"She says, 'You can't repeat the past.'
I say, 'You can't? What do you mean, you can't?
Of course you can.' "

©Bob Dylan, *"Summer Days"*

MY FAVORITE STOP LIGHT

"Then the coal company came with the world's largest shovel
And they tortured the timber and stripped all the land
Well, they dug for their coal till the land was forsaken
Then they wrote it all down as the progress of man."
John Prine, "Paradise"©

When I was young, my family lived on the east side of Washington Heights in upper, upper Manhattan. That was before the neighborhood began a quick descent from "wonderfully diverse" to gritty and then to treacherous, before rising Lazarus-like, to become the gentrified bastion of diversity that it is today. In 1959, in order to escape the oppressive heat and the boredom, we began to spend summers at a small bungalow colony in the picturesque, sleepy hamlet of Livingston Manor, about two hours northwest of the city. I was four and a half years old. At about that time, the State was completing the "Quickway" portion of New York State Route 17, which provided much faster and safer access to the Catskill Mountains, where Livingston Manor and its sister town of Roscoe sit quietly in the northern and least touristy corner of Sullivan County. For ten weeks each summer, I happily played the role of Jewish Huck Finn, fishing the crystal clear trout streams, hiking twisty trails, and chasing fireflies in the dense evening fog.

Each year, we would depart for "The Manor" in late June, my folks' classic Olds' '88 packed to the gills. I vividly recall relishing the fact that from the moment we turned onto the George Washington Bridge at West 179th Street until my dad steered into our bungalow colony some 115 miles later, we would not pass a single traffic light. That is, except for one. Seven miles southeast of Livingston Manor lay the even smaller hamlet of Parksville, which like The Manor, had a single traffic light. But while the light in The Manor was a "normal" light, controlling the near-absent traffic rolling through town, the Parksville stoplight was different. For when the Quickway was built, instead of constructing an overpass over low-lying Parksville with the usual exit and entrance ramps, the State dumped its new highway right down onto the center of town. This in effect created a grade crossing for Route 17, to be forever (or so we thought) controlled by Parksville's single traffic light, which, as luck would have it, was already right in place. That traffic light, the only one on the Quickway, controlled traffic for the two lanes in each direction going up and down the Quickway in addition to local traffic traveling perpendicular to the highway, from one side of town to the other. Most of the time, the light would be green for traffic flying up and down the 65 MPH highway and red for cross-town traffic. Even when it was red for the Quickway, it seemed that it had become so much a part of the local topography that we did not much mind stopping there for a moment, to quietly take in the peaceful scene. (Point of semi-relevant information: the average person will spend about two weeks of her or his life waiting for traffic lights to change).

At the start of the summer of 1963, my two brothers and I were crammed, as usual, into the Olds, barely tolerating each other for the two hour trip, while boxes of clothes and knick-knacks encircled and further encroached upon our small bodies. Full of nervous energy, we were even antsier than usual as we slowed to a stop at the red light at Parksville. But something was different that year. As we waited and waited for the light to change, we noticed a small free-standing building on the right side of the road. It was freshly painted red and white and the large sign read "Dari-King." My youngest brother, David, was barely 3 years old but had no difficulty comprehending the meaning behind the large painted ice cream cone that beckoned from the side of the structure. We were enthralled.

To be clear, the region already had several excellent ice cream establishments. There was the truly legendary Poppy's Pancake House, located right in "downtown" Parksville itself, perhaps a couple of hundred yards from where we sat at the light. Poppy's featured not only pancakes and a diner-ish menu but also terrific ice cream (topped off by "The Kitchen Sink," guaranteed to satisfy an entire table of starving camp counselors). The Manor was home to "Frosty Cup," a seasonal shack that made "Blizzards," the best thick shakes I have ever had. We could never have predicted that Poppy's, Frosty Cup and other local competitors would not make it out of the 1970's. We also had no way of knowing, as we stared wide-eyed from the car, that we were in the initial throes of what would be our 49 year love affair with "Dari-King," or as it eventually came to be called after its owners, "Fiddles."

Fiddles was no fly-by-night operation. As of this writing (2013), the Fiddle family has been living in Parksville for five generations. Jacob Fiddle moved up from Manhattan in the 1920's to become the Parksville postmaster general. His parents ran a hotel nearby called The Fiddle House. Mandi Fiddle Bergenfield still looks after the small, historic synagogue, which currently operates only on an "as needed basis." Over the years, the family opened, closed and sold numerous local businesses, but none had a longer run than the Fiddles ice cream parlor. The shop was open from March to October and employed 3 full-time and 11 part-time local folks, many of them students, and all of whom were cheerful, friendly and well-groomed. It drew business from transients, locals, and the many summer camps in the area. The transients, of course, were composed predominantly of folks driving through, and perhaps forced to come to a full stop by that trusty Parksville traffic light. After a tiring two-hour drive from the city, or just prior to embarking upon a depressing two-hour ride back to civilization, a quick stop at Fiddles was the ultimate impulse purchase. The combination of irresistible product and insufficient willpower made pulling over a no-brainer. Fiddles even catered to the strictly observant Jews from local bungalow colonies and summer camps by obtaining Rabbinical Kosher certification for their ice cream.

Dave Batt, at Fiddles, in his ice cream eating days. © Aaron Eidman

Fiddles served other kinds of food but make no mistake, it was the ice cream that drew the customers. The flavor and texture of the soft-serve had a uniquely smooth and rich quality. I always ordered the same thing: a medium chocolate cone with chocolate sprinkles. I ate it while reading the local magazine of real estate offerings, which were always stacked neatly in the corner of the shop. Occasionally, especially if it was early in the evening, we would sit outside at one of the tables, the Catskill Mountains looming overhead. Inevitably, we would become entranced by the light traffic stopping and starting at the whim of the only traffic light along Route 17.

As the years turned into decades, Parksville fell on hard times. The hotels died out, many summer camps closed and local tourism decreased. Then Parksville fell on even harder times. The main drag, a couple of blocks south of Route 17, became nothing but parallel rows of abandoned stores and decrepit buildings. The tall "Poppy's" sign now stares down upon an empty lot. Yet Fiddles managed to carry on, albeit with a shorter open season, thanks in no small part to the accidental marketing ploy of the Route 17 stoplight just yards away. And if times had changed, it was comforting to know that the quality of the ice cream had not. In addition, the low prices at Fiddles were a subtle reminder that good people stood behind this business: many of the local folks might not have been able to join in the fun had the Fiddles family actually charged what ice cream of similar quality fetched at other places. It was no wonder their customers remained fiercely loyal: as my brothers grew up and raised families of our own, our children, now mostly grown, considered a stop at Fiddles to be a mandatory part of the "country" experience.

I am uncertain when I first noticed, but a number of years ago, I observed that one of the decades-old "Route 17" signs suddenly had a companion alongside it. The new sign read "Future USA 86." A short time later, roadwork began. We soon learned that Route 17 was being brought up to Federal standards in order to become part of the official Federal highway system. As of this writing, this work is still ongoing. I imagine that by the time this book is finished, so will be the Parksville section of USA 86; in the long-term, this will probably be a money-saver for the taxpayers of the State of New York. In order to federalize the highway, it needed to be widened at certain areas and – as it turned out – it was no longer permissible to have a grade crossing with a traffic light right smack in the middle of it.

Therefore, a new section of road was built over Parksville, thus eliminating the anachronistic stoplight. When I first learned that this would happen, my immediate concern was not for the environmental havoc that the long-term construction would certainly wreak or for the years of potential traffic delays. Instead, I lamented that the new road meant a slow, painful death for my favorite ice cream place.

Had the government merely opted to obnoxiously confiscate the land upon which Fiddles sat via eminent domain, the family would have been entitled to receive fair compensation. But the government chose the path of least resistance: it left Fiddles alone and built an elevated section of highway road, just south of the old grade-level crossing. Since no physical land was taken, no compensation was offered. The fact that a small business that had managed to survive the vicissitudes of the Catskills economy for 49 years was left to wither away was of no import. Even though Fiddles is now located close to the main highway, Fiddles is now hard to find, even when an old customer takes the time to exit the new road at Parksville. In 2012, the family gave it a go, opening for the summer season, in spite of the fact that travelers were no longer being transported through the stoplight right to the store's front door. With business decreased by 80% in 2012, the 2013 season and the anticipated jubilee celebration of Fiddle's initial opening, was not to be. The family has offered the business rent-free to any hearty soul willing to take a chance, provided that the tenant pay the real estate taxes. So far, there have been no takers.

THROUGH THE PAST DARKLY:
MTA HIGH SCHOOL

"When some loud braggart tries to put me down
And says his school is great
I tell him right away
'Now what's the matter buddy
Ain't you heard of my school
It's number one in the state'"
Brian Wilson & Mike Love, "Be True to Your School"©

Between 1968 and 1972, I attended a high school known as Manhattan Talmudical Academy. Its official name was slightly less presumptuous, but more of a mouthful: Yeshiva University High School for Boys in Manhattan. The official name mattered little because everyone simply called it "MTA," which differentiated it as the slightly tamer version of its Brooklyn counterpart, "BTA." MTA was (and still is) an all-boys school, and back then, there were approximately 135 students in each grade. It was located in Washington Heights, on Amsterdam Avenue and West 185th Street. In the 1940's and 1950's, my maternal grandparents owned a candy-store one block north while my father attended MTA (but that's a whole 'nother story).

The student body ran the gamut of the modern Orthodox Jewish world, with some students hailing from revered and learned rabbinic dynasties while others came from non-observant families who had recently decided to embrace a different path. Most, like myself, were from somewhere in between. Some kids went—or more likely, were sent—there because of the school's superior academic reputation.

Helping out, as loudly as possible, during a janitors' strike. © *Daniel Wohlfarth*

MTA was impressively ensconced within a castle-like fortress of a building constructed in the 1920's. Like any other castle, the block-long building contained a confusing labyrinth of corridors, passageways and catacombs. The many architectural quirks shaped the students' experience there. For example, the building had a gym in its basement, which, according to an MTA urban legend, was supposed to have been a pool until impenetrable bedrock was encountered during construction. So, instead, we wound up with a gym that had an infamously low ceiling, reaching barely 3 inches above the top of the basketball backboards. On account of the low ceiling, generations of yeshiva boys grew up with permanently-skewed, line-drive jump shots that would inevitably clang off of the front rim.

Even by 1968 standards, the classrooms, offices and auditorium were unintentionally retro in design and technology. There was a single elevator and leave it to bored, creative yeshiva kids to turn that into an amusement park ride. In other words, there was no shortage of opportunities for major and minor mischief. Being the wise-guys that we were, my friends and I took advantage of all of them.

MTA, at that time, was divided into two distinct divisions. In the Talmud Division ("TA"), guys studied Talmud, the arcane, difficult written collection of Jewish oral law, also known as Gemara, for 3 ½ hours each morning. [The Gemara was written in Aramaic and compiled in approximately 500 C.E. It is actually an elaboration, recorded in an elliptically obscure style using the Socratic Method, on the six written volumes of oral law called the Mishna, which had been compiled approximately 200 C.E. In the Gemara, a Rabbi may make a comment, perhaps adding a detail or clarification, to one of the laws of the Mishna. Invariably, he (and it is always a "he," never a "she") will be met with one of two interjections: (a) that's obvious, so why are you even bothering to say anything at all? Or (b) how do you know that? Then, they're off to the races, so to speak, playing all manner of rabbinical and intellectual mind games.] Following a full morning of Gemara, the TA kids had lunch and in the afternoon, they attended secular classes plus one class of Hebrew language, finishing up at 6:15 p.m. Then, they would commute home via public transit or carpool, to destinations throughout the City or beyond, to begin a long night of homework.

I was in the other division, known as TI, as in "Teachers' Institute," for reasons that were never explained to us and remain a mystery. In TI, we studied Gemara for a mere 1 hour and 45 minutes each morning, followed by an equivalent period of general Jewish studies, in subjects such as Torah, the Prophets, Psalms, Jewish History, Jewish Laws, etc. Since we did not have the Hebrew language class in the afternoon, we got out nice and early, at 5:25 p.m. In order to accommodate students from out-of-town who dormed during the week and went home on weekends, we had no school on Fridays but we did have a "half-day" on Sundays, meaning until 3:30 p.m.

According to the official school manual, students were required to wear jackets and ties. We dutifully followed orders on the first day of classes. Alas, as with so many other things, we then took our cues from the upper classmen and never wore the jackets again. Ever. The ties were another story, a remnant of a bygone era, a rule that was strictly enforced by the school's brand new administrator, George Finkelstein. One student, Abe Feld, conformed to the letter if not the spirit of the law by wearing the same tie every day, week in and week out, year in and year out. He kept it in his locker, pre-tied, ready to be haplessly tossed over whatever clashing, plaid-pattern flannel shirt he wore that day. Well, it was a look.

George Finkelstein had been elevated from office boy to administrator within a few short weeks prior to our entry to MTA, following the sudden death of legendary administrator Norman "Jap" Abrams. At that point, George was not a Rabbi, he was merely a "Mr." I well recall one of the older kids from my Queens car-pool, telling him, *"Oh come on, to me you'll always be good old George."* And like I said, we tended to take our cues from the seniors and juniors. Perhaps to compensate for his youth and smooth face, George comported himself in a serious, officious and even grave manner. As we progressed through MTA and found ourselves spending more time (involuntarily) in his office, I found it somehow impossible to take George seriously, in spite of his sober, almost funereal mien. There was something a little off about him, something that did quite not compute within this fortress of cynical, Jewish male bonding.

Maybe he just took himself too seriously but I don't know, I never felt as if he was someone I wanted to talk to or hang out with. Put simply, he could never have been considered a confidante.

During my first two years in the TI Division, I fell in with what became a solid, tight-knit group of guys, one or two of whom I knew from elementary school. I am no longer close with many of them, but the strong ties of MTA will always bind us. For example, Steve Harris and I crossed paths in the legal world after not having seen each other in 35 years, that is, since he left MTA after our sophomore year and it was as if we were still the great friends we were back then.

Most of the teachers and administration viewed the TA guys as the serious students and the TI guys as rebels. But that was OK; we held our own scholastically and probably had more fun. I was usually in class with my best friend Danny, my Queens pal Howie Warter, the quietly brilliant Vic Fallek, the aforementioned cool Steve Harris, future caterer Abe Feld, math whiz Elia "Dorf" Weixelbaum and class jock Bruce Wenig. These guys made the overall stuffiness of the place tolerable and sometimes downright whacky. Once or twice, a brilliant iconoclast such as Jeff Levy or Avi Appleton would switch into our class, just to mix things up and to agitate the TI Rabbis.

Unfortunately, after our sophomore year, the administration purged our class of many of its most interesting personalities, on undisclosed grounds that reportedly involved anything from 'religious indifference' to 'academic insufficiencies.' We lost fashion maven Steve Harris and point guard Howie Miller to YHSQ, another Jewish high school in the area. Howie Warter left for public high school and class clown Alan Weinberg was never heard from again. All in all, about 20 were sent packing, leaving behind many funny memories. I still remember the day in 10th grade when Harris asked Rabbi Goodman whether one is allowed *"to go to a hospital with a nun"* and Weinberg yelled out *"only if you're really hard up!"* Victor Botnick, who once put glue into the lock of our biology room door in order to cause postponement of a test (and it worked!), was also sent packing. Botnick carried over his "fixer" mentality into real life, working his way into the fringes of the New York City political world, before predictably and tragically spiraling and crashing.

After the purge, it was never quite the same but we stuck together and did the best we could. I inherited Steve Harris' double-sized locker (with mirror inside!), located in the basement. One day during my senior year, George Finkelstein saw me sitting on the bench alongside the open door of my locker (with the New York Rangers schedule taped beneath the mirror). He told me that I was not supposed to have a double-locker and that I must immediately report to the school secretary, who would reassign a standard locker to me. I did the prudent thing and ignored the order. Nothing ever came of it. At the time, it only struck me as slightly weird to encounter George down in the basement locker room. During my three prior years at MTA, I had never seen him there or knew him to venture down to the basement. In light of subsequent revelations, perhaps it was not so strange, after all. But I will explain that, all in due time...

In any event, as juniors, we kept at our shenanigans. We joined some seniors in a strictly off-the-record basement hockey league and we actually recorded some statistics. We also had unfettered access to the locked gym, thanks to Abe Feld's bootleg key, the one with the words *"Do Not Duplicate"* engraved thereon. When we were really bored, we snuck around the catacombs leading to a walkway over the auditorium, from where we would occasionally disturb the tests being administered down below. For a while, we even rode on top of the elevator, a crazy activity that we learned from upperclassmen. Harry Bruckner used a book jacket to neutralize the elevator bell beneath the elevator. Then, someone would stick a comb between the elevator doors, in order to pry them open to stop the elevator in between floors, so that we could climb on top. While on top of the elevator, one could control its movements, causing teachers to miss their floors. Ultimately, the school caught on and some of us were hauled into the school's security office where we were confronted with the key piece of evidence against us: Bruckner's dusty book cover. Eventually, the school installed "anti-comb devices" and the party was over, undoubtedly for the best. So despite having lost many of our friends after our sophomore year, we did make the best of it.

Our morning sessions were led by rabbis, some of whom, the "good guys," did not seem to resent teaching us, despite the gap between their approach to Judaism and the approach of many of the TI students. Because we spent so much time learning Gemara and due to the difficulty of its often inscrutable subject matter, I always had a "good season" when my Gemara teacher fell into the "good guy" category. That was true during my freshman year with the lovably oblivious Rabbi "Schwady" Schwadron, a part-time lawyer, who was so easy-going that when the school suddenly needed an extra English teacher, he gave that a try as well. By contrast, my Gemara teachers during my sophomore and senior years, were unable to relate to us and our increasingly rebellious teenage ways in any meaningful manner and could not hide their contempt. These were lost seasons, at least for me.

Standard-issue MTA nicknames were par for course, but some teachers may have resented this more than others. For example, I am positive that Rabbi Goodman, did not mind the fact that he was known as "Noodles." It gave him a certain cachet. On the other hand, I had heard that a year or two before we arrived at MTA, then-administrator Norman "Jap" Abrams held a private heart-to-heart with a class on behalf of the pink-cheeked Rabbi Ryback. He quietly explained to the students in his heavily accented voice *that "it is nawt respectful to call your Rebbe 'bebby-fess'; a grunn man should not be called bebby-fess..."*

I guess this would be the right spot to throw in a shout-out to Rabbi Hesh Fishman, who taught us non-Gemara Jewish Studies during our freshman and junior years. If we performed well during his fast-paced studies of Torah, Prophets, Psalms and his Trivial Pursuit-like survey of rabbinical history, we were assured that a good part of his class would be reserved for a free-flowing "bull session," where we would dissect the issues of the day, ranging from the plight of Soviet Jewry to the passing arm of Joe Namath. On occasion, during lunch, if you still had the stomach for the pounding that he liked to inflict under the boards, you might do battle with Rabbi Fishman at either the outdoor hoops or in the gym.

After lunch, our general studies teachers were recruited from two distinct pools. Many of the earlier classes were taught by Orthodox Jewish teachers, most of whom also taught Jewish Studies classes during the mornings. Some, like Rabbi "The Big D" Dulitz for English and Mr. Hagler for American History, were famous or notorious, depending upon one's point of view, for being extraordinarily competent, demanding and well-informed. There were others, such as my 10th grade English teacher, a self-professed compulsive neat-freak, who was fond of espousing views that were slightly to the right of his contemporary, Archie Bunker.

By the late afternoon (but never on Sunday), the school was quietly infiltrated by a group of moonlighting teachers, who had already completed their shifts at various NYC public schools including Bronx Science, which back then was considered the jewel of the New York City public school system. (After my buddy Mike Blumenthal graduated from Stuyvesant High, Stuy may have surpassed Bronx Science; then again, it was always said of Mike the he was "MTA at heart.") For these public school teachers, their couple of laid-back hours at MTA must have been a nice transition between the regimented structure of the public school system and their return to civilian life at home.

Many were memorable characters, including Mr. "Rudy" Bernstein who entertained bored seniors with memory tricks, sleight of hand and even some Shakespeare. Joel "Seigs" Seigerman not only gave us his own capsule reviews of the Fillmore East shows, but once brought to class, and actually ignited, a substance that *"was not marijuana but smells exactly like it,"* so that we would be able to flee the scene of the massacre if we were unlucky enough to encounter that distinctive smell again, in real life. Seriously, that really happened during my junior year. The following year, in a landslide vote, we ended up dedicating our senior yearbook to Seigs. Then, there was the ever-genial Mr. Miller, who did not require the handful of seniors registered amongst the juniors in his chemistry class to actually attend class. He gladly turned a blind eye while we played hockey right outside the chemistry lab. Once a month or so, we'd thank Mr. Miller by quietly slipping him a six-pack of Miller High Life. What can I say, this was only about two years after Woodstock and as the Rolling Stones remind us, *"things are differ-ent today..."*

Even though we enjoyed ourselves, it was not all fun and games at MTA. Far from it. I must stress that the place was permeated by a strict, rigid and often puritanical sensibility that really got under our skin. It was not just the fact that sanctions were imposed upon any kids who were found to have gone to the Ramaz Dance [a prom-like scene at a neighboring less-Orthodox, coed Jewish high school], or that some of the Rabbis would run their hands over our backs to see if we were wearing tzitzis [fringes attached to undergarments required of Jewish men], or that we had Sunday classes on the day of the Salute to Israel Parade. I understood and accepted that many of the teachers and administrators would forever view the world through the myopic lens of their own narrow experiences and upbringings. What bothered me more was that our views and opinions, mattered little, if at all, in the eyes of the teachers and staff. They were dismissive, condescending and belittling of any opinion that did not fit squarely within the four corners of the orthodox yeshiva world. In the overall scheme of things, we were seen as little more than recruitment fodder for Yeshiva University and were expected to fit the mold of the future yeshiva college student. It was the rare kid, such as Jeff Levy or David Langer, who had the guts to speak his mind and actually make it through the four years.

During our junior year, our Gemara teacher was Rabbi Macy Gordon. "Macy" or "The Mace" was one of the more well-known and controversial figures in the school. Our 1972 high school yearbook, the Elchanite, contained the following entry: *"Not satisfied with establishing a personal relationship with only his talmidim (students), Rabbi Gordon makes an effort to come into contact with more students of the Yeshiva, and his guidance and friendship always leave their mark. Besides giving a T.A.-like shiur (Talmud class), the rabbi also gives a Hebrew course in which students study various materials that they would not ordinarily take up."* Well, that barely scratched the surface.

On the one hand, Macy was a classic authority figure, his bald head and closely-cropped beard easily commanding respect or fear, depending upon the student's personality and background. It was a poorly-kept secret amongst the MTA student body that Macy had a god complex. Even Macy played along with it. One morning, a student flipped the light switch in a dark classroom, exclaiming, *"Let there be light!"* Macy interrupted him, stating, *"Hold on, that's my line."* It was also well known that Macy took pride in knowing everything that was going on "behind the scenes." Because of Macy's god-like omniscience, I never lied to him on Sunday mornings when he went around the room, asking each of us how many times we had attended shul that shabbos. It was way better to honestly answer "one" than to lie and say "three," only to have the Mace activate his secret, extra-sensory hot-line to my local Rabbi. Macy knew who was dating who (most of us were not dating anyone), he knew who had been at the Grateful Dead concert the night before his midterm exam and he knew which senior had tipped me off to an obscure Talmudic commentary on the day when I had nonchalantly offered a surprisingly brilliant answer to one of Macy's brain twisters.

Macy's Gemara class, or shiur, was a somewhat tense hybrid of the Socratic Method and third-degree interrogation. We were expected to combine a facility to read and comprehend the literal flow of the Aramaic text with the ability to quickly answer questions and engage in a free-flowing discussion. The aim of his class was to discern what was really on the minds of the rabbis who debated the minutiae of Torah and Biblical law, between 1,800 and 1,500 years ago. We were also expected to be able to read and understand the obtuse commentaries to the Talmud and he would grade on our ability to do so, during high-stakes oral "recitations." I well recall Macy calling upon one of my classmates and asking him whether *we should go through the motions or just dispense with the formalities in favor of the customary zero.* My friend nobly fell on his sword, opting for the latter.

Not surprisingly, some were not taken with Macy, with his authoritarianism or his intimidation tactics. However, like many or even most, I found his class extremely interesting and probably learned more Talmud and more about how to learn Talmud than at any point during my yeshiva years. Thanks to him (Him?), I finally understood that Talmud was a link, perhaps the key link, in an ongoing chain, or more accurately a web, connecting our Biblical roots to the great Torah academies of Europe in the second millennium.

Perhaps I was predisposed to like Macy because he and my dad had been high school classmates at MTA during the late

1940's, when Macy, a resident of Boston, resided in the high school dormitory. If anything, I found his efforts to engage with us on a more personal level to be refreshing after our distant, sarcastic and hostile Gemara teacher from our sophomore year. My brother Steve was in Macy's class two years later and Macy sensed Steve's ambivalence, memorably telling him, *"Steve, you're on the fence. I'm going to give you a push and you're going to go one way or the other."* To be sure, there were some kids who wound up on the wrong side of Macy's fence. Or who started out there. But most of us were happy to interact with a teacher who was actually interested in learning what we were all about, even if the idea was for us to buy into his program and not the other way around. So, we all had fun going to Macy's house for a Chanukah party (he had discontinued his Purim parties two years prior after the guys had gotten into his liquor cabinet and…well, let's just say that not all of them were able to hold their liquor too well). I spent a shabbos or two with friends in Teaneck, where Macy was the respected Rabbi of the only shul then existing there, and we visited him at his home on Shabbos afternoon where he received us in his stylish smoking jacket. Many years later, after he had moved to Israel, Daphne and I visited him there and shared lunch with him in Jerusalem.

In December 2012, The Jewish Daily Forward, in an interview with former YU President and Chancellor Norman Lamm, broke the story about a major scandal at MTA. For some reason, I had allowed myself to imagine that my religious, all-boys high school had been miraculously immune from the scourge of sex abuse that had plagued the Catholic Church and so many religious institutions and schools. This plague had only recently taken down the most famous and powerful football coach in the history of college football and rocked Penn State to its very foundation. The cloak of secrecy and veil of immunity that had long protected abusers everywhere had been gradually disintegrating and dissolving over time. And then, suddenly, it was time for MTA and by extension, Yeshiva University, to feel the heat of the sudden exposure of shameful deeds long hidden from the public eye.

After thinking about it, I did not find it difficult to believe the accusations against George Finkelstein. He always seemed to be hiding something behind that stiff and stuffy demeanor. Certainly, during my tenure at MTA from 1968 to 1972, there was no talk of any improprieties at the school. Not that I was aware of, anyway. Back then, I never heard of any sexually-charged wrestling matches or humping, groping and punching, which were now reported to have occurred in George's office and at his home. It does appear, however, that at least one incident is alleged to have happened in 1971, while I was still at the school. This, of course, was news to me. I was also recently told of a "mutual pushing" incident that he attempted to initiate in the locker room, about 4 years after I had graduated. This naturally reminded me of my unusual encounter with George down in that same locker room, as I mentioned earlier.

At some point after we graduated, complaints escalated. The higher-ups got involved and must have found the accusations to be credible, because the door to George's office was removed, although he was permitted to stay on. In 1995 he was, in effect let go, but permitted to effectuate a seamless aliyah to Israel, leaving behind not only his lofty perch at MTA but his position as a pulpit rabbi in Washington Heights. Yeshiva University and MTA swept the mountains of dirt beneath the rug where it all remained hidden but festering for a couple of decades.

I found the revelations about Macy more surprising and tougher to take. There is some indication that the allegations, while fewer in number, dated back further and are certainly far more shocking. Sure, I had endured his above-the-shirt tzitzis checks but I didn't find anything creepy or uncomfortable about them. I just assumed Macy wanted to know if I was wearing tzitzis, like he wanted to know everything else. The Macy allegations, which contained elements of sadism and physical abuse, were beyond my comprehension. I mean, I knew this man. I had spent time in his home.

Just to be clear, I did not dismiss these allegations as being untrue or as being the revenge of bitter former students. For one thing, as I had learned while handling a couple of lawsuits involving sexual abuse of minors, these type of accusations are most often true. Not always, but almost always. Second, I have some reason to believe that Macy, as a kid, was subjected to the type of seemingly benign but ultimately humiliating hazing that could easily have morphed into sexual abuse, if taken a couple of steps further. Finally, when push came to shove, Macy did not even bother to categorically deny the horrifying accusations, instead saying that he did not recall such events having taken place.

Perhaps Macy's proclivities were the causative factor behind his somewhat tumultuous family life. His departure both from MTA in 1984 and from his prestigious pulpit in Teaneck, ran on a parallel track to George Finkelstein's similarly hasty exodus. Of course, no one blinked when he gave it all up in favor of aliyah and the opportunity to finally live the dream. Isn't that what we are all supposed to be doing? As things turned out, 6,000 miles and 20 years proved to be not nearly enough distance or time in order to outrun the past.

On January 29, 2014, in the case entitled *Mordecai Twersky, et al, v. Yeshiva University, et al,* Judge John G. Koetl of The United States District of the Southern District of New York, docket number 13 Civ. 4679, dismissed the ensuing lawsuit brought on behalf of 34 former MTA students against Yeshiva University, who claimed that they had been abused by George Finkelstein, Macy Gordon and a friend of George's, while the school looked the other way. The court did not decide the merits of the suit.

Rather, the case was dismissed because, in the court's view, it was brought after the expiration of the statute of limitations.

Prior to the revelations, I viewed my high school as a cloistered, narrow-minded and insular institution that despite itself, produced a graduating class of outstanding, often brilliant students. It was a place where I learned to compete and where, for the first time, I was comfortable being perceived as a bit of an outsider. Down the road, all of that served me well in my profession. It was and remains part of who I am, more for the better than for the worse. Now, I know that there was a whole other side to the place, of which I was blissfully ignorant. There was a side to the school that brought shame, fear and sadness to many of my contemporaries. I cringe at the thought that an old friend, who attended MTA shortly after I did and is now one of the country's most influential and forward-thinking Rabbis, arrived at school each day fearful of the abuse that he might have to endure. At least he landed on his feet (and maybe for this reason, he chose not to join the lawsuit).

I can only hope that the other victims are no longer suffering as a result of what happened to them at my school. I hope that they too are leading productive and happy lives. I will almost certainly never know if that is the case. But even if I knew that to be true, it will be impossible to reminisce back to my MTA years in the same, innocent way that I did before the revelations. The scandal has transformed my personal relationship with MTA from a nostalgic one to something very different and infinitely more complicated. Because every time I try to focus on the friendships, antics and even learning that I experienced there, I end up thinking about what may have been taking place behind closed doors in certain parts of the school. And I am deeply saddened by the knowledge that while most of us left MTA unscathed or even strengthened, some of our classmates spent their MTA years as victims and departed its big iron doors with a deep sense of shame or even misplaced guilt. Some of us have even asked ourselves whether perhaps, we were blind to what was going on right before our eyes, in which case, we would bear some measure of actual, non-misplaced guilt. And if I no longer feel nostalgic or whimsical about the place as I did before I learned of the scandal, it is worth remembering that our classmates and friends who were victims, never felt that way about the place.

BY THE TIME I GOT TO WOODSTOCK
(THE TOWN, NOT THE FESTIVAL)

"Can you hear that singing? Sounds like gold.
Maybe I can only hear it in my head.
Fifteen years ago they owned that road.
Now it's rolling over us instead.
Richard Manuel is dead."
Jason Isbell, "Danko/Manuel"©

A long time ago, Van Morrison sang a song entitled "Almost Independence Day." Granted, the title "Almost Labor Day" might lack the same whimsical flair but was nevertheless applicable to the situation at hand: it was just a couple of days before Labor Day weekend, work was light and Daphne was visiting her folks in Israel. The weather was sultry and I was feeling antsy so it seemed a perfect time to attend to a bit of long-unfinished business in Woodstock, NY. I had my mind on spending one day there, then driving the scenic route over and through the Catskill Mountains, ultimately winding up at my folks' summer place in G-d's country, the tiny hamlet of Livingston Manor. I had a general idea as to a Woodstock itinerary but I purposely left it fluid because I suspected that despite my nearly 35 minutes of exhaustive research, some of my intended destinations might resist being easily found. So, at 8:30 a.m. on a bright and clear Wednesday morning, I hit the road, armed with a GPS, Waze, a google of printed downloads, a dog-eared, pre-publication copy of Howard Sounes' "Down the Highway: The Life of Bob Dylan" and several antiquated road maps dating from the mid 1980's. The soundtrack was going to be the *"Love for Levon"* tribute concert double CD, supplemented by my first-generation iPod, which contained roughly 8,000 songs. This was a solo trip and I figured that ought to get me through.

By way of backstory, you should know that way back in 1967, Bob Dylan's bass player, Rick Danko, rented a pink house at the end of a long country road, in Woodstock, NY. (The 1969 Woodstock Festival, of course, did not take place in Woodstock but in Bethel, about 60 miles away). Many of you already know all about this but perhaps a few of you do not, so I'll continue on with the key details. Rick and the other members of Dylan's back-up band, who later became "The Band" lived in the pink house. Hence, the house's famous nickname, "Big Pink." During the summer of 1967, they supported Dylan musically and spiritually, while Bob and the band informally played in its basement about 150 cover songs, traditionals and new Dylan songs, while Garth Hudson kept an old reel to reel tape recorder rolling. These home recordings were later referred to as "The Basement Tapes." The informal sessions took placed so that Bob would have something to do while he continued his physical and psychological convalescence following his motorcycle mishap of one summer earlier and to provide material for other artists to cover, which would keep the Dylan cash train happily chugging along while the genius was off the road. Some of the recordings made in the basement of Big Pink were goofy and trivial. Others were and remain amongst the greatest compositions in the Dylan canon. Most of the original compositions defy categorization but dug deeply into the folk, blues and country traditions. All were recorded in primitive fashion. For some time, The Basement Tapes existed only as a wild rumor.

The following summer, on July 1, 1968, The Band released its debut album. It contained original material that had been conceived, arranged and honed (but not recorded) in the basement of Big Pink along with covers of three choice Dylan basement originals. The Band's record was called "Music From Big Pink." Some of the Dylan tapes made in the basement were soon purloined, surfacing as rock music's first bootleg recording, called "The Great White Wonder." It was sold on wildly colored vinyl albums in the back of sketchy head shops.

All of this sent shockwaves through the psychedelic world of late '60's rock music, with the pop music world's leader suddenly having veered off in a drastically different direction. In 1975, Columbia Records officially released many of the best Basement Tapes recordings but the entire kit and caboodle, six CDs worth, wasn't put out until 2014. The history, aftermath and impact of what went down in that basement during the summer of 1967, is the subject of many books and countless articles —but as my Talmud teacher likes to say when a fascinating but tangential question is posed: *"that is not for now."*

Big Pink (the house) has remained remarkably unchanged in the 48 years since Garth Hudson turned on his tape recorder. It is currently owned by a musician and his wife, who maintain the hallowed downstairs as a recording studio. But with the rest of the house having recently been listed as a "vacation rental," I was reminded that the *"times they are (truly) a changin"* and who can tell what might lie at the end of the proverbial "long and winding road"? If I wanted to stand at the threshold of this holy site, then, as Hillel sort of said, today was a better time to try than tomorrow.

By the time I exited the New York State Thruway at Saugerties, I needed to focus on my whereabouts, so I turned off the "Love for Levon" concert CD I was listening to. (Of course, I had already been able to confirm my initial impression of the sound on the recordings: it was sub-optimal, with the too many instruments compressed into a mushy mix. While dependable veterans, such as Mavis Staples, John Prine, Greg Allman, Jorma and Joan Osborne/David Bromberg more than held their own, especially on the quieter, more soulful songs, none of the performances approached the originals in musicianship, feeling, texture or any other way. The younger artists seemed to have little sense for the material.) I quit multitasking, a necessity at my age, and turned my attention to the road.

My intensive research had revealed that the street name where Big Pink is located had been changed and in fact, was now a private road. The alterations of the street name and house number were probably effectuated in order to thwart sad nostalgia cases like me. I punched in the old address, which I fortunately remembered, and my first generation GPS failed to recognize the house number but luckily, did recognize the old street name. I figured that was as good a place to start as any. I drove along that street, really a small country road, starting from number 4, looking for a number in the 2000s. The road climbed, became even narrower and was as twisty and tortuous as any country road I had ever traversed in the northeast — and I have driven a few. I thought of all the car wrecks that The Band members were reputably involved in, including the one where bass player/vocalist Rick Danko fractured six bones in his back, preventing The Band from touring after release of "Music From Big Pink." Now it all made sense.

After what was probably a mile or two (but felt like many more), I was at the top of a mountain and I could see the end of the road. There was still the occasional house tucked deep into the woods but it had gotten pretty desolate. There was a dirt road cutting in on the left with a hand-painted sign. The sign bore the name of the private lane. I made the left and it became darn clear that I was now on private property. I remained ever alert and vigilant for what I understood from my research was a cranky neighbor on the left. I was thankful for the silence of my hybrid's electric engine. The Big Pink owners had published a blog, seeming to welcome unobtrusive and respectful visitors to the site and asking them to keep to the right side. The entire private lane was perhaps 100 yards long and as I neared its terminus, on the right was the unmistakable pink ranch house that I had seen so many times on album covers, photographs and T-shirts. In fact, the house seemed so familiar, it felt as if I had been there before. There was no one around so I parked, got out and just stood there, taking it all in.

The pink house was majestic in its simplicity. I tried to conjure up mental pictures of Sun Studios (where Elvis did his thing), Hitsville USA (the home of Motown Records), Gold Star Studios (where the Wrecking Crew reigned) and Fame Studios (home of the Muscle Shoals sound), each austere in its own right. But all of those legendary edifices were single-mindedly dedicated to making the great music that was created within their walls. Big Pink was different. It entertained no such grand notions or elaborate plans. It was and remains merely an oddly-painted home at the end of a quiet lane, where genius and happenstance casually met and decided to hang out for a single season. The rest, as they say, is history. In 1985, when my beloved Uncle Leslie passed away just shy of his 50th birthday, he left an intimidating collection of about 1,500 classical and opera records. Hidden amongst all of that high culture were perhaps half a dozen pop recordings. One of them was The Basement Tapes. Uncle Leslie always had class. I did not want to overstay my welcome at the Big Pink house, so after a few minutes, I climbed back into my car, feeling very, very glad that I had finally visited the place where it all went down.

If visiting Big Pink made me feel good, the feeling would not have lasted long had I made no attempt to say a silent "thanks" to a couple of its former inhabitants, who created such timeless music and whose legacy will forever reside right there in Woodstock. I could write a lot, an awful lot, pages and pages in fact, about Rick Danko and Levon Helm, but again, that is simply not for now. Besides, the sadness of the back-end of their lives is in such disproportion to the joy that I derived and still derive from their music. So I prefer to leave it all unsaid except what specifically relates to the matter at hand—my own quest. I wound my way down from the backroads of Woodstock and onto its main drag, Tinker Street, in search of a florist. Jews typically leave a small stone at a gravesite as a symbol of having visited and having remembered the departed but for this occasion, flowers seemed appropriate. The doorway to the local flower shop also served as the entrance to a high-end chocolate shop and I figured that this might be my only opportunity to purchase a $10 bar of chocolate from a well-dressed young woman with striking blue hair. Besides, I needed the energy to power me through the next leg of my journey, as the sun was now high in the late summer sky and it was unseasonably warm. When I asked the long-haired, 60-ish year old guy in the flower shop for directions to the cemetery, his near-smile conveyed a sense that he was onto me and that he had sold a few of these gravesite bouquets before. With (delicious!) "small- batch" handcrafted brown butter milk chocolate in one hand and the flowers in the other, off I went.

I made a tiny error in assuming that Levon had been buried in the small Woodstock Artists Cemetery, where many of the town's illustrious residents (and founders) are buried. I should have known that Levon Helm, a populist if there ever was one, would be buried across the street, in the main Woodstock Cemetery, amongst the common folk. I had little difficulty locating his final resting place, which is in front of a well-maintained wooden fence adorned with musical notes, flower boxes and a wooden cut-out of Big Pink. The gravesite continues to be memorialized by Levon's many fans and friends, with messages written onto stones and markers. Both the Canadian and state of Arkansas flags were planted firmly into the surrounding soil. Still, even though Levon hailed from Bill Clinton's home state and found his musical voice and style in the Great White North, he chose to be buried in the small upstate New York town that he had called home since the middle '60's.

I had parked outside the cemetery and walked in. While inside, I noticed that aside from me, there was not a (living) soul in the well-kept, local cemetery, with its views of the Catskill Mountains, except for one black car parked a short distance away. I scoped out what I thought was a good place for my flowers, and set them down along with a small stone. I summoned up the mental and sonic images of when I first saw Levon, along with Dylan and The Band, on January 16, 1974, in Landover, Maryland. I remembered how his pneumatic, metronome, country drumming drove the entire show and how his powerful, throaty baritone easily cut through the arena's acoustics. I thought about when, many years later, he signed his autobiography for me, inscribing it (and telling me) to "keep stout." I felt thankful that I had also been privileged to have seen him perform again, many years after that, at his home/studio/barn during one of his "Ramble" shows. Channeling the unnamed protagonist from Dylan's "Isis," I "said a quick prayer and I felt satisfied..." Then, I went off to find Levon's Band-mate and compadre, Rick Danko.

It might sound foolish but for the first time all day, I was gripped with a sense of urgency, which I still do not fully understand. It probably had something to do with my firm belief that Rick was not only the most underrated member of The Band but one of the most overlooked and under-appreciated musicians of my era. Why do I say that? Again, NFN (not for now) but feel free to ask me sometime. For now, let me simply state that what made The Band special, aside from pure talent, was the unique contribution of each of its members. Robbie Robertson symbolized its ambition and vision. Garth Hudson was its virtuosity and sound. Levon brought the passion.

Richard Manuel represented its soul. Rick Danko was the spirit. That spirit (along with his gorgeously lonesome voice and original bass lines) was devoted to two things to the exclusion of all else: making great music and having a good time. As a result, Rick did not have the life he might otherwise have had, had he dedicated his attention to a few other areas, beginning with health and business. (By the way, I definitely would have paid my respects to the equally talented but tragically and fatally flawed Richard Manuel but alas, Richard is buried amongst his people, near his place of birth, up in Stratford, Ontario.)

So I set off looking for Rick Danko's gravesite, in the general vicinity of Levon, which was where the ever-truthful Internet had led me to believe I would find it. About fifteen or twenty minutes later, I was still wandering about in the hot sun, engaged in a not-quite-aimless but fairly unsystematic search for Rick. I guess I was expecting something that would stand out amongst all the standard-issue, drab, grey stones, just as a jumpy Rick stood out whenever he approached the mike for one of his unforgettably plaintive vocals. I checked my remaining bouquet and it seemed to be standing up to the heat a lot better than I was. I was about to make an executive decision whether to abandon ship or to begin searching every tombstone in the place, methodically, section by section, row by row. Stubborn as ever and with Dylan's "Tombstone Blues" buzzing around in my head, I was strongly leaning towards the latter. I had already eaten the entire chocolate bar because I did not want it to melt in the hot car and I figured that a power surge would soon be kicking in.

Just then, the black car that I had noticed earlier, idled up next to me. In it was a couple, just about the right age for this sort of nutty endeavor and the man asked me, *"By any chance, are you looking for Rick Danko?"* I guess they had noticed me lost in my thoughts next to Levon. They told me where to look, which was in an entirely different section from Levon's (conflicting with my online intel!). Former baseball catcher Tim McCarver likes to say that when he and his teammate Hall of Fame pitcher Steve Carlton relinquish their mortal coils, they will be buried 60 feet and 6 inches apart. I had mistakenly assumed that it was a foregone conclusion that the tightest rhythm section in rock music would spend eternity in close proximity.

Even with the helpful directions from the likeminded folks in the black car, I did not locate Rick Danko easily. They had pointed me to a certain section and told me to look for a Canadian flag, where I expected to find an impressive headstone that bore proper testament to one of my favorite musicians. I did a slow, walking tour of that cemetery section several times, each time a bit slower, to ensure that I did not walk right on by it. Then, in the second row back from the path, I spotted a small,

Though he lived haphazardly, the great Rick Danko
deserved a better final resting place. Photo courtesy of the author.

tattered Canadian flag, barely upright. To its left was a footstone, flush with the earth, which read, "ELIZABETH DANKO, JULY 18, 1943-AUGUST 2, 2013, FOREVER IN OUR HEARTS." Elizabeth was Rick's second wife and she was seen in Levon's recent film "Ain't In It for My Health." There was footage of Elizabeth private jetting around with The Band during the heady days of the 1974 Dylan/Band tour. There were also grim and sad scenes, as Elizabeth was being interviewed nearly four decades later, while residing in a senior home in Woodstock, under obviously modest and sad circumstances, long after Rick had died. I put my flowers just to the right of Elizabeth's footstone and then turned my attention to the two footstones just below hers.

Below Elizabeth's was a similar footstone, just as unobtrusive, with the inscription, "RICK DANKO, DEC 29, 1942- DEC 10, 1999, FOREVER YOUNG, FOREVER LOVED." (Footnote for the footstone: Rick was actually born on December 29, 1943 not 1942 but that was a fairly innocent error, based upon a mistake on Rick's birth certificate.) Next to Rick's footstone were empty cans of Miller Lite and a CD. People had put down a few pebbles and someone had thoughtfully left the entire top from a case of Foster's Beer, which looked like a footstone of its own albeit a colorful one. To the right of Rick's footstone was a third one, this one reading, "ELI DAMIAN DANKO, NOV 23, 1971- MARCH 3, 1989, HIS SONG LIVES IN OUR HEARTS." Eli was Rick's son from his first marriage. He died while in college after a binge drinking episode. Since the three Danko footstones were flush with the earth, grass had begun to grow around and over the edges and there was some dirt on them. I tidied them up a bit and took a few photographs. Then, I remembered Rick's broad, goofy smile aboard the "Festival Express" train (great movie!), leading (the late) Janis, (the late) Jerry Garcia, (the late) John Dawson of NRPS and (the still living, as of this writing) Bob Weir in a raggedy version of "Ain't No More Cane." I recalled that amid all that star power, it was clearly Rick's party.

I had one more stop to make before I left the Woodstock Cemetery: I went to look for the caretaker. Instead, I found his father, Alan, a severely disabled but engaging Viet Nam vet and we spoke for more than half an hour about some of the things he had learned since moving to Woodstock in 1957. He told me that

Paul Butterfield, perhaps the world's greatest white blues harmonica player, was also buried there. Alan put me in touch with his son Shea and I later spoke to Shea about potential improvements to the Danko burial site. It seems that there <u>was</u> a headstone there, at least for Rick, but that Elizabeth did not choose it or like it and had it removed. In the ensuing days, I contacted two of my friends and we agreed to try to get a suitable headstone for the three Dankos. We quickly discovered that this is difficult to do in the face of family and management politics and history. (Before I went on my way, Alan graciously permitted me to take his photograph and it turned out to be an amazing depiction of the man, which I might have published here except that doing so would be both a violation of Alan's privacy and of Section 51 of the New York State Civil Rights Law.)

Afterwards, I was feeling a bit dejected and out of sorts. I decided it was time to leave and to regroup with my thoughts at (according to the internet) the best local coffee shop, which turned out to be 25 minutes away, down 10 miles of winding country roads. I sat for quite a while, gathering my wits and studying a map, while drinking iced decaf in a section of Saugerties, NY known as Barclay Heights. I still had some unchecked items on my agenda and given my sub-par sense of direction, I needed to plan the most sensible routes. Daphne always wonders how I ever find my way anywhere when she is not around, but the secret is that I am okay with occasionally getting lost. Once, while fly-fishing alone on an unfamiliar section of the Ausable River outside of Lake Placid, NY, I got turned around and had extreme difficulty navigating my way from streamside back to my car. Before too long, I was caught somewhere between utter confusion and outright panic. (And if you think I overreacted, I suggest that you read "Lost in the Wild," by Cary Griffith, an excellent account of hikers and campers losing their bearings close to civilization and getting desperately lost.) But in Woodstock, NY, with a car, cell phone, phone charger, GPS and maps, I felt confident I would make it home in one piece.

Feeling somewhat rejuvenated, I decided to visit the spot where The Band stood in 1969 when Elliott Landy shot the classic photograph for the cover of the eponymous second album, referred to by some as "The Brown Album." John Joy Road looked different than in the photo and I realized that at some point during the past forty-six years, it had been paved. Time does have a way of changing everything... Well nearly everything— to this day, it is still my all-time favorite record, just as it was back in 1975, when it was the subject of my term paper for a Pop Culture course I took at Queens College.

Next, I got back into my car and drove to Striebel Road, off of Route 212. I recalled the large, block-letter New York Post headline announcing that rock star Bob Dylan had been badly injured when he fell from his Triumph motorcycle. That headline appeared on July 30, 1966, a day after the event, when I was 11 and 1/2 years old. If in fact, the mysterious motorcycle crash did occur (again, NFN), this was where it most probably happened. If it did. Finally, I spent some time tooling around the beautiful Byrdcliffe Artists' Colony but was unable to locate the two homes where Dylan lived back in the late '60's and early '70's.

Before too long, it was time to go. I wanted to take in the splendid views on the drive back to Livingston Manor while the light was still good. And if you must know, when alone, I always allow some additional "getting lost" time, just in case. So I carefully wound my way back onto Route 212 before hanging a right onto 28. At Big Indian (the town, not the person), I turned left. Then, for the next sixty or ninety minutes, I seemed to be suspended between the lush, rolling splendor of the Eastern Catskills and the streams and lakes region of its western side.

Barely a single car passed in either direction during the full length of that long stretch. It was beautiful.

I drove through Frost Valley and past the access point to the Slide Mountain trail. I stopped to take a photograph of a field of flowers in front of a lonely farmhouse with the tree line to its back and rows of gentle mountains further off in the horizon, meeting the blue sky. In just a short while, I would be at my folks' place in Livingston Manor, undoubtedly checking my voice-mail messages. But having played hooky for a day without a doctor's note was exactly what the figurative doctor had ordered.

Dr. Efrem "Effie" Nulman on Woodstock:
Over the past 40 years we return regularly to Woodstock. We rejoice in the serenity, the music and the beauty of the mystical woods & mountains. We honor the great history of respect Woodstock has to all manner of artistic effort, achievement & spirit. We feel blessed to carry the spirit of Woodstock within & gratified for the peace it brings.

NOVEMBER 22, 1963

"I can't remember if I cried
When I read about his widowed bride.
But something touched me deep inside,
The day the music died."
Don McLean, "American Pie"©

I am writing this on Friday, November 22, 2013. It is eerily fitting that today is a Friday because 50 years ago, November 22, 1963 also fell on a Friday. There is a short list of days when everyone recalls where they were and what they were doing. September 11, 2001 is probably number 2 on that list. For most anyone born before the mid-50s, the event that occupies the top spot on that fateful list occurred 50 years ago, on November 22, 1963, when President John F. Kennedy was assassinated. I am not sure whether I am more surprised by the precipitous passage of a half century of time or by the fact that I am still moved and saddened by the terrible events of that surreal afternoon and its aftermath. Back then, I certainly could not have foreseen myself sitting at a computer, a month shy of my 59th birthday, still mulling over the shockwaves that were set off by the blast of the assassin's gun.

Fifty years ago, I was a month short of 9 years old, in the 4th grade at Yeshiva Rabbi Moses Soloveichik, an Orthodox Jewish elementary school located in the Washington Heights section of upper Manhattan. Since that time, I have come into

36

contact with numerous grade schools but for my money (or more accurately, my parents' money), YRMS remains the best. I'm not really sure what its secret of success was but I believe it had something to do with its roster of excellent, traditional teachers and a parent body that supported the teachers and did not interfere. That year, I certainly benefited from a pair of old-school teachers. In the morning, my Jewish studies teacher was the dignified and learned Dr. Grynberg, a stickler for proper pronunciation. He focused on teaching us to read and understand Rashi, the main interpreter of the Torah. For general studies, my teacher was Mrs. Gurtov, straight out of central casting, circa 1935, with her grey hair tied tightly in a bun as she conducted inspections of our polished shoes, scrubbed fingernails and (hopefully) clean necks before beginning her unique lessons, such as comparing and contrasting the industrialization of Pittsburgh, PA to Bombay, India.

Once the clocks fell back off of daylight savings time in late October, dismissal on Fridays took place at about 2:00 pm in order to allow everyone to reach home in time to prepare for Shabbat. After dismissal on that Friday, I was in front of the school on West 185th Street, amidst the crowds of hyper kids and parents, all zipping along in different directions. I was slowly making my way eastward, to my cousin Eddie Friedman's house for my weekly Cub Scout den meeting. I wasn't exactly rushing because Cub Scout meetings were not all that thrilling. At the den meetings, the host mom would supervise some sort of scout-related activity, although it was never as cool as we imagined it would be when we first signed up. (i.e., lots of arts and crafts and very little fire-building and bear-tracking.)

Before I could extract myself from the crowded sidewalk, I bumped into another 4th grader, a large boy, named Mark Spitzer. (A couple of months earlier, in September, Spitzer had unilaterally assumed the captaincy of our class' punch ball team during recess and me, being the smallest kid in the class, had to prove myself to him, before I was permitted to play. By Rosh Hashanah, I was batting third, playing shortstop and telling Spitzer what position to play.) Spitzer told me that an upperclassman with a transistor radio, the accessory of choice at that time, had just told him that the President had been shot in the leg. My brother Steve, two years my junior, confirms that while he was outside of school at that time, he heard the same rumor, from our older friend Danny Metzger, who was in the 7th grade. There was nothing else for me to do at that point but to continue on to Eddie's apartment, located a couple of blocks away, between the school and my home.

The Friedmans were just one of several sets of my grandma's relatives, who lived in the Heights, all within a few blocks of us. Eddie's father, Artie Friedman was my grandmother's first cousin, and Eddie's grandmother, who I knew as Aunt Becky, was my mother's great aunt. Aunt Becky lived with Artie and his family until she passed away. This was old-world living in the new world and my brothers and I loved every minute of it, as we were constantly being doted upon by one relative or another. Artie Friedman was a jovial, fun-loving guy, married to Anne. They had three kids: Eddie, who was three months older than me, Michael, who was the same age as my brother Steve, and their baby sister, Roseann. They also had a Rhodesian Ridgeback, named Beauty, who grew from a cuddly little puppy into a ferociously protective beast who kept strangers, visitors and close relatives at a safe distance from the baby.

During the summers of 1957 and 1958 when I was 2 and 3 years old, before my parents had discovered their second home in the Catskills, our family and the Friedmans rented summerhouses together for a month on Lake Taconic in Columbia County. We have some great, if somewhat faded 8 mm film of Artie and my father horsing around in the lake. In one scene, my mom is seen relaxing on the steps leading up from the dock to the house, disconcertingly oblivious, as her toddler sons, Steve and I, run back and forth along the narrow dock without life preservers on. (Today, Child Services routinely

Cousin Eddie & Author
Photo courtesy of Florence & Seymour Eidman

strips parents of their parental rights for lesser acts of non-supervision.) Some of my earliest memories involve being up to my neck in that lake, pulled along by a string attached to a faded red, moth-eaten life preserver. I attribute my life-long aversion to swimming to those wonderful, lazy days of forced immersion in freezing water. I also remember playing with Eddie in the rowboat that was tied up to the dock, arguing about who would get to "row" with the oar that was on the lake-side of the boat.

But back to November 22, 1963... When I arrived at Eddie's apartment, the TV was on and I immediately learned that President Kennedy was not surrounded by his glamorous, young wife and powerful, dashing brothers as he recuperated in the hospital, from a minor injury to the leg. Instead, we were informed by Walter Cronkite that John Fitzgerald Kennedy, the 35th President of the United States and the youngest man to have been elected to the office, had already been officially declared dead after having been shot in the head. The rest of that day is a total blank. My mom tells me that the scout meeting was canceled.

Most of the next 48 hours remain a blank as well. The next thing I remember was watching TV in my grandma's bedroom in our rambling apartment on West 192nd Street, a little before noon on Sunday morning. We were watching the sole suspect, Lee Harvey Oswald, wearing handcuffs and being led away by Federal marshals. We watched history unfold and the memory remains as shocking today as it did fifty years ago when we first witnessed it in living black and white. The thing happened so quickly, catching me off-guard somewhere between disbelief and fascination. In what seemed like a flash and before I was able to gather my thoughts, my parents swooped in, turned the TV off, grabbed my youngest brother David who was 3 ½, and hustled all three of us out the door and to the local movie theater. If I recall, we caught a decent Lassie flick. Suffice it to say, they did not take us to "The Birds" or even to one of our favorite Godzilla flicks—and definitely not to "The Manchurian Candidate."

I assume that schools were closed on the day that JFK was buried because when I close my eyes and concentrate, I still hear that awful, slow, solitary drum beat, I still see the flag-draped casket upon the open wagon and the black, rider-less horse. I distinctly remember that this was the first time that I ever wished that something was just a bad dream and that the world could revert back to how it was a few days before. Unfortunately, this sad feeling of despair, of wanting to turn back the clock, is one that all of us experience, every once in a while, throughout our lives. Only this time, even my child's eyes discerned that the entire nation and much of the world wished to G-d that it would awake from the same collective nightmare.

The short-lived presidency of John F. Kennedy stirred America from its post 1950s malaise. Despite some foreign policy blunders and personal flaws, President Kennedy had managed to instill an aura of hope in the country. His cold-war stare-down of Khrushchev, his dedication to the space race and nuclear non-proliferation, his moving speeches about civil rights and his ability to use inspirational rhetoric to unite the country led us to believe that great days were just around the corner. We

40

will never know if JFK would have been the man to heed the warnings of President Eisenhower and stand up to the military-industrial complex, instead of allowing the Vietnam War to tear the country apart for another decade. With his sudden and violent death, history turned on a dime.

Whatever residual innocence that might have been transferred over from the 1950s, it most permanently died along with the President. Despite the many historic and lasting achievements of President Lyndon Johnson's "Great Society", the death of John Kennedy ushered in an era of escalating war, government distrust, conspiracy theories and paranoia that engulfed the country for many years. An emerging optimism and brightening instantly turned into a deep pessimism. It was as if the blast of Oswald's rifle had let loose pent-up dark and violent forces throughout America. A shadowy pall of social unrest and uninspired leadership descended, culminating in race riots, economic downturn, more assassinations and the violent deaths of 58,000 Americans and hundreds of thousands of Vietnamese. It was a national shroud that took some 30 years to lift.

As I suggested earlier, people's memories of life-altering events are inextricably intertwined with where they were, what they were doing and who they were with. Shortly before 9:00 a.m. on September 11, 2001, I was told that a plane struck the World Trade Center. At that precise moment, I was about to push the "play" button of my office cassette machine, all psyched to hear a recording of a radio broadcast of Dylan's brand new album, "Love and Theft", for the first time. As things turned out, it would be weeks before I would get around to hearing it or even wanting to. 38 years before that, I was with my cousin Eddie when I found out that the President had been killed. I will always remember being with Eddie at that moment. I also remember birthday parties and Chanukah parties with him, in addition to the Cub Scouts and those summers when we were little boys, playing on a dock.

It was at about the time of the JFK shooting that Eddie began to complain of headaches. He was only 9 years old. A year later, my folks told me that Eddie had been diagnosed with a brain tumor. I saw him a few times after he got sick and I didn't need any grownup to tell me that things were very serious. I just knew. Soon enough, I was in the fifth grade, and our terrific teacher read a book aloud to us: John Gunther's "Death Be Not Proud," a heart-wrenching account of the futile fight waged by the author's son against a brain tumor. I may have been too young to connect the events of the book to what was happening to my cousin, in real time, but I gained an understanding of the battle. My mom tells me today that Eddie was getting chemo but these were still the pioneering days of chemotherapy and I don't know if the treatments shrunk his tumor or afforded him any relief. The Beatles and Stones were huge by then and Eddie wanted to learn to play guitar. I recall overhearing my parents talking about how Eddie's folks got him that guitar but that he was no longer able to see well enough to learn how to play it. Nobody needed to spell out to me where this was going.

My mom tells me now that Eddie's mom, Anne, asked my father to bring a siddur [prayer book] to the hospital so that Annie could pray while sitting with Eddie. Anne, a convert to Judaism, embraced our religion. But afterwards, she could not help but wonder if the terrible events that befell her innocent son were a form of divine retribution for her abandonment of the religion of her birth. I remember Anne, now long deceased, as a kind person and good mother and she did not deserve to suffer such guilt.

One quiet, sunny morning, when I was 11 years old, my father walked with me up our block on West 192nd Street, towards the building where our cousins Sam and Fay Bart lived. He was dressed in a suit. There was no one else on the street. He told me, "God had to take Eddie." I felt sad, but not surprised. Much like Don McLean, I can't remember if I cried. I probably did not want to in front of my father. I remember stealing a quick glance at the blue sky over Audubon Avenue and knowing that at least the suffering was over. I do remember that. I am alone now. I am crying now.

After the killing of JFK, the country moved on, at least in a manner of speaking. It moved on as a person might move on after suffering a severe, disabling injury. Hobbled, debilitated and limping—but still alive. And after Eddie's passing, his family continued on, as best as any family could after the loss of an 11 year-old child. But like the country after 11/22/63, it was never the same.

Myron Baer Remembers:
After school dismissal, my mother took me to the library and as the news broke, it was the first time I had ever seem my mother actually cry...German Jews just didn't do that. It was a moment in time burned into my mind as if it had happened yesterday. We watched the whole event on a black and white TV right through the funeral.

SUGAR BLUE PLAYS
ROSA'S LOUNGE IN CHICAGO
(AND IT'S MORE BITTER THAN SWEET)

"Well the south side of Chicago
Is the baddest part of town
And if you go down there
You better just beware
Of a man name of Leroy Brown."
Jim Croce, "Bad, Bad Leroy Brown"©

The summer of 2014 was winding down and our two youngest sons would soon be returning to college. If we were going to spend some time together before then, it was now or never. Over the years, we had already exhausted most, if not all, of the desirable locales within easy driving distance. Since none of us had been to Chicago and the boys and I wanted desperately to visit Wrigley Field, the Windy City was a popular choice. And, having been to Maine the prior year, an urban vacation didn't seem like too shabby an idea.

The trip, a whirlwind 4 and ½ days, exceeded our expectations. We hit the touristy hot spots, grabbed a show at the fabled Steppenwolf Theater, caught some great comedy at Second City, ate really cool food (spicy fish tacos and kosher smoked bar-b-que) and browsed old record stores where I found (for $4.99!) a used copy of Dave Mason's "Alone Together" with the psychedelic "marble" vinyl. And if I was to say that for a baseball fan, Wrigley is a shrine to be cherished as long as the great game is still being played, then I would be underselling it. This ballpark even impressed Daphne, and we all thoroughly enjoyed a meaningless August contest between the ever-rebuilding Cubbies and the Milwaukee Brewers.

When we first blew into town and were settling into our VRBO pad just off the hipsterish Wicker Park neighborhood, our son Jonah made it clear that we would be hitting a couple of blues clubs. I am sure we would have done that anyway, even if we had we been kid-less for the trip. But I was happy that we were all on the same page because if Wrigley is a baseball fan's idea of a pilgrimage, then checking out the blues in Chicago is of similar holy significance for the blues fan. It's a sorry fact that for all of its cosmopolitan abundance and breathtaking scope, there is not much of a blues scene in New York City these days. At the cavernous and glossy B.B. Kings' Blues Club in the heart of Times Square, tourists are fed a steady menu of mainstream rock and pop acts but precious little blues. The real hard-core blues clubs, such as Dan Lynch on the lower east side and Manny's Car Wash uptown, have been gone for years. So when we found ourselves rocking out amid a packed house of blues fans at Kingston Mines, Chicago's largest blues club, it was a welcome reassurance that the blues are not dead. Since we had a full schedule of touristy events lined up for early the next day, we stayed for a couple of sets and left hours before the 4:30 a.m. closing time.

After seeing the overflowing crowds scrambling for tables and dance floor space at Kingston Mines while a couple of local bands did their thing, I was happy that we had advance reservations to see blues harmonica semi-legend, Sugar Blue at Rosa's Lounge. When Daphne had read to me the list of acts playing in town that week, that name rang a bell. I vaguely remembered Sugar Blue as being the guy who played the distinctive harmonica riff that formed the backbone of the

Rolling Stones' huge hit, "Miss You", which led off their last truly great album, "Some Girls", way back in 1978. Google quickly confirmed that sure enough, this was the guy. Born and raised in Harlem, the former James Whiting had a show business mom and renamed himself after seeing the title of a Sidney Bechet recording. He traveled to Paris in the 1970's to try make a name for himself and eventually met the Stones, who recruited him to play on a couple of tracks from "Some Girls". He has enjoyed an interesting, varied and well-regarded career, has recorded many albums and even taken home a Grammy. I was surprised to discover that Sugar had even recorded an obscure tune with Dylan that eventually saw the light of day when it was included on the first of Bob's official "Bootleg Series" releases.

So, needless to say, I was pretty psyched.

The show was at 9:00 pm, with doors at 8:00 pm and since one of the ubiquitous local Uber drivers had warned us that Rosa's was tiny, we planned to arrive no later than 8:20. Traffic was a bit lighter than expected and as it turned out, we arrived at Rosa's at 8:10. The club was not located in the downtown area or in a funky neighborhood, like Kingston Mines was. In fact, this part of town seemed too quiet, on the verge of sketchy. The façade of the club was composed of faded wooden boards with two small cut-out windows and a hanging sign that read "Rosa's Live Blues 7 Nights". Below that was the word "Dancing", as faded as the wood. We tried to open the door and when it did not open it dawned upon me that we must be at the wrong place, possibly an old, long-abandoned, former location. Glancing quickly over my shoulder, I saw that thankfully, our Uber driver was still curbside and had not abandoned us to whatever fate awaits tourists who don't know their way around a city famous for an abundance of guns and gun violence. [I cannot say enough good things about our trip to Chicago but the fact remains that in 2012, it was the only city in the country that had more than 500 homicides and that over July 4th weekend this year (2014) it experienced 60 shootings. And this comes from a New Yorker.] But a split second before my imagination ran away from me (another "Some Girls" reference), the door to Rosa's swung open and we were greeted by an attractive young lady, who apologized for the locked door and escorted us inside.

Rosa's Lounge is indeed, an intimate little club, with a few small tables in front of a barebones stage and bar along the

Never judge a book by its cover.
Photo courtesy of the author

side. The sound board is at the foot of the stage, stage right. Amongst the many photos adorning the walls were a couple of shots of a local politician who wound up going places. These were pictures of Barack Obama, who visited Rosa's while on the campaign trail. Rosa's was opened in 1984 by an Italian immigrant who was blown away after meeting some of the blues legends in Milan. He came to Chicago and named the place after his mom, who helped him run it. The young woman who had let us in, Amberly, had been managing Rosa's for a while. Amberly had grown up "in the business", as her father was a guitar player. She developed a strong affinity for the blues and for Bob Dylan. We agreed to disagree as to Bob's skill with the harmonica, but as I pointed out to Amberly, her derision was unfairly influenced by years of listening to live shows from true harp masters such as Sugar Blue.

We noticed that even though it was now well past 8:30, we were the only ones in the room and Amberly asked if we were the ones who had actually bought the advance tickets (at the righteous price of $8). I would have preferred a white lie at that moment, but the ever-truthful Daphne, admitted that it was indeed us. She then proceeded to ask Amberly, "do *these shows ever sell out?*" At that moment, had she known us better,

Amberly had the perfect opportunity and right to make some crack about Pipe Dream Productions (our perennially under-performing concert promotion business). But all Amberly was able to muster was something about how during a nice summer in Chicago, like in New York, folks look for every possible reason to stay outdoors. I couldn't help but picture the hundreds of people grooving and dancing at Kingston Mines the night before...but just then, at 9:00 on the button, Sugar Blue came on stage.

Sugar Blue has his own band and many of his fine band performances are available on You Tube. He was currently in the midst of a month-long residency of weekly acoustic duo shows, featuring himself on vocals/harp and Harry Hmura on guitar. I found out later that Sugar had met Harry in Paris at the same time he met the Stones. So this was a long-term relationship. They opened with the oft-covered "Key to the Highway" and quickly made us forget that it had been "oft-covered." I had never heard Sugar sing and his vocals were excellent, even surpassing the lead-singers from the impressive local bands we had seen the night before. His harmonica playing was first-rate, and it was easy to see why part-time harp players such as Dylan and Jagger were happy to step aside for him, at least for a moment. As for Harry Hmura, this veteran player was simply the best acoustic guitarist that I had never heard of.

Still, there was something vaguely off-putting about the set. Unfortunately, the first part of the set was marred, to some extent, by the house sound, which had way too much "top-end" (as in treble and high-frequencies) making Sugar's harmonica too high and piercing. More significantly, Sugar's stagecraft and demeanor made us uncomfortable and it was impossible to warm up to him. His tales leading into one blues song or another inevitably involved some level of domestic hostility bordering on violence (or at the very least, hostile miscommunication) between him and his obviously long-suffering wife, e.g., *"I hate when you're doing that......doing what?......what you're doing right now, you know what you're doing..."* There were tales of long drinking sessions with fellow harp player, Billy Branch and it dawned on me that Sugar may have had more than a few to drink before showing up that evening. Not that you could tell from his stellar performance. But when Amberly brought him water, he pointedly complained that she was not bringing him liquor, and replied, *"Folks, that's Amberly. Spank you, I mean thank you Amberly."* Sugar's introduction to "The Hoochie Coochie Man" included more details about the hoochie and the coochie than we needed to hear. Yet, when he finally got around to playing it, his version would have done Muddy Waters proud.

About a third of the way through the set, the young and apparently newly-hired sound tech showed up, walked right over to the soundboard and adjusted the too-trebly harp, downward. The house sound improved immeasurably. During the remainder of the set, the kid continued to fine-tune the sound. Each time, Sugar would eye him warily and warn him not to touch anything. Each time the kid made an adjustment, the sound got better. Each time, Sugar sounded more threatening. The strange thing was that the kid was not messing with the sound coming from Sugar's on-stage monitors. Sugar could not possibly be hearing the house sound, at least not as we were, so I chalked this up to the old-time bluesman not trusting the new kid on the block, especially when that kid failed to pay proper respect when he showed up late.

We decided to split after the first hour-long set. At its peak, there were maybe 15 people in the house during that set, including us. I talked briefly with the traumatized sound-tech and assured him that he did good work, at least according to my ears. And after all, after seeing hundreds of concerts, including so many of our own productions, it's reached a point where, while we may not be trained sound-techs, we sure as hell can tell when the sound is right. On the way out, Jonah admired the awesome, Chagall-ish, Rosa's Lounge T-shirts that were for sale but unfortunately, they were sold out of his size.

Amberly wanted to know what we thought of the set and I told her how impressed we were with the music but that we were a bit put off by the somewhat surly and intimidating stage presence of Mr. Blue. To her credit, Amberly, who was the undeserving object of one or two of Sugar's discomfiting remarks, took to his defense. She argued convincingly that Sugar is a "genuine blues guy" and that these guys sing and play the blues for a reason and that they are who they are. That week, I was reading a book by Amanda Petrusich about obsessive collectors who search for rare blues records and it contained the following passage:

> *"With few notable exceptions, blues music was rowdy and social, and its creators led brash, lustful lives. They drank and roamed and had reckless sex and occasionally stabbed each other in the throat."* (©Amanda Petrusich, "Do Not Sell at Any Price", 2014, Chapter Four)

Indeed, in this day and age, it is worth remembering that there is more to the history of the blues than an aged and universally beloved B.B. King, amiably chatting up the crowd with stories about how he saved his prized guitar, Lucille, from a house fire, before firing off his classic intro to "Thrill is Gone." While reading Ms. Petrusich's book, I listened to many of the recordings made in the 1920's and 1930's by the likes of Charley Patton, Geeshie Wiley, Blind Blake, and Blind Boy Fuller. These giants used the heartache, poverty and racism they experienced each day as fuel to inform and improve their art. Ultimately, we must accept a real bluesman such as Sugar Blue, who continues to deliver the goods to audiences large and small, for what he is, warts and all.

Interestingly, the intimidating Mr. Blue swung by just as we were leaving and wanted to know whether we had enjoyed ourselves. His offstage presence was as humble and friendly as his onstage demeanor was surly and intimidating. We talked for a bit and I decided that I did not want to be the ten millionth person to ask him what it was like to record with the Stones. But I did ask whether he recalled which Dylan song he had played on. Sugar replied, that he *"can't remember the name, something about a baseball player."* I asked him if the song was "Catfish" and Sugar enthusiastically responded *"that's the one!"* So, as things turned out, Dylan was into Sugar before the Stones were, since Bob recorded "Catfish" in 1975 during the sessions for the "Desire" album. This insignificant song is an ode to baseball pitcher Catfish Hunter, who ©*"used to work on Mr. Finley's farm but the old man wouldn't pay, so he packed his glove and took his arm. And one day he just ran away......."* It was thankfully left off the album but came to life when it was played each night of the Rolling Thunder Tour by bass player Rob Stoner. When the Bootleg series was released, I assumed that it was Dylan playing the deep, mournful, bluesy harp on "Catfish". I guess I should have read the liner notes, which credited the harmonica work to "Sugarblue" (sic). That's Dylan for you, always way ahead of the curve and always knowing how to pick musicians.

ORLANDO'S RECORD SHOP

"They had a hi-fi phono and boy, did they let it blast.
Seven hundred little records, all rock, rhythm and jazz."
Chuck Berry, "You Never Can Tell" ©.

The New York Times ran a story last week about the opening of the American flagship branch of the British music retail giant, Rough Trade, in Williamsburg, Brooklyn. This was a newsworthy event from a business, cultural and real estate perspective because conventional wisdom holds that record stores are going the way of dinosaurs—or at least the way of Blockbusters. Rough Trade's Williamsburg store will consist of 15,000 square feet of "repurposed" warehouse space. In fact, it will contain many "repurposed" shipping containers, one of which will become an in-house coffee shop. There will also be a sizeable performance venue within the store. One of the owners has been quoted claiming that this new mega-store will "complement" existing, smaller record shops and that the new behemoth will "help them." If he means, "help them go out of business," I agree. But such is life in ever-expanding Williamsburg, circa 2013.

The first record store I ever frequented was Orlando's Record Shop, which was located around the corner from my Jewish elementary school, on St. Nicholas Avenue, the main drag in Washington Heights. It inhabited roughly 800 or so square feet of purposed storefront. On Fridays, school ended early and a good part of my 6ᵗʰ grade class would invade Orlando's, en masse, in order to check out the latest hit singles from the British Invasion, Motown and the other occupants of the Top 40 charts, circa 1965 and 1966. I, along with my friends Danny, Myron and Manny as well as a few of the "hipper" girls, had discovered the secret pleasures of AM radio a year earlier and by now, its seductive appeal had infiltrated most of our extremely sheltered class of Yeshiva kids. It wasn't as if we were trying to spread the word or anything—we would have preferred to keep it all to ourselves. But with TV shows such as "American Bandstand" and "Where the Action Is," not to mention "Ed Sullivan", it was no longer possible to keep it under wraps. So by 1966, even the geekiest and nerdiest members of our class had probably heard the latest hit single by The Dave Clark 5.

Orlando's Record Shop was a typical neighborhood record store of that era, with Orlando perched in a corner behind the counter overseeing rows of 45 RPM singles lined up on tables within the aisles, in non-descript cardboard boxes. Several of the big hits were posted on the wall. The place did not stock many albums, which were just beginning to gain market traction at the time. When we wanted to check out the new albums, we would go to Woolworth's, which was just down the street. There, we could gaze longingly at "Rubber Soul," "Pet Sounds" or compilation albums from the many bands whose singles we favored, such as Gary Lewis & the Playboys, Paul Revere & the Raiders, Herman's Hermits and Jay & the Americans. But at Orlando's, singles—those magical 45's with the big holes in the middle, many ensconced in their soon-to-be-collector-item slipcases—were the order of the day.

In order to play a "45," you need to insert a spindle adapter, which is generally a round plastic insert, often yellow, which fits into the large hole in the middle of the record. Then, the small hole in the middle of the adapter fits snugly over the spindle and onto the platter of the turntable. [Daphne bought me a tie with a pattern composed of the classic, yellow spindle adapters, an item that is identifiable only by members of a certain generation. I once wore the tie on the final day of a jury trial. After voting against my client (and by extension, against me!) a member of the jury, a lovely woman of about 60, felt compelled to explain to me what the yellow things on my tie were. Thanks.]

50 Years later, this 45 & the "red box" remain classics.
© David Eidman

Now, getting back to the Friday afternoon visitations from the 6th grade of Yeshiva Soloveichik, let me say that it was an interesting dynamic. Orlando, a balding Latino (back then, we probably said "Puerto Rican" even though we had no idea where Orlando was from) of about forty, was an unpredictable, sometimes combustible mix of geniality and grouchiness. I may have been young but I was not oblivious and I easily detected that he did not look forward to these mini-invasions at all. That was because these young Yeshiva boys and girls were usually loud, somewhat unruly and always broke. Invariably, thirty or forty kids who had been locked up and under-stimulated all week were suddenly released into the wild. They would charge into the small store and proceed to rifle through all the record bins, mixing up the order of the records (which, admittedly, were not in great order to begin with). And then, just as suddenly, they would depart, again en masse, empty-handed except for their over-sized school bags, to catch the various buses that traveled along St. Nicholas Avenue en route to upper

Manhattan and the Bronx, in order to arrive at home before shabbos.

During the week, my brother Steve and I, along with one or two friends, tried to visit Orlando's during less busy hours. We were amongst his youngest regular customers and were, as far as I knew, his only (paying) customers from Yeshiva Soloveichik. Listening booths, to sample new singles, had been de rigueur for record shops in the 1950's but had mostly gone out of style by the mid-'60's. Orlando's did not have any and frankly, I can't think of any stores that still had them at this point. But as I recall, if you were a regular customer, if the store was not too busy and if you asked politely, Orlando would play a single for you on the portable record player next to his cash register. Orlando sold us many classic singles, such as "Paperback Writer"/"Rain," "Paint it Black," Lou Christy's gorgeous "Lightning Strikes" (which still gives me chills, just thinking about it), Paul Revere's "Kicks", (with its classic opening guitar riff), in addition to number one hits by the Lovin' Spoonful, the Mamas & the Papas and the Supremes. And then there was the Stones' "Have You Seen Your Mother Baby Standin' in the Shadows," with its famous, shocking, hysterical and seriously collectible dust jacket depiction of the band in drag, which, of course, we did not appreciate at that time and soon threw away. And many, many others.

These singles cost 80 cents each in 1966 dollars, which is equivalent to $5.93 today (2016). That is an awful lot of money to pay for just two songs, one of which (the "flip side") was often crummy. But without tape recorders, let alone the Internet and computers, and with much less product flooding the market, music was not viewed as the disposable and limitless commodity that it is today. It had real value that is difficult to explain in modern terms. Look, if you wanted to hear Sonny & Cher sing "I Got You Babe," you could turn on the radio during the two months when it topped the charts and you would probably hear it every hour. After that, if you wanted to hear it again, you'd need to own the record. There was no other way. So record companies were able to charge for that privilege. Just like the classic song by The Association, my brother Steve and I cherished these singles and stored these gems in a small red case that our Mom bought for us. Many of them, along with the red case, survive to this day, in our younger brother David's home. Not sure how that happened. One or two may even still have the original dust jacket, including The Lovin' Spoonful's "Did You Ever Have to Make Up Your Mind?"

During the summer of 1966, my family spent the summer at a small Jewish bungalow colony in The Catskill Mountains, as we did every summer from 1959 through 1970. Had it not been sold, we would probably still be spending the summers there. At some point that summer, our mom had to make a trip back to the city for a couple of days and we stayed behind with our grandmother. (Our father would come up from the city on weekends). Apparently, Mom did not want to return from the city empty-handed, so she paid a quick visit to Orlando's and asked him what the hottest new single was. When she returned to the mountains, she brought with her a shiny new copy of the Stones' "Mother's Little Helper," no doubt the highlight of a slow summer.

Despite a curmudgeonly exterior, Orlando was a good guy and knew his customers well. My friend Myron may have been the only 6th grader in the world with a charge account, shelling out 10 cents per week towards his latest single, which he was allowed to take home only if he stuck to the installment plan. One of the highlights of my week would take place on Friday afternoon, after all the kids barreled out of Orlando's to run to catch the bus, after buying nothing. Orlando would wait until all the kids were out the door and silently signal for my brothers and me to come back. Then, he would quickly slip us copies of "Go Magazine," the free handout that covered the latest pop news, and which Orlando had stashed behind the counter, away from the hordes of freeloading browsers. Thanks to this gift, I would know which hit singles had a "bullet," what the Beatles were wearing and what's what with each of The Monkees. I wonder if Rough Trade, with its 15,000 square feet of repurposed glory, will offer its young customers that kind of personal service.

MEAN MIKE NATURE AND
THE SUMMER OF 1975

"Oh, I miss the singing front porch banjo nights,
And when friends come by to pass the time away
And when the winds that chill the Berkshires in the night
Heading east through Massachusetts toward the bay."
Arlo Guthrie, "Won't Be Long" ©

January 1975 was cold and gloomy. My brother Steve and I had been spending winter break between college semesters holed up in the room we shared, playing the newly released "Blood on the Tracks" over and over. I was biding my time until I left on a Queens College trip to the swanky ski resort community of Stamford, NY. One morning, my mom came into my room to tell me that she had just registered my youngest brother David in the teenage program of a brand new camp that was opening that summer in Pennsylvania, and that Steve was signing on as a counselor. Nice for my brothers, but for me, the big news was that this camp was looking for a full-time nature counselor and that I was on the short list of candidates. In fact, given that they were looking for an observant Jew who was comfortable in the great outdoors, I was the only candidate.

During the prior four summers, I had worked at Camp Raleigh in Livingston Manor, NY, where I had made many close friends and had experienced all sorts of teenage adventures. But as the summer of 1974 wound down, there was no doubt that things had gotten stale at our beloved summer haven. It was around that time when we began to hear rumors that Mr. Honig, the larger than life father of Steve's friend Witzie, was close to fulfilling his lifelong dream of acquiring his own camp. Five months later, when my Mom took that phone call, we learned that the new camp was being called Camp Oren.

If owning a camp fulfilled Mr. Honig's great dream, that phone call fulfilled one of my modest teenage dreams. Even though I had moved up the seniority ladder at Raleigh, I never attained enough insider status to land a coveted position as a member of the "sh-t staff." Those are the specialty staffers of whom it is said: "They don't do sh-t around here!" Admittedly, part of the problem was that I didn't play any of the specialty sports well enough to teach them. The main perk to a "sh-t staff" job was very simple: you did not have a bunk full of spoiled, bratty kids cramping your style all summer long. As a member of the sh-t staff, you were a gifted savant, rendering lessons and wisdom in your particular sphere of expertise to one bunk of kids at a time. Of course, when the hour was over, you relinquished permanent custody of the little rascals to their overburdened and undercompensated glorified babysitters, who were technically on duty from 6:45 am until curfew, with barely one period off. Sh-t staff members were higher up on the totem pole than mere counselors—and they damn well acted that way.

I already knew all I would need to know in order to handle Nature Counselor duties. In fact, while at Camp Raleigh, my pals Danny, Myron and I rotated, taking bunks of kids on overnights in addition to our normal duties as bunk counselors. We had assumed the added duties for two reasons. Sure, we loved to get into the woods and to sleep outside once in a while. But we also loved to get away from our own hyperactive, demanding bunks of kids, not to mention the tiresome and ever-repetitive camp night activities. So when my mom informed me that Johnny Halpert, the director of the new camp, was willing to employ me as Nature Counselor with no other (official) duties at all, it was music to my ears. I put "Blood on the Tracks" back on and returned to sleep.

There is something special about getting in on the ground floor of almost anything—and that is certainly true when the

Author preparing for overnight.
Photo courtesy of the author

fledgling endeavor is a summer camp. One of the perks was that we were not hamstrung by any dumb, longstanding traditions; on the contrary, by virtue of our automatic seniority status, we got to make up the rules as we went along. Of course, the flip side was that things tended to be a bit disorganized and haphazard and we definitely spent a lot of time flying blind.

When I arrived in camp, several days ahead of the campers, it became immediately clear that I was no longer in Camp Raleigh. For starters, whereas Raleigh was a picturesque, perfectly laid-out camp of about 400 campers and staff, Oren was built for about half as many campers and was spread rather slap-dash over a virtually tree-less plain. It lacked both a lake and a gym. From an aesthetic perspective, its sole redeeming feature was a pretty stream which bisected the camp. The other major difference was geographic. Raleigh was situated in the cool air at about 2,000 feet above sea level just a few miles from some pretty Catskill towns. Oren, on the other hand, was at a modest altitude of 700 feet in Nicholson, Pennsylvania, a G-d forsaken little town of about 600 souls, 20 miles north of Scranton. The evenings, as well as the days, tended to be quiet, hot and sticky.

I entered that summer in a good place. I had completed a very successful junior year at Queens College, and I had a solid group of friends, in and out of school. Between my low-pressure gigs as a Torah reader and bingo worker (not a typo), I always had a few bucks in my pocket. There was great live music everywhere, at small and large clubs, theaters, arenas, stadiums, and even at school. (As a matter of fact, just before camp, we all sat second row center for The Rolling Stones at MSG, and watched Keith break in new member Ronnie Wood.) Near the end of the semester I had started dating a cute art major I had met in the college caf. While the summer intervened before that could get anywhere, it still contributed to my good mood. (Cue The Happenings singing "See You In September.") So I was all set for a great summer.

I first met Oren's camp director, Johnny Halpert, in 1968 when he was my 9th grade gym teacher and the coach of the high school junior varsity basketball team. (This was before he gradually worked his way up to head coach of the college basketball team at Yeshiva University, where he remained for some 42 years and attained iconic status.) One of Johnny's goals at the new camp was to have a basketball team that could not only compete with the Jewish powerhouses, like Camp Morasha, but also with some of the better non-Jewish camps, such as the classy Tyler Hill. With that noble goal in mind, Johnny recruited some big names from the small and insular world of Jewish hoops, including my high school classmate Bruce "Pistol Pete" Wenig. Johnny even imported some public school talent, including a quiet kid from Francis Lewis High School in Bayside named Richie. Perhaps Johnny's ultimate free agent signing was the nearly mythical figure of Stuie Poloner.

Stuie enjoyed unanimous acclaim as the greatest hoopster ever produced by the Yeshiva world. Even if he was no longer gracing the courts at the advanced age of 27, it was assumed that his name, gravitas and legend would suffuse every inch of the camp (I cannot believe that made sense to us back then). The ever-modest Stuie's easy going demeanor was in keeping with the general mood of the place, as he spent most of the summer preparing himself psychologically for the upcoming birth of his first child. And then there was the chronically moody Albie Faber, another aging but speedy former YU star, who had been brought over from Raleigh to run the kitchen and play point guard. Maybe not in that order.

As for Mr. Honig, it was refreshing to see a camp owner out there with the common folk every day, reveling in the embodiment of his dream. Instead of barricading himself in an air-conditioned office, Mr. Honig, ever the jolly raconteur, held court amongst the counselors, at virtually any time of day or well into the night. On visiting day, my parents took me home so that I could take the Law Boards the following day. And there was Mr. Honig, all 350 pounds (at least) of him, huffing and puffing as our car rolled down the dirt road on the way out of camp, calling out, *"Don't worry about him, we'll get him some jet-propelled roller skates, he'll be able to catch up to those ambulances...."*

The Nature Counselor gig was pretty much whatever I was willing to make of it. I began with an inventory that included one cumbersome, two-sided axe and a $100 budget to purchase camping equipment. I used this extravagant budget to buy 8 cheapo sleeping bags and a small tent (for storage, not for sleeping). I brought my own Coleman lantern, stove and sleeping bag, and called it a day.

Once I was set with the gear, the next order of business was to figure out where the outdoor sleepovers should take place. Since no one had even the vaguest understanding of the surrounding areas, I took off alone one hot afternoon into the woods. Equipped with a compass, mosquito repellant and the aforementioned axe, I walked aimlessly through unfamiliar territory. There were no trails as far as I could tell. I walked up the side of a small mountain. I arrived at a plateau and lo and behold, seemingly out of nowhere, I walked right into a small clearing that had obviously served as a campsite, complete with ready-made stone fire pit and cut-off tree stumps for seats. It was almost too good to be true. Although there was no trail leading back down to the camp, I blazed a path, marked it well and it served us nicely throughout the summer.

Probably due to the dearth of alternative evening excitement, my overnights always drew some interesting late-night guests, from amongst my friends, the camp staff and administration. People brought up guitars and I often had a steak stashed in the cooler for after the kids fell asleep, courtesy of one of my pals in the kitchen. As fate would have it, it rained so frequently, that more overnights were canceled than actually took place, but I think we managed to complete seven of them. Remember, we had no tents. I slept close to the fire on an air mattress, while the kids huddled together beneath the stars, in a tangle of sleeping bags. One night, after the boys fell asleep, my brother Steve, who was the bunk counselor, noticed a fat skunk walking on top of the sleeping bags while the kids were sleeping soundly. Soon, the skunk had his nose inside of the open bag of potato chips that one of the kids left atop his sleeping bag. While the skunk munched, the kid started to wake up, stretching out his arms. We warned him not to move. The skunk stopped for a moment, stared at Steve and me and began to lift its tail. Discretion being the better part of valor, we slowly started to back away. We figured that if the kids were going to get skunked anyway, there was no reason we needed to get sprayed as well. Thankfully, at the last moment, the skunk lowered its tail and slinked back into the woods.

My job as Nature Counselor did not begin and end with the overnights. In addition to setting up camp fires and taking the younger kids on mini-hikes, my duties also included various odd-jobs and loosely defined 'nature' tasks. We fished a little in the stream, catching a few decent brown trout (I even remember losing one big one after a spectacular leap). Then there was the time that a parent brought five gerbils to camp and I was instructed to build a cage for them. Somehow, they were constantly escaping and it seemed as if I spent half my summer searching for them in the shed only to have them escape again. I also recall building camp signs for the road leading to camp, a task which more than taxed my modest artistic skills.

One rainy day, some genius decided that the small children of married staffers should get a tutorial from the Nature Counselor. The babysitters decided they did not want to hang around while I enlightened their spoiled charges about the local flora and fauna. So, to get these 4 and 5 year olds to behave while under my tutelage, the babysitters introduced me to the kids as "Mike" and told them that they needed to behave themselves because I was *"very, very mean."* After that, throughout the summer, whenever the little darlings saw me in camp, they would scream, *"Hey Mean Mike! How mean are you today!?"* And I would have to huff and puff and pretend to be the angriest person in the world and the kids would laugh hysterically. That summer, all of the sh-t staff, in fact, became known by their job titles, so in addition to Mean Mike Nature, we had Joel Karate, Jill Office, Barbara Swim, etc.

I happily admit that I really did not have to do much of anything that summer. I'd typically roll out of bed around 9 a.m., sneak past Albie and scrounge something from the kitchen, then hang out with my friend Jill Office, in the office for an hour or so. When it wasn't too hot, I'd play some ball and then I'd walk back and forth across the expansive, empty field, carrying my trusty, double-sided axe, just for appearance sake and in order to look occupied. Once in a while, I'd overhear Johnny Halpert saying to his assistant, Effie Nulman, who was my main running mate that summer, *"Get Eidman to help you."* Then I would sigh because I knew some pain-in-the-neck chore awaited us, some real work, such as carrying/dragging the heavy wooden Aron Kodesh (the ark which held the Torah scrolls) several hundred yards, from the shul to the tennis court, so that services could take place outdoors.

Of course, my main duties, such as they were, fell within the natural world and the administration, notably Johnny, took a broad view of that. One rainy afternoon (of course), everyone was eating lunch and from the dining hall window, we saw a strange sight. The field was being invaded by extremely large pigs. Now, these were not of the cutesy, pot-belly variety. These dark creatures stood over 5 feet at the shoulder and appeared to be wild. I was staring through the window in rapt wonder when I heard, *"Where's Eidman? WHERE'S EIDMAN!?"* Now, I'm not sure what exactly Johnny wanted me to do but the next thing I knew, I was standing by myself in a muddy field of pigs.

Now I may have gone out there without a clue but I did not go out unarmed: on the way, I grabbed a heavy fallen branch, and stomped it down to club-length. When I approached the 'bay of pigs,' I saw that they were not dark but were instead extremely muddy and that maybe, just maybe, they were not wild at all. They say that pigs are smart creatures, more intelligent than dogs. Because I didn't know what else to do, I walked to the front, so that all the pigs would notice me, holding my Fred Flintstone club very conspicuously. The pigs had left a deep, muddy path which I followed back through the woods. And wouldn't you know it, they began to follow me, one by one, in a straight, orderly line, single file. After about a mile and half we eventually came out at a farm. And that was where I left them. Why the pigs decided to make a break for it that day will remain a mystery.

The next time I heard the *"Where's Eidman!?"* call to action, I happened to be standing on third base. It was during the Tisha B'Av staff softball game and Mr. Honig himself had just hit a scorching, low drive, all of 6 inches off the ground, straight into centerfield. There, the ball took a drastic 90 degree turn to the left. I remember thinking that I had seen bad bounces before but never one quite that bad. But something else was happening at the exact same moment. A second, distinct object was bouncing randomly, once, twice, three times, this way and that, randomly circling the spot where the ball had originally hit. After three or four convulsive, comical bounces, the object stopped bouncing and lay still on the outfield grass. That was when we realized that Mr. Honig's blistering drive had struck a large rabbit that now lay dead in centerfield. That's when I heard the dreaded call of *"Where's Eidman!?"* Apparently, providing the rabbit with a decent, respectful burial was also within the job description of Mean Mike Nature.

Maybe because it was a smaller camp, maybe because of the pioneering project, maybe because we didn't have the greatest facilities, maybe because people hadn't had enough time to form cliques yet... or probably because of all of those things, Camp Oren had a certain happy-go-lucky spirit. It had a freewheeling feel, sort of like we were in an episode of M*A*S*H but without the Major Burns and Hot Lips Hoolihan characters. Dylan's "Basement Tapes" were released that summer to much hoopla and acclaim and they were played constantly over the camp P.A. In fact, instead of waking up to Reveille or some stale announcements, the first thing we would hear in the mornings was Richard Manuel and The Band singing *"I had a hard time waking this morning, I had a lot of things on my mind..."* And if you didn't like the music emanating from the HC hut, you just walked in and changed the cassette—a level of trust and egalitarianism I had never experienced at camp before. I enjoyed the camaraderie and cheerful atmosphere so much that I did not use all of my days off—it was more fun to hang out in camp than to leave it and maybe miss something.

I preferred to remain in camp because there was always some whacky thing or another going on (not to mention, the camp was located in Nicholson, PA, not exactly a hub of activities). And, lest I forget, my wheels were out of commission as I had crashed my Mom's car while returning from taking the law boards, when I swerved to miss a deer on a country road. On one of the few days when I did leave camp, I visited Camp Hillel to see the girl I had recently started dating. She caught me unawares, sneaking up behind me and covering my eyes, in that flirty "Guess who?" game. Then she really caught me unawares by telling me that she had returned to her old boyfriend who was with her at camp. But I was having such a great summer, I was not even phased by this turn of events, not in the least.

Sometimes, the whacky stuff happened on its own and other times, we helped it happen. Due to a shortage of bunks on the main campus, the sh-t staff was stationed across the river, in mildew-infested quarters, hidden amid deep woods. We accessed our shack via a shaky wooden bridge across the stream. The bridge was missing many of its slats, so that you had to play a risky game of hopscotch every time you crossed it, especially after dark. Well, one night, bored with the usual roller skating night activity (and with the same extracurricular activities, for example a counselor taking down a misbehaving camper with the old "pull the shirt over the head" hockey maneuver, preferably in front of a bunch of girls), I accepted the challenge to roller-skate across the bridge. To be honest, I did not think it would be that difficult, as I had become a fairly accomplished roller skater, but there was only one way to find out.

Before I knew it, a small crowd assembled streamside while I took off, skating towards the main campus side of the narrow bridge. Every few feet, I had to jump, both feet at the same time, over a missing section of bridge and continue rolling on—the most literal type of *"rolling on a river..."* It was a clear night and the dew had made everything, including the wood, wet and slippery. I was nearly across when I landed from a jump and my wheels skidded. The next thing I remember is my body dangling upside down, with my face in the cold, surging water and my legs hanging onto the side of the bridge. I heard people laughing hysterically. Unable to extricate myself, I had to wait helplessly until two members of the kitchen staff came to my rescue. Luckily, this was before the days of cell phone cameras and You Tube.

As Nature Counselor, I also dodged a bullet right near the end of camp, when I was put in charge of mounting a huge "1975" wooden sign on a wire frame and then, lighting it on fire as a spectacle for the campers. This ritual was an unfortunate carryover from Camp Raleigh and it was part of the big, schmaltzy, end-of-summer extravaganza. I had done this several times at Raleigh, where I had been furnished with heating oil to soak the carved wooden numbers, which were wrapped with cotton. This would allow the wood to burn slowly, cleanly and evenly. Predictably, no one at Oren had any heating oil but they had plenty of gasoline and we all figured it would do the trick. I filled up a waiter's bus box with about 6 inches of gasoline and let the numbers soak for a good long time, and mounted them on the wire screen. After dark and with the entire camp gathered around, I struck the match, and lit the display just at the bottom of the "1." Instead of the flame spreading gradually to the other numbers, there was a gigantic boom! It threw me back a few feet and when I regained my footing (not to mention my composure), I was relieved, and also somewhat alarmed, to see that "1975" was indeed burning. Heck, it was a veritable inferno, with flames shooting towards the darkened sky. But that wasn't all. The bus-box, which still contained about six inches of gas, was now also ablaze, flames leaping twelve feet or more into the air. To my utter horror, I observed that the bus-box was situated a mere fifteen feet, perhaps less, away from the arts and crafts shack. I silently called in every heavenly favor that I might conceivably be owed, as we moved everyone a respectful distance away from the conflagration. It was touch and go for a solid ten minutes but ultimately the gas burnt itself out and the arts and farts shack survived. All that remained of the bus-box was a hard sheet of gray plastic, permanently seared into the cement on which the box had rested: a memorial to a nice idea gone awry.

Plenty of other unusual occurrences transpired that summer, including an invasion of midges, a kid who threw a rock into a nest of wasps, a counselor who was demoted to janitor because he told a camper to *"shut up"* after the camper had said that *"Bob Dylan is stupid,"* a mud bowl Color War football game and the transformation of the camp into a convention of village idiots. It was that kind of summer. Perhaps the highlight of the summer was a full-fledged rock concert, with a band led by my pals Sol Merkin and Dov Kahane, and which featured concert hall ambience, including avant garde/classical walk-in music, a light show and sleazy ticket scalpers.

Finally, for better or for worse, the story of The Summer of 1975 cannot be told without an account of the Camp Oren 'Marijuana Massacree' (sic). Admittedly, the passage of nearly 40 years makes this incident seem more innocent and less regrettable than it actually was but I still have plenty of regrets. As Arlo Guthrie would have said, it all started some 40 summers ago, on a summer afternoon when it was too hot to play ball. I was sitting on the porch of one of the bunks, with another sh-t staffer and a couple of counselors. Everyone was quiet, staring down at the floor. When he couldn't take the awkwardness anymore, the other staff member finally looked up and said *"Eidz, do you want to come?"* I responded obliviously: *"Where?"* When everyone got quiet and uncomfortable again, I instinctively knew "where" and said "Ohhhh..." Then, we were off to the woods.

What I did not know until then was that the staff member on the porch had recently returned from a quick visit to the city with a pound, yes a pound, of quality grass. It was paid for communally at a rate of $20 per man and was being stored in a large, plastic trash bag in the woods. It was available on an as-needed basis, no questions asked, 24/7 or more accurately, 24/6, since we rested on shabbos. As the summer rolled merrily along and we slid into the dog days of August, the trips to the woods became more and more frequent. We established a rule or two, in particular, that the endless supply should not be shared with any campers, waiters or junior staff. But "establishing" and "enforcing" are two very different things and word began to reach me through the grapevine that people were looking the other way while this 15 year-old CIT and that 16 year-old waiter were getting high. I should have known that it was just a matter of time before the sh-t, or the weed as it were, would hit the fan but I guess I was having too good of a time to care.

Before I knew it, the camp calendar was quickly winding down and I had still had not used all my allotted days off. A staff member with a tricked-up van offered a bunch of us a ride outside camp to parts unknown so I decided to go along for the ride. We stayed out the whole day, returning at dusk to a strange sight. There was Johnny Halpert's right-hand man, my friend Effie standing in the middle of the dirt access road leading to camp. He waved us to stop and it was immediately clear that something was terribly wrong: He informed us that one of the underage pot smokers had gotten caught and had already been sent home. As my future criminal procedure professor would say while discussing the futility of the exclusionary rule, *"Once the cat's out of the bag, the cat's out of the bag."* By the time Effie filled me in on the gory, sordid details of the 'massacree,' Johnny already knew everything, including the who, what, where, etc.

At that very moment, law school was starting to seem more and more remote, even though my Grandma had recently notified me that I had done well on my law boards.

I was glad to have missed out on being an eyewitness to all the drama and trauma of the days' events but I was disappointed about missing the comic moments of the ordeal. Apparently, an angry and betrayed Johnny demanded that Effie conduct shuttle diplomacy between the camp administration and the marijuana miscreants, some of whom were Effie's friends. Johnny demanded that the offensive and illegal weed be turned over to him, and the matter was resolved quickly and quietly in exchange for amnesty. After all, there was less than a week remaining in camp. Effie soon marched, evidence in hand, into Johnny's office. Johnny was expecting Effie to reach into his pants pocket and to extract a crunched up tissue with a few crushed leaves inside. So when Effie ambled into the office, extra-large trash bag at his side, poor Johnny nearly passed out. Of course, I was not spared from all the ramifications of the 'massacree,' as anticlimactic as they were. The bottom line was that for the last few days of camp, the Oren 7 were treated as outcasts and criminals by the camp administration. (It should also go without saying that 1960's teachings and writings of drug revolutionaries such as Timothy Leary and Ken Kesey had gained virtually no traction upon mainstream orthodox Jewry circa 1975 and that we were decades away from the legalization movement. I mean, it was not until the following year that Peter Tosh recorded his classic "Legalize It" album. In our narrow corner of the globe, it was assumed that anyone caught with "drugs" in camp would be thrown out and forever labeled an addict, a pariah or worse.) Suddenly, we could not wait for camp to be over.

There was one final, spontaneous act of defiance that occurred during the big banquet, which took place two nights before the end of camp. The Eilat Duo was there, playing simcha music, while folks danced around. Suddenly, the Oren 7 converged into its own tight circle, shoulder-to-shoulder, spinning like crazy across the lawn while the accordion and clarinet played. I glanced at the perimeter and noticed Johnny's wife watching what she must have considered to be the ultimate act of chutzpah, if not outright depravity, but she just stood there simmering.

The 'massacree' left me wracked with guilt. I had known Johnny for a long time, I liked him and I had let him down. In those days, if a camp earned a reputation as a "druggie camp," it was well on its way to going out of business. Oren closed two years later after a run of only three summers. I believe the 'massacree' had little or nothing to do with this, but in my eternally guilty heart I have to know that this incident during the camp's inaugural summer was not helpful and for that I am sorry. Still, my lingering guilt is vastly outweighed by the many warm and happy memories that I carry with me from the summer of 1975.

In life, most things are part of a continuum, a chain or an arc connecting a series of events. Once in a while, there is an exception to that rule. For instance, in the music business, most concerts take place as part of a carefully routed tour, but every once in a while, a band may play a single show, unrelated in location or time to any other shows. They call that a "one-off." During the summer of 1975, Bob Dylan was busy working on his "Desire" album, a "one-off" if there ever was one: different and unrelated to anything else he ever recorded, with musicians he never worked with before or since, recording songs mostly co-written with a writer he never worked with before or since. It turned out great.

Well, for me, Camp Oren was a "one-off". I was there just for that one lazy summer, in a neck of the woods that I never returned to or wished to return to. For the most part, I hung out with a new crowd, the vast majority of which vanished from my life shortly afterwards. But the ephemeral nature of those relationships in no way diminishes the magic of that summer and I suspect I am not alone feeling this way.

Dov Kahane's Summer of 1975:
We did a canoe outing on one of my 'days off.' Your job was Nature Counselor and you were kind enough to take me at my word that I knew what I was doing in a canoe. Luckily you did not let me take it out alone but offered to go along. One of the many problems at Camp Oren was the fact that there was no lake. Instead a river runs through it. So doing a canoe outing meant letting the current take you easily downstream and then paddling like hell to get back upstream to where you launched. Well, for some of the strapping basketball ball 'jocks' this activity was a piece of cake. But for me, this salmon-like rite was a challenge. I recall that - owing partly to the unusually strong current that day and partly to my paddling abilities - we capsized and somehow managed to get back to camp, soaked but in one piece. I had a great time and I am convinced that you saved my life that day.

Dov Kahane & Steven Eidman
Photo courtesy of the author

THE WORLD'S GREATEST GAME

"Got a beat-up glove, a homemade bat, and brand-new pair of shoes
You know I think it's time to give this game a try.
Just to hit the ball and touch 'em all, a moment in the sun
It's gone and you can tell that one goodbye!"
John Fogerty, "Centerfield" ©

Many years ago, I was watching a baseball game on TV and a former relative who shall remain nameless, entered the room. He glanced at the TV, looked at me and sneered: *"The game of the masses."* Although the man's intention was to convey his utter contempt for the game, I relished his observation. In fact, a large part of the beauty of baseball, in my view, is that it **is** a game for everyone—or more accurately, anyone who lets it into his/her heart.

That incident occurred over 30 years ago and football has long since surpassed baseball as the nation's most popular spectator sport. With its point spread and weekly schedule, it is the perfect vehicle for betting, office pools and all sorts of fandom activities. Meanwhile, the gradual migration from rural areas to the inner-cities fueled the growth of basketball as the preeminent participatory sport amongst young athletes. But whether it takes place on a field, a court, in a stadium or on a playing board, no game or sport has surpassed baseball for the depth and totality of the sporting experience.

Do you remember the very first time that you attended a

major league baseball game? If not, do you recall the first game that you attended last season or a game you took in after not having been to one for a long time? I will never forget my first game: walking through the tunnel leading to the stands at the old Polo Grounds in upper Manhattan, excitedly looking for Willie Mays, only to emerge in front of the largest and greenest expanse of grass that I could imagine. I remember marveling at the perfectly smooth red-clay of the infield and pitcher's mound. It was a day game and everything was contrasted against the cloudless deep blue sky. Having only ever watched professional baseball on a black and white television, this was truly a sight to behold.

On a purely aesthetic level, before a single pitch is hurled, baseball immediately distinguishes itself by the fact that each park is its own unique picture postcard with its own special charm. (Well, almost every park… Perhaps the charms of "The Trop" down in Tampa Bay or the new Yankee Stadium have been lost on me.) Football fans, no matter where they are, are looking at a rectangular field of identical dimensions, surrounded by a large oval-shaped cement bowl crammed with people. Basketball arenas are basically glorified gyms. But when a fan settles in at Kauffman Stadium in Kansas City, he or she will look out on a unique landscape; that vista will be different than the one facing the fan sitting at PNC Park in Pittsburgh or the fan at Flushing's Citifield. I must admit that golf courses are similarly unique, but that is where the comparison ends between the two sports!

As for the pace of the game, part of baseball's greatness is the lack of a clock. (OK, golf too). You play 9 innings. It could take 2 hours. It could take 4 hours. Usually it's somewhere in the middle. Of course, this comes with its pitfalls. Today's egocentric baseball players have applied the proverbial brakes, dragging out games to unprecedented lengths. Batters are constantly stepping in and out of the batter's box and are unsealing and resealing the Velcro on their batting gloves after each pitch. (I love you Dustin Pedroia, but I'm talking about you). Some pitchers act as if they would rather do anything in the world except throw the ball back to the catcher. They walk down the second base side of the mound and back, play with the resin bag, make the catcher run through the signals five times, throw over to first base two or three times to keep the runner close, then signal for the catcher to come out for a chat. Maybe after that, they'll throw a pitch. Or maybe not. Managers make 5 or 6 pitching changes per game, sometimes more. The break in between each half-inning is twice as long as it used to be. It all adds up. (For reference, the final score of the 7th game of the 1961 World Series was 10-9 and featured several pitching changes; yet it was played in 2 hours 37 minutes. Today, that is a 4-hour game, no question.)

Having said all that, it's important to remember that baseball is a pastoral game played in a pastoral setting (OK, again, just like golf). What's the big hurry, anyway? To get back to the damn computer? As Earl Weaver, aka the Earl of Baltimore, put it: *"You can't sit on a lead and run a few plays into the line and just kill the clock. You've got to throw the ball over the damn plate and give the other man his chance. That's why baseball is the greatest game of all."*

If the word "pastoral" sounds somewhat old-timey and antiquated, think about this for a second: even though today's athletes are unquestionably faster and stronger than in prior generations, baseball's standard infield, with 90 feet between each base, remains the most perfect and consistent dimension in sports. Should a batter hit a ground ball to shortstop, and should the shortstop manage to field it cleanly and make an accurate throw across the diamond, the batter will be out in 2013 just as he was in 1913. But should the shortstop bobble the ball, then other specific factors—the reflexes of the shortstop, his composure, his arm strength, the runner's speed and the first-baseman's stretch—will determine the "out" or "safe" call. Same today as in 1913. 88 feet would not work and neither would 92 feet. Exactly 90 feet between each base, in every ballpark, yesterday, today and tomorrow.

Conversely, just as baseball derives some of its charm from the uniqueness of each ballpark's architecture and environs, some of the game's magic is due to the diversity of the dimensions and shape of the outfields in each MLB park. Some outfields are symmetrical, some asymmetrical. There might be a tall wall along left-field, looming ominously close to home plate, or perhaps a hill in dead centerfield, or even a thick patch of ivy in the centerfield wall (where one ball once went in but two came out). Yankee Stadium used to have monuments to its dead heroes in its outfield. Can you imagine if some chessboards had more spaces than others did?

Now, I want to address this *"game of the masses"* business. Baseball is most certainly a game of the masses in the sense that it has been and is still enjoyed by the 'common folk,' including people of lower socioeconomic status. On a cold, windy afternoon in Wrigley Field, the Bleacher Creatures might even be said be "huddled masses." Sadly, with the advent of pricey new ballparks, crowds at the games are necessarily a bit more upscale than in prior generations. To be fair though, baseball has always had more than its fair share of worldly, intellectual admirers. Hemingway was a huge Cubs fan and wrote about it from time to time. Pulitzer Prize winners David Halberstam and George Will both wrote multiple books about baseball.[1] (And of

---

[1] None of their books are amongst my favorite baseball books, however: too pompous for my taste. My favorites, instead, include Roger Kahn's "The Boys of Summer", Art Hill's "I Don't Care if I Never Come Back" and Bill James' "Historical Baseball Abstract". I also recommend Whitey Herzog's "You're Missing a Great Game". Also, if you want to read an irreverent, hilarious look at life in the minor leagues, there is the non-fictional account of pitcher Dirk Hayhurst, "The Bullpen Gospels".

course, there's the book that you are now holding in your hand.)

Part of baseball's magic lies in its capacity to be enjoyed on its most simplistic level or on a level of sophistication that even life-long professional "baseball people" do not fully comprehend. For a novice, it may just be a game of balls, strikes, outs, runs and innings. In fact, one can spend a lifetime enjoying the game on that level and arguing about who was better, Williams or DiMaggio, Mantle or Mays, Harper or Trout. But should one care to scratch the surface, the game is a bottomless pit of planning and strategy. At its core, the game is a struggle between the pitcher and batter, with "the count" functioning as the rope in the tug of war. Keith Hernandez's wonderful book, Pure Baseball, focuses in large part, on how the count affects not only the battle between the pitcher and batter but all other aspects of on-field strategy including the running game, infield defense and outfield positioning.

Willie Mays sliding home, past Phillies catcher Smokey Burgess.
April 17, 1952, Polo Grounds, NYC. © AP Photo, used by permission.

Studies have found a high correlation between chess players and baseball fans and it is easy to understand why. Just imagine this fairly pedestrian situation: home-team leading 2-1, bottom of 7th, man on 1st base (a fast runner), no one out. Here are just a few of the factors that will play into the decision of what type of pitch the catcher should call for: the batter's and pitcher's strengths, which hand is dominant for either one, the pitcher's control, who is on deck, how many pitches the pitcher has already thrown, what pitches the batter has already seen during this at-bat and during prior at-bats, the speed of the runner on first, the catcher's throwing ability, the batter's propensity to strike out or to put the ball in play, whether or not a relief pitcher is already "warm" up in the pen and more.

As such, the manager of the team at bat will need to sift through an equally exhaustive list of factors just to decide what he should have the man on first do: should he attempt to steal, should they put on a hit and run play, or just play it straight up? The manager might think to himself: by starting the runner on a hit and run play, the batter will have a nice hole on the right side of the infield to shoot for and will probably not ground into a double play. On the other hand, a runner in motion might distract a focused batter and may also be a dead duck in the event the batter fails to make contact. And that is just one example…

In addition to in-game strategy, baseball teams are constantly involved in contentious decisions involving both short and long term planning. The planning revolves around the question of what types of players are most likely to produce winning results. This affects the composition of the team's roster, its lineup and even its farm system and player development. Thanks to a field of study known as "sabermetrics," both the planning and strategic aspects of the game have undergone a revolution during the past 30 years. The best-seller and major Hollywood film, "Money Ball," touched on some of that. For example, smart teams and managers no longer automatically lead off with a speedy batter, unless that batter has a demonstrated ability to reach base frequently. That is because, thanks to sabermetric godfather Bill James, we now know that the most important offensive skills, by far, are the abilities to get on base and the ability to hit for power. As the saying goes, "you can't steal first base" and the corollary to that is that you can't steal second base either, if you have not reached first.

Therefore, smart teams will lead off with a batter who has a high on-base percentage even if that player is not a stolen base threat. An example of a recent shift in game strategy is that we see fewer sacrifice bunts and stolen base attempts than we did years ago, that is, less "small ball." This makes sense because it has now been proven that it is not worth giving up an out in exchange for advancing a runner one base. After all, each team is afforded only 27 precious outs per game. Better not to waste one. Similarly, sophisticated analysis and modern metrics have influenced how pitchers are used, how fielders are positioned and even how ballparks are constructed. [They have also proven, beyond a moral certainty, that Derek Jeter has been a lousy fielder for years.]

But the democratic nature of baseball goes beyond its unbiased appeal to plebeians and aristocrats alike. Firstly, I daresay that baseball is also the most culturally diverse of the major American sports. With the increasing influx of players from Latin America and East Asia, diversity continues to increase.

Secondly, unlike football and basketball, professional baseball is often played at its highest level by normal-sized people and not by pituitary freaks. (Yeah, yeah, just like golf.) Willie Mays and Hank Aaron both went about 5'10" and played their careers at no more than 180 to 185 pounds. Pitchers tend to be on the tall side but the great Pedro Martinez will no doubt be waltzing into the Hall of Fame in a couple of years at 5'11". [2016 update: And so he did.]

Thirdly, baseball is a true team sport. In football, a star quarterback will have a dramatic effect on a great majority of his team's offensive plays. In basketball, a superstar will exert an even greater influence upon a game's or even a season's outcome. For example, when Kareem Abdul Jabbar joined the Milwaukee Bucks for the 1969-70 season, the Bucks increased its win total from 27 to 56, an improvement of 29 games over an 80 game season. The rookie Larry Bird was primarily responsible for a 32 win improvement in the Celtics record. In baseball, no single player can exert such a disproportionate influence upon the game. Batters take their turns in order, and each one generally has four or five opportunities per game. Starting pitchers pitch in a rotation, so when a Justin Verlander or Clayton Kershaw dominates a game, he will not be pitching again during the next four days. Mathematical calculations that are way too complex for me, have proven that should a team be fortunate enough to add Willie Mays or Hank Aaron to its roster, the team might be picking up 7 or 8 additional wins, perhaps 9, over the 162 game season, a significant but not earth-shattering impact. And while football and basketball are viewed as "team games" because the games seemingly rely upon plays involving a multiplicity of players, it is actually baseball that emphasizes the uniformity of opportunity during the course of a game. After all, Michael Jordan always took the last shot (except for that one shot by John Paxson) and the star quarterback will always have the ball in his hands with the game on the line. In baseball, even the smartest manager cannot arrange for Jeter, Ortiz, Mays or Clemente to always take the key at-bat. [In fact, just as this book was going to press, the baseball world sat transfixed as game 7 of the 2016 World Series came down to a 10th inning at bat, featuring Michael Martinez (career B.A. of .197) vs. Mike

Montgomery (career record of 8-11 with 3.51 E.R.A.).][2]

When steroids infected major league baseball, the public's visceral opposition was overwhelming. I believe that the source of all the anger was two-fold: first, rampant steroid use wreaked havoc upon the record books, which no sport holds in as hallowed esteem as does baseball. In fact, no sport comes close. When I grew up, numbers such as 714 (then 755), 2130, 511, 56, and 61 were so much more than mere digits. They were mountain peaks, scaled by the greatest of the greats. But the steroid scandal didn't just destroy many of the records that we long held dear (not to mention devalued the careers of stars who chose not to cheat). I believe the scandal also chipped away at our belief that baseball players were not 7 foot freaks or 300 pound monsters and that just maybe, with different circumstances and some more practice, you too could have been Jacoby Ellsbury. Or at least Dustin Pedroia.

Despite the steroid scandal and the long games and the crazy salaries, baseball remains great because you "still got to play the games." That means that no matter how the "experts" might size up a pending season or even a game, they really have no way of predicting, with any degree of certitude, what will occur once the home plate umpire yells "play ball." I've been writing this essay during the 2013 baseball post-season and virtually none of the games have gone "according to form."

Take the ALCS between Detroit and Boston. In Game 1, at Fenway, the Tigers' number 3 starter beat Boston's top pitcher, John Lester. In Game 2, also in Boston, Detroit's presumptive Cy Young award winner, Max Scherzer, had a 5-1 lead after 7 innings, thanks in large part to a shaky start by Boston's Clay Buchholz, who was nursing a sore shoulder. Boston came back in ultra-dramatic fashion to tie the series. In Game 3, in Detroit,

---

[2] As to whether Terry Francona should have inserted Martinez into a tie game at the bottom of the 9th inning as a defensive replacement for a far superior batter is a conundrum best left for another time.

the Tigers' ace Justin Verlander, who had been unhittable during the playoffs, lost 1-0 to John Lackey, who missed all of 2012 following elbow surgery. The next day, Doug Fister, Detroit's fourth best pitcher, dominated former Cy Young award winner Jake Peavy. Then, when neither Sanchez nor Scherzer was able to deliver a victory for Detroit, the series was over. The NLCS ended when the transcendental Clayton Kershaw, who may win the NL MVP award, lost to a rookie Cardinal pitcher by the score of 9-0. Then, the World Series began and things got even crazier. So far, the series is tied 2-2, with the last two games having ended on an obstruction call and a pickoff call. No post-season game had ever ended in such fashion.

Now, I know that I am not Roger Angell or Roger Kahn or Red Smith. If after reading my essay, you remain skeptical, walk over to your computer and google George Carlin: Football vs. Baseball. Maybe that will do the trick. See you at the ballpark.

The Stein Brothers Chime In:
It's the only game with no clock. The strategy changes on each and every pitch count, and the true aficionados have time to analyze and appreciate that fact during the pace of the game.
-Neil Stein, M.D.

Baseball, more than other sports mimics life and societal relationships. There is elementary/high school, etc. levels and then minor league before you qualify for your advanced degree. Anyone can play it well, no matter the physical size ,etc.
The game is not time-limited...MAN decides when it ends-not a clock. No other sport has as many schedule changes or cancellations-the sport is HUMAN .As we get older we all realize that time is racing and we are losing control of it. The pace of the game allows the observer at home or at the park to control his time too.
The sport is wholesome AND SAFE.
-Aaron Stein, M.D.

MY DAY JOB

"Bernie tells me what to do,
Bernie lays it on the line.
Bernie says we sue, we sue,
Bernie says we sign, we sign."
David Frishberg, "My Attorney Bernie" ©

Maybe it can be traced to Walter Matthau's character in "The Fortune Cookie," aka "Whiplash Willie," the get-rich-quick scheming lawyer. The doltish William Hurt character in "Body Heat" sure didn't help. And even the great Paul Newman in "The Verdict" first enters the film as a pathetic alcoholic has-been, trying to sign up a widow at a wake, before redeeming himself by winning a righteous but difficult medical malpractice case. Talk about sleazy! We can even look much further back to the Bard of Avon himself, Bill Shakespeare, with his *"the first thing we do, let's kill all the lawyers"* line. [And the last thing I want to do here is to get involved in the debate as to whether the context of that suggestion actually transformed the line into a pro-lawyer comment, or whether that argument is merely a shameless exercise in self-serving trickery, concocted by a clever trial lawyer.] Certainly, the endless cacophony of lawyer ads on TV, radio, the internet, subway cars and urinals must, by now, have reached some sort of tipping point. At least, I hope that it has. Recently, I was in a doctor's waiting room and noticed that most of the ads on daytime TV began with the phrase "Have you

84

been injured?" I kept thinking that everyone was looking at me. It was embarrassing. Even thirty years ago, Robert Klein lampooned the sorry state of affairs with a shtick that began *"Have you been injured? Do you want to be injured? Do you know anyone who wants to be injured...?"* (To be fair, Klein also satirized his $300 per hour divorce lawyer, whose stuttering speech impediment was costing Klein a small fortune.) And my brethren of the plaintiffs' trial bar wonder why it has become virtually impossible to seat a decent, open-minded non-jaded jury!

As of this writing, I have been a personal injury and medical malpractice lawyer, always for the victim, for over 36 years. Now I suppose that every job and occupation has some disconnect between its public image and its self-image. But for me, that disconnect has become a gaping chasm, as wide as the Grand Canyon. Once in a while, even I start to believe the bad

The author at work. © Fred Ajaj

reviews and the disconnect between the public image and self-image starts to narrow—such as when I read a survey and discover that the public rates the trustworthiness of my ilk slightly below politicians and slightly above telemarketers. Then, it's time for a reality check. So, in that vein, here is a "Top 10" list, not in any order, of what makes my line of work unique, gratifying and/or socially worthwhile.

1. <u>WE HELP PEOPLE WHO HAVE SERIOUS PROBLEMS</u>. Every one of my clients has gotten a bad break (literally or figuratively) and needs help. Often, something really terrible has occurred. A cop was ticketing a truck and was hit by an oncoming car and he will never work again. A teen was abused by a priest for 3 years. Parents were just getting to know their healthy 3 week-old baby boy and just like that, found out that the child will need round-the-clock medical care for the rest of his life because a part-time doctor did not recognize meningitis when he saw it. A nurse shattered her calcaneus (the bone in the heel of the foot) when she stepped off of an unmarked display platform at a high-end Manhattan store. A young speech pathologist was helping a friend deal with a leak on the roof of the friend's building and wound up falling off its unguarded edge. The difficult and emotional years of litigation are all in service of winning some monetary compensation, usually paid by an insurance company. This money will make the lives of these clients or their survivors no less painful but can help alleviate the severe financial challenges that accompany their physical setbacks or loss of a breadwinner.

2. <u>WE ONLY GET PAID WHEN WE ARE SUCCESSFUL</u>. Personal injury lawyers are paid via 'contingent fee retainers.' That means that we receive a portion of the settlement or verdict that is paid. Put another way: my client only pays me if and when I recover money for her. If a case

is unsuccessful for any reason, I am not paid at all, no matter how much time I have spent on the case. That is true even if the case was won at trial but was lost on appeal. If a case has gone all the way through trial, we're talking about hundreds of hours down the tubes (plus expenses, which can run into tens of thousands of dollars). For standard personal injury cases, my portion generally comes out to 1/3 of the recovery after reimbursement of case expenses. Sometimes it is less. For medical malpractice cases in New York, the fee is generally substantially less and depends upon the amount of the recovery. In addition, the lawyer must wait until the very end of the case to get paid. Since most cases (virtually all major cases, in fact) take years to complete, the personal injury lawyer is always concerned with cash flow and must plan and project several years ahead of time.

3. <u>NO TRIAL LAWYER WINS THEM ALL</u>. I should not have written above, "<u>If</u> a case is unsuccessful...," — "<u>When a case is unsuccessful</u>" is much truer to life. Any lawyer who says that he has not lost a case is not an experienced trial lawyer. The insurance, business and medical communities have vast resources at their disposals and have no difficulty in retaining top-notch legal talent and well-credentialed experts. They win their share of cases. So, every one of our cases is a bit of a gamble for the lawyer. Currently, injury victims lose about half of the general personal injury trials that go all the way to a jury verdict, while medical malpractice trials result in losing verdicts at least 70% of the time. Bottom line: no recovery for client (a common occurrence) means no fee for lawyer.

4. <u>THE TRIAL LAWYER AND THE CLIENT ARE "PARTNERS."</u> Because of the contingent fee arrangement, we, unlike lawyers in most other areas of practice, have a mutuality of interest with our clients. Some lawyers get paid

on a "flat fee" basis. This can serve as a disincentive to work as diligently as necessary or to put in the hours needed to best represent the client. Most lawyers get paid on a "per hour" basis. The more time they put into a case, the more they will earn. However, this arrangement does not always benefit the client either. For instance, it is in the financial interest of the insurance defense lawyers, who are generally paid on an hourly basis, to file frivolous motions and try to delay the resolution of a case, which benefits the insurance company at the expense of the client. By contrast, under the contingent fee arrangement, there is no incentive on the lawyer's part, to "churn" a file by doing unproductive, repetitive or needless work. The lawyer has an incentive to achieve the best possible result because the better the client does, the more the lawyer earns. And since the lawyer does not earn anything until a recovery is obtained for the client, the lawyer has an incentive to finish the case. There is an inherent unity of interest built into the relationship, instead of an underlying conflict of interest.

5. A TRIAL LAWYER GENERALLY ADVANCES THE CASE EXPENSES. Personal injury litigation, like other forms of litigation, requires significant expenditures in order to support and finance each case. Funds must be advanced for medical records, expert reports, deposition transcripts, court filing fees, expert testimony and a host of other expenses. Should a case go to trial, these "disbursements" typically run into the tens of thousands of dollars and are beyond the means of most individuals. In the vast majority of cases, these expenses are advanced by the lawyer, in the belief that same will be reimbursed at the end of the case, out of the settlement. It is also understood that should the case go south, it is not likely that the funds will be reimbursed to the lawyer by the client. Most personal injury lawyers rely on lines of credit from banks, at their own risk (and at a rate of

interest), in order to fund case disbursements.

6. <u>A POOR CLIENT CAN AFFORD THE SAME HIGH QUALITY OF REPRESENTATION AS A RICH CLIENT.</u> Because the client does not pay a fee until the settlement comes in and because the fee is based upon a standardized percentage, an indigent personal injury client can afford the same high level of representation as a wealthy client. In order to get her foot in the door, the only thing a client needs is a worthy case. Consequently, the contingent fee system helps level the playing field between the unlimited resources of an insurance company and an ordinary person. There are very few arenas in life where this is the case. Brilliant and nationally-recognized trial lawyers represent poor people every single day. I feel safe in asserting that the cream of the matrimonial and criminal bar, amongst other specialties, cannot make the same statement. It is not their fault; it is just that the system of paying lawyers in the United States makes it virtually impossible for premier lawyers in those fields to regularly take on clients who cannot pay steep hourly fees throughout a protracted litigation. The contingent fee system that governs personal injury litigation truly puts the pauper on equal footing with the prince.

7. <u>THIS SYSTEM FILTERS OUT BAD CASES</u>. Because the personal injury lawyer will not be paid unless the case is successful, he has a disincentive to accept a frivolous or even a weak case. It is simply too financially risky to do so. Why litigate a case for four years or more, advance thousands of dollars in expenses and expend countless hours on a matter that will not eventually earn a fee? After all, to quote Hyman Roth in Godfather II, while it may be *"the business we have chosen"*, it is still a business! Unfortunately, I could (but won't) write a separate essay about the frivolous defenses that insurance lawyers put up against good cases. So,

contrary to what certain interests group might have you believe, the contingent fee arrangement helps keep bad cases out of the system.

8. <u>WE HAVE TO KNOW A LOT OF STUFF.</u> A personal injury lawyer must develop a host of interdisciplinary skills. The license may read "juris doctor" which means "doctor of law" but we also play the role of writer, orator, investigator, physician, medical researcher, pharmacist, physical therapist, social worker, psychologist, mechanic, biomechanical engineer, economist and confidante (sometimes all in the course of the same case). [If you believe that this statement contains even an ounce of hyperbole, just ask me about my former client Chris's case. Or try imagining cross-examining a board-certified oncologist without a good working knowledge of cell division, doubling time theory and chemotherapy.] Speaking of interesting extracurricular lawyer-skills, I once litigated against two insurance defense lawyers who were both amateur magicians. I was a little extra careful with those guys, who I didn't really trust anyway.

9. <u>SOCIETY BENEFITS FROM OUR WORK.</u> Trial lawyers hold corporations, insurance companies, drug companies, manufacturers, builders, landlords, hospitals and other powerful institutions accountable. As a result, we promote positive changes in society. Personal injury litigation got the Corvair deathtrap off the road and exposed the dangers of the Ford Pinto's exploding gas tank. Dangerous drugs such as Vioxx would still be reaping millions of dollars in corporate profits at the expense of patient lives, if not for the deluge of lawsuits that brought Merck to its financial knees, if not its senses. The National Football League and its helmet manufacturers continued to fudge medical data and to deny the connection between football and brain trauma, until trial

lawyers made it no longer possible for them to do so. Hopefully, this will result in a safer game with better equipment. Consumer products, the workplace and the environment have all been made far safer as a result of litigation, which has proved far more effective than legislation in encouraging corporate America to do the right thing (or at least, punishing it for doing the wrong thing).

10. HOPEFULLY, OUR CLIENTS OBTAIN REASONABLE COMPENSATION, BUT THEY ARE NEVER "WINNERS." Although I aim to obtain "reasonable compensation" for each and every client, there is simply no such thing as "adequate compensation" for a very serious injury. During a closing argument, I once told the jury the true story about how casino mogul Steve Wynn, due to a severe eye condition, tore a big hole through a valuable painting, while showing it to a potential buyer. The hole was repaired without a trace but the puncture wound reduced the value of the picture from $139 million to $94 million. When dealing with property, in this case, mere canvas and oil, we have no qualms about assigning seemingly arbitrary values to inanimate objects. Thus, I have no doubt that had the value of this diminished masterpiece been presented for determination, the jury, after hearing expert testimony, would not have been squeamish about coming in with a $45 million verdict. Yet, when dealing with flesh and blood, bone and tendon, pain and sorrow, life and death, too many people confuse monetary justice with greed or vulgarity. I have been in the business for over 36 years; I am still waiting to meet my first client who would not trade her settlement, however generous, for her pre-injury state of good health.

I asked top trial lawyer Stavros Sitinas to tell me what he says to a badly injured client; he decided to jokingly channel "Whiplash Willie" and reported that he says: "Trust me, you're hurt."

FRANCIS DEWITT AND KINFOLK

"One day I looked up and he's pushin' eighty,
He's got brown tobacco stains all down his chin.
Well, to me he was a hero of this country
So why's he all dressed up like them old men?"
Guy Clark, "Desperados Waiting for a Train" ©

Francis Dewitt was the caretaker of Paradise Lake Bungalow Colony, where my family spent twelve summers, from 1959 through 1970. I believe he worked there before we arrived in 1959 and I know that he continued on well after the owner, Phil Beller, summarily closed the bungalow colony in 1970 and then sold off most of the property several years later.

When I first met Francis, I was all of four and a half years of age and he seemed to me as old and ragged as the mountains in which he was raised. Looking back, it is obvious that this picture was skewed by the distorted lens of a child's eye. As Archie Bunker would have said, Francis had *"fought in the big one, W-W-2"* and was part of the allied force that, along with De Gaulle's French troops, liberated Paris on August 25, 1944. Although neither garrulous nor nostalgic, Francis did enjoy recounting the spectacle of the crowds lining the streets of Paris, with women tossing, shall we say, 'personal effects' at the passing soldiers. One can only imagine the impression that such a wild scene left upon a young man from the tiny hamlet of

Livingston Manor, NY. In any event, simple math tells me that he could not have been all too ancient in 1959.

Francis & my dad, Seymour, 1982. Photo courtesy of Florence & Seymour Eidman.

Francis Dewitt came from solid Dutch stock, who settled in Livingston Manor, located in the western Catskill Mountains about 92 miles northwest of New York City, as the crow flies (115 miles if you are not a crow). Several Dewitts fought during the Civil War and are buried in the local town cemetery, including John Dewitt, who deserted in July 1863, while on a march near Funks Town, Maryland. After WWII, Francis returned home and married cousin Marge, who was every bit as tall, lean and straightforward in her manner, if not quite as reticent, as he. As far as we kids knew, they had two children, Donald ("Donnie") and Marie. It wasn't until much later that I learned there was more to it. Donnie and Marie were in fact the offspring of Marge's sister who was confined to a psychiatric hospital. Francis and Marge took the kids in and raised the simple but friendly Donnie and the shy and challenged Marie as their own.

In 1955, New York City, after purchasing land and destroying four small towns in the abutting Delaware County, opened the Pepacton Reservoir, to serve the growing demands of thirsty city denizens. The Pepacton was a half-hour's drive from Francis' Livingston Manor trailer-home, hard on the banks of the Wilowemoc Creek. After enduring a harrowing visit to "Green-witch Village", as both he and Bob Dylan pronounced it, for a physical, Francis landed a job working the locks at the gigantic upstate reservoir and dam. While today's Jewish summer camps feature trips to unfathomable destinations such as China, we would spice up a slow week at the bungalow colony with a trip to the reservoir, where Francis would arrange for a short tour. I can still picture him, a long, lean figure walking the narrow wall along the top of the dam.

But it was through Francis' other job, as caretaker of our beloved bungalow colony, that we really got to know him and it was impossible not to notice his decency, humility and dignity. Paradise Lake Colony was a small, intimate place of perhaps 15 or 16 modern-orthodox Jewish families. Many were holocaust survivors or descendants of survivors. Though the sentiment was rarely expressed, all believed they were incredibly fortunate to be spending summers together, amongst fast friends, while lodged in Spartan quarters in the mountains. While the men returned to the city during the week, the moms gamely made the best of their rustic environs, squeezing in some mahjong and scrabble amongst the domestic chores. Meanwhile, we kids were kept occupied in an on-site day camp and we created plenty of mischief in the evenings. Francis was a quiet but constant presence throughout the day.

In the early morning, as the sun prepared to rise high in the sky, Francis would rearrange the sprinklers throughout the lawns and fields before heading off to the reservoir. In the beautiful late afternoon light, Francis was a solitary figure, riding his lawnmower, back-and-forth, across the green fields.

He would usually be wearing his uniform from the reservoir: standard green work shirt, pants and cap. Even today, the smell of freshly-cut grass in the late summer afternoon causes my mind to flash back to that sight. Sometimes in the afternoon, if there were tasks to be performed at one of the bungalows, Francis would stop and say hi to Esther Metzger and her group, while they were *"scrappling"* (as Francis would say) in front of bungalow 9 or to some of the kids who he came to know so well. He had an uneven, tilted gait, due to the several toes that he had lost during the war. However, the missing parts of various fingers seemed to have little effect upon his dexterity and I recall him tying fishing knots with no difficulty. He also built a cage for our snakes in no time at all, with a wood frame, screening along the sides and a sliding door on top.

Francis was a large man of prodigious strength, and was always able to do whatever needed to be done. I remember late one afternoon, after day-camp had ended, when one of our gang summoned him because a colony of bees was swarming around a beehive attached to the bottom of the bench of the heavy wooden picnic table on which we had been playing cards. These tables, with long benches attached, required perhaps a half-dozen healthy adults to move even a short distance. While we were jabbering on and on about wasps, hornets and bumblebees, Francis lifted the corner of the table well off the ground with the stubby remains of a single, partly chopped-off finger, peered at the underside of the bench and said two words: *"Yup, yellerjacks."* We then got to watch Francis burn the hive, which proved mildly entertaining, if a bit gruesome. But Francis didn't shy away from ugly situations like this. When a normally reclusive red fox wandered down during broad daylight, right in front of the Wohlfarth and Aumann bungalows, Francis knew that this must have been a diseased animal. He silently approached the fox, carrying the world's largest wrench. He uttered not a word. With one swing, the fox was history. And sure enough, lab testing proved that the poor animal had been suffering from distemper. Somewhere, in one of my parents' drawers, there is a photograph of Francis walking off, expressionless, carrying the fox by its tail, with the humongous wrench in his other hand. Even as an adult, I remember moments of astonishment at his physical prowess: In June 1974, when my friends Danny, Myron and I rented a bungalow for a week of fishing, I recall Francis easily moving the refrigerator right across the kitchen floor with one long, outstretched arm.

While we kids secretly marveled at Francis' feats of strength and bravery, the adults respected his dedication to his work and his quiet, good cheer. He happily sampled Jewish food, especially challah and he sometimes sat around our bungalow on a Saturday, talking about his work or family. Actually, I was never able to understand much of anything he said. He spoke with a deep, indistinct rumble, struggling with the pronunciation of many words. Maybe part of his tongue had gotten blown off in WWII, as well. He would talk fishing with my dad, and inevitably, it came across as "…..*at the Willo-willo-willo…..'cross the street……big brown trout…..*" Francis had both the patience of Job and the muscle power needed to row all day and fish the huge expanses of the Pepacton. He was proud to show off the occasional monster trout that his endless hours of stamina produced. My dad tells of a bitter-cold November day, when Francis lost what might have been a record-setting musky on the St. Lawrence River. After the fish ferociously struck the large wooden plug, it ran so hard that the gears of Francis' fishing reel melted, with a puff of smoke blowing from the reel into the frozen air. Although this was the only bite that Francis had during this entire chilly road trip, he accepted his fate as he always did: silently and stoically.

During those years, we knew Francis' "son," Donnie Dewitt, as an amiable, gawky, goofy country teenager, about 8 years my senior. Because he was a teenager, in our eyes, he had a certain aura, even if we kids had accumulated far more sophistication and education in far fewer years. When the British Invasion hit, sure enough, Donnie showed up at the bungalow colony with an electric guitar. It never occurred to us that he had no idea how to play it or even how to turn it on. So when we begged and begged him to play something at our end-of-the-summer talent show, Donnie became the original air guitar guy, singing The Beach Boys, while a record player played the music behind a curtain. [Later, my good friend/wise guy Manny Adler pointed out the multiple non-sequitur aspects to Donnie's singing of "Carrie Anne," when Donnie kept singing the chorus as *"Hey Carrie Anne, what's your **name** now, can anybody play?"*, instead of *"....what's your **game** now, can anybody play?"*.] Good-natured Donnie accompanied us on many a fishing trip although to my knowledge, no one ever witnessed him catch a fish. Or lose a fish. Or get a bite. I know that he knew you needed bait in order to catch a fish because of an incident, which I was told took place on the Willowemoc, when he absconded around a bend with all of the worms, leaving his "fishing buddies" high and dry. When the others finally tracked him down, they grabbed Donnie, who couldn't swim, and dangled him over a deep pool in the creek. Pleading for mercy, the best that Donnie was able to muster was *"I'll give you all my split shot"* ("split shot" are small fishing sinkers) in exchange for a reprieve. I was never told how that situation played out, but Donnie did survive to fish another day. And after yet another fishless day for Donnie on Stump Pond, it was Donnie and not Yogi Berra, who declared with typical acceptance, *"Stump Pond stumped me again."* About 45 years later, I found myself driving along the Stump Pond road but for the life of me, was unable to locate the turn-off to the little lake. When I called Manny Adler to tell him about my outing and my frustration, his response was, *"Well, I guess Stump Pond stumped you again."*

After Paradise Lake closed, we continued to see Francis, his nuclear family and the extended Dewitt clan, albeit less often, during our excursions in and around the area. In 1983, my dad was shopping for his own trailer to put onto Elm Hollow Road. While at Dreher's Hardware Store in Roscoe, my sister-in-law Diane remembers being startled to see my brother Steve engaged in a spirited conversation with a *"slim, local woman, of Amazonian height, whose pants were hitched well above her waist."* That encounter served as Diane's introduction to Marge Dewitt, who she heard whispering to Steve in a conspiratorial tone, *"I hear that your Dad is looking at a double-wide."* After the house, or more accurately, the single-wide trailer known as The Eidmont came to be, my father became close friends with Francis' cousin, Balsey (short for Balsam, obviously). This was particularly ironic because we had come into contact with Balsey decades earlier—an encounter we barely survived. My dad had decided to rent a boat for us to do a little poaching on Mud Pond, a small, under-fished lake with oversized perch. (Another Dewitt, Perry, had a pond that was rumored to be stocked full of trout, but that was too daunting an excursion, even for dedicated poachers such as us). Just as the fishing on Mud Pond was getting good, a large local man unceremoniously signaled for us to row back in and proceeded to escort us from the lake at the point of his rifle, while his shorter sidekick was muttering something that sounded a lot like *"shoot 'em, shoot 'em!"* It turned out that that the large rifleman was Francis' cousin, Marshall Dewitt. (He was not an actual marshal as in "Marshal Dillon," but he sure acted like one.) When the account of our apprehension spread to Francis, he explained that the smaller man must have been Marshall's brother, Balsey, "the runt of the Dewitt family". Balsey, not exactly a midget at 5'10", claimed in later years, that *"if not for all their feudin', the Dewitt's would've owned the whole valley."*

Ironically, thanks to Balsey, who continued on as caretaker for Mud Pond throughout his life, we were able to (secretly) fish there from shore up until Balsey passed away. A couple of years before the Mud Pond (near) Massacre, Francis and my father survived another misbegotten Mud Pond adventure when half-way through an otherwise uneventful fishing trip, my father's inflatable rubber raft blew up, with a "bang!" That was when my father discovered, to his great relief, that unlike Donnie, Francis knew how to swim. The drenched and weary anglers returned to our bungalow colony and recounted their riotous tale of woe to a hero's welcome. By sheer coincidence, on that very day, there was a major naval disaster. The headline in the next day's Daily News read: *"Boat Blows Up, 2 Missing, Assumed Still Alive."* With some creative editing, our mom cut out and replaced the word *"Missing"* with the word *"Fishing"* and that newspaper hung on the wall of our bungalow until the day that Phil Beller sold it out from under us.

Francis, Marge, Donnie and Marie continued to dwell in their trailer, along the shore of the Willowemoc, in the section known as Hazel. Sadly, neither Donnie nor Marie survived their 50's, although Francis and Marge lived into their 80's. At least two of Balsey's sons also resided in that neck of the woods. One is Balsey "Dean" Dewitt, a former airline pilot, who, after a disastrous (non-Sully) emergency ocean landing en route from JFK Airport to St Maarten in 1970, retired from the airlines and became a math instructor at Sullivan County Community College. A well-reviewed account of what was the first open-water ditching of a commercial jet, can be found in *"35 Miles From Shore: The Ditching and Rescue of ALM Flight 980."* Dean still lives in the fine home that he built for himself on Mud Pond Road, close to where his dad lived. Another son of Balsey, Danny, spent quite a bit of time fishing with my dad on Tennanah Lake, while holding forth on a variety of controversial topics, including the Arab-Israeli conflict, where, thankfully, he and my father shared many a somewhat right-of-center point of view. Danny was a great friend to my father and a big help during the period when my father's vision was impaired. He also adopted my nephew Alex's dog when it became clear that she needed a country lifestyle and an attentive but firm owner. Unfortunately, Danny died way too young.

It is probably true that the Dewitts will never get to *"own the whole valley."* Nevertheless, members of the current generation continue to populate the region, including Dean' son, "Little Dean." His trailer, with its confederate flag flying, is on Elm Hollow Road, just a short way's down from my folks' place. {Update: As of the summer of 2015, I am pleased to report that the aforementioned symbol of the Confederacy is no longer in evidence. And as the saying goes, that is a good thing.}

MY GREAT GRANDMOTHER

"So if you're walking down the street sometime,
And spot some hollow ancient eyes,
Please don't just pass 'em by and stare
As if you didn't care,
Say, 'Hello in there, hello in there, hello'"
John Prine, "Hello In There" ©

Bubby with her grandson, & my uncle,
Marty Teller, in 1944. She was 61.
Photo courtesy of Florence Eidman

When I was a child, my great-grandmother, Tillie Bodian, lived with us until her death when I was about 9 years old. Her real first name was "Alte," which is Yiddish for "old one," a name that was given to her to confuse and ward off the evil eye after the premature deaths of her older siblings. "Tillie" was an Americanization, sort of. She was the mother of my maternal grandmother, Fannie Teller, who also lived with us. Since we called our (virtually) American grandmother "Grandma", my brothers and I called our (extremely) eastern-European great-grandmother "Bubby," which is Yiddish for grandma. It's been close to 50 years since Bubby's passing but she was a presence, and I remember her

101

vividly.

Although my Bubby was "only" 81 when she died, I think of her as the oldest person I could ever imagine. She never walked without her "shteken" (Yiddish for cane) and moved across our spacious apartment in Washington Heights at a glacial pace. She spent most of her time seated at the chair in her room, quietly looking out the window. One of my friends realized that she had passed on when he walked up the street one day and he didn't spot her sitting in the window. By contrast, my dad is now (in January 2014) close to 82, G-d bless him, and he still drags and stretches the stubborn cover onto his boat with the agility of a teenager. (Perhaps a stiff teenager, but frankly, I cannot do it.) And my father-in-law, G-d bless him, is still spry at 93. I think in that respect, times have really changed: 81 truly is the new 61!

Bubby was from a town of about 10,000 called Terebovlya (Trembowla in Polish), in what was then the Austrian empire and is now the Ukraine. When economic and social conditions turned dismal for many of the Jews there, various members of my mother's family began joining the flood of Jewish immigration to the States. In fact, during the decade following the 1903 Kishinev pogrom in Russia, 1 million Jews immigrated to the USA. First, my great-grandfather came over and after testing the waters of these fine shores, sent for my bubby in 1906. She was 24, and was already the mother a two year old—my grandma Fannie. Of course, they could never have predicted how much worse life for the Jews in Europe would get. In 1942, the Nazis liquidated the Jewish population from Trembowla and in 1943, over 1,100 of the town's 1,486 Jews were murdered by Germans in a nearby village.

My Bubby lived in the US from when she arrived in 1906 until her death in 1963. She never learned English, preferring to speak only in Yiddish. She came from a very religious Jewish family and remained quietly devout throughout her life here in the States, even though her four kids did not. She davened [prayed] regularly and when she died, I was proud to receive her High Holiday prayer books. On the inside cover, written in a childish, tentative scrawl, was her American name: "Tillie Bodian." I remember her tending to her plants and cooking for the Jewish holidays in her old-world, eastern European style. She made a kind of white blintz called "verenikas" for Shavuot. We loved when she baked individual small challahs for us kids and made her "raisin wine" to drink on Passover. (I have not drunk or seen "raisin wine" since she died and I believe the recipe went along with her.) Before Rosh Hashanah, our only bathtub was temporarily off-limits because Bubby had a live carp swimming around in it, which would be served during one of the meals. Her only true "Americanism" was her love of professional wrestling: she would sit with us and watch as Bruno Sammartino, Gorilla Monsoon and Cowboy Billy Watts tossed each other around the ring (and sometimes outside of it).

Unlike almost all of my friends, I had American parents, so English was always the primary language in our home, not just for the kids but for the adults, as well. Although we were fairly fluent in Hebrew by the age of 5 due to our Yeshiva day schooling, we never formally learned any Yiddish. So when my parents or grandparents didn't want us to understand what they were talking about, they would shift to Yiddish—their secret code. And of course, when my folks or grandma spoke to Bubby, it was always in her native tongue, which my father spoke well and my mom spoke haltingly. Although I never became fluent in Yiddish, over time, I was able to decipher some key phrases. I was the "groisser" as in the older one, David was the "kleiner" or small one, and Steve, ever the middle child, was the "anderer" — the other one. But my younger brothers were, well, younger, so the linguistic confusion produced unusual, and occasionally hilarious, results. Bubby was constantly looking for her "shteken," her cane, which was often left hanging from the top of one door or another. I recall going into our corner grocery store, Lippers, during Christmas season, with my mom and Steve, who must have been about three years old. When he saw the oversized candy canes among the display of holiday cheer, he exclaimed, "I want a Christmas shteken!"

Bubby had a soft spot for us kids, even when we acted up. Steve was a particularly rambunctious child, but lucky for him, Bubby was always his great protector. Steve often used little David as an outlet for his wild streak. Inevitably, you would hear my mom yell, *"What happened?!"* and David, just learning to talk, would struggle to answer back, *"Teedy [Steven] happened!"* My parents, like others of their generation, would often then apply the old "spare the rod, spoil the child" theory of discipline. My kind-hearted Bubby, on the other hand, did not similarly subscribe. Before my parents had a chance to corral the perpetrator, Bubby would start yelling at the top of her lungs, *"Shlugimnisht, shlugimnisht, shlugimnisht!"* [*"don't hit him, don't hit him, don't hit him!"*] One day, Steve and I were with our mom at the Lippers' store. Mrs. Lipper reveled in the fact that I was attending a Jewish day school and she asked Steve (who was still just a toddler and had not yet started school) if he knew his Jewish name. Without batting an eyelash, Steve said, *"Yes, my Jewish name is 'Shlugimnisht'."*

I am sorry that Bubby did not live longer. I don't know if she would have been capable of walking to shul for my bar mitzvah, in fact, I doubt it. But I can say with confidence that she would have been proud. In college, I took a couple of semesters of Yiddish and it would have been fun to try it out on her. Maybe I would have learned about what life was really like for my mother's side of the family, and their Jewish community, in Eastern Europe during the 19th century — real "Fiddler on the Roof" stuff. Still, thanks to my Bubby, I was the only one of my friends who experienced four generations under one roof, and she played a key role in our unique family dynamic.

SHABBOS WITH THE
ALLMAN BROTHERS BAND

"Well, the train to Grinder's Switch is runnin' right on time
And them Tucker Boys are cookin' down in Caroline,
People down in Florida can't be still
When ol' Lynyrd Skynrd's pickin' down in Jacksonville
People down in Georgia come from near and far
To hear Richard Betts pickin' on that red guitar".
Charlie Daniels, "The South's Gonna Do It" ©

Jelly Roll Morton famously boasted that he "invented jazz" but in fact, few, if any, musicians can rightfully claim to have created a specific genre of music. Music, art and culture just do not work that way. That does not mean that certain artists are not the undisputed leaders or even fathers of the movements with which they are associated. When Gregg Allman was told that the Allman Brothers Band was at the vanguard of the "southern rock" movement, he disparaged the term, declaring it redundant and comparing it to "rock rock." But Gregg's protestations notwithstanding, ever since he and his elder brother Duane came out of Jacksonville, Florida in 1969, the Allman Brothers Band were and remain the heavyweight champions, if not the actual creators, of that distinctive branch in the rock world's family tree. In five days, I will be seeing the great, venerable band for what will likely be my final time at The Beacon Theater and very possibly, my final time, period.

The Brothers began hitting The Beacon in 1989 and their extended annual March runs at the City's premier rock venue have long been a cherished part of the New York City musical calendar. I can't say I have been there every year, but I can say that I have been there often enough to have witnessed many changes in personnel and in vibe over the years. For instance, I have seen them play the Beacon with, without, with and ultimately without Dickey Betts and his fire-red Gibson. All told, there have been 222 Beacon shows before the current run and I have probably seen about 20 of them (although I bet that our pal Ray Glenn has been to about 215 of them.)

Alas, boys and girls, once upon a time, it was not so easy, so commonplace and so darn convenient to see the Allman Brothers Band. Certainly, it was impossible to see them in such a "user-friendly" venue as The Beacon. I'm talking about how we've gotten spoiled catching the ABB for annual weeks-long residencies, in a 2,800-seat Broadway palace, with state-of-the-art sound, perfect sightlines, new seats, full bars, almost-sufficient restrooms and more official memorabilia than you could afford. Let's not forget that this was a band that along with The Dead and The Band, drew 600,000 people to the upstate backwater boondocks of Watkins Glen, NY during the summer of 1973. I could just imagine what the "amenities" were like there. My first Brothers show was one huge hassle—probably making today's treks to Phish shows seem like a walk in the park—but there was no choice back then. Actually, it never would have even occurred to us that seeing a band as great as The Allman Brothers was supposed to be easy; the sweltering heat in a blighted locale-that was the way the deal went down.

As best as I remember, it was during 1972 when the brothers Eidman began to hear the brothers Allman on FM radio. The band's distinctive double-lead guitar coursed through WNEW staples such as "Whippin' Post," "Statesboro Blues" and "One Way Out." By 1973, I had become a serious concert-goer, thanks to being 18 and in possession of a driver's license, not to mention my parents' generosity with their car keys. 1973 saw me catch up with Traffic, the Dead, Faces, the New Riders and a few other stars of that majestic era. On September 27, 1973, dorky Don Kirshner featured The Allman Brothers Band on his vastly underrated show "Don Kirshner's Rock Concert.[1]" Unlike most rock music, the performance came across surprisingly well on the little black and white TV in our bedroom and we were hooked[2].

It was not until 1974 when we finally got our chance to check them out live. It was going to be two nights, Friday and Saturday June 7 and 8, at Roosevelt Stadium, a decrepit, former minor league ballpark located deep within the armpit of pre-gentrified Jersey City. We had never been there before but we knew that The Dead and The Band, amongst others, had previously graced this dilapidated venue. Given the enormity of Duane's talent and legend, we were well aware that we had forever missed our opportunity to see the ABB at the peak of its prodigious powers. At this point, most of our favorite rock performers had peaked already.[3] But that was OK; we were

---

[1] I believe that it was also on Don Kirshner's show that I first discovered the astounding stage presence and intense style of Van Morrison, whose music I had heard for years but not fully appreciated. So, thank you very, very much, Mr. Don Kirshner!

[2] Ironically, when I recently watched the 23 minute performance (and you can see it on You Tube), I was struck by the relatively tepid quality of the band's performance in what were still the doldrums of the post-Duane and Berry Oakley period. (Founding members Duane Allman and Berry Oakley had died in motorcycle accidents in 1971 and 1972). For a real treat and assuming that you can bear the frustrating cinematography, check out the original band, with the brilliant Duane Allman, on September 23, 1970 at the Fillmore East, also available on You Tube as of this writing.

[3] In fact, by the time I first saw Dylan (1974), The Rolling Stones (1975), The Band (1974), Traffic (1973) and probably The Grateful Dead (1973), they were also beyond their creative and/or performance zeniths. (I did

excited and were not going to miss seeing one of these ABB shows.

There was one major logistical issue with June 7 and 8, 1974. Those dates fell on Friday and Saturday nights, so it was virtually impossible to see either show without violating Shabbos. At that time of the year, Shabbos began at about 8 pm on Friday and extended to about 9 pm on Saturday night. But "virtually impossible" is not the same thing as "impossible" and we knew we could figure out a way. We managed to score 4 tickets for the Saturday night show. I was going to go with my brother Steve and his friends Alan "Schuch" Schuchalter and Sol Merkin. (Sol had a con artist's knack for finagling our last ticket to the best shows but I'm not sure how Schuch got to come along for this ride.) I was 19 and my brother and his friends were 17, so I didn't need to be reminded by my mom that if anyone was going to be the responsible adult on this trip, it would be me. Well, maybe I did need to be reminded.

Roosevelt Stadium was a "general admission only" type of place, with "festival seating" throughout the infield and outfield. Given the fact that "festival seating" is concert-speak for "no seating," leaving Queens after shabbos seemed too risky. As fate had it, a family friend owned some real estate near the concert venue, in a neighborhood that was still more than a quarter century away from the beginnings of gentrification. In fact, it was probably still several decades before the word "gentrification" had entered the lexicon. We were given permission to use a vacant apartment in one of his buildings there; it was unfurnished and probably had no electricity, but

---

see Springsteen at his absolute best, in February 1975, well before the Boss replaced drama and spontaneity with scripted shtick. And it is very difficult to pinpoint a specific high-point for the venerable Neil Young, who I caught on his Rust Never Sleeps tour and the one before that. And if Billy Joel is still your thing, I saw him way before his peak, at Max's Kansas City in November 1973.)

what was the big deal? We'd bring sleeping bags and a cooler of food and we'd be good to go. After Friday night dinner, we could walk over to the Stadium and hang around, taking in the vibe and listening to the music from outside. Then on Saturday, we'd be able to observe shabbos, in a manner of speaking, which in this context meant not driving, not using electricity and eating chicken that we bought on Friday morning at our favorite kosher take-out place.

Steve and I were given the thankless task of driving to Manhattan in brutal Friday afternoon summer traffic to pick up the other guys. We were in my mother's cherry red 1972 Buick Skylark with the white vinyl top. While my parents knew exactly what their eldest sons were up to, the Merkins and Schuchalters were under the impression that their children were spending shabbos in the friendly confines of the Eidman home, where the worst thing their boys might conceivably do was to get to shul late or G-d forbid, play tennis on shabbos. While it is said that ignorance is bliss, the fact remains that it is still ignorance. So, off we went, on our excellent adventure.

In this pre-GPS and pre-google maps era, it took quite a while to slowly navigate our way to our weekend pied-à-terre in the unfamiliar environs of gritty downtown Jersey City. We reached the building—a dingy walk-up—about a half-hour before shabbos. We schlepped our stuff upstairs and I flipped on the light switch. The good news was that, lo and behold, the electricity worked. The bad news was that as soon as the lights went on, a myriad of creepy and crawly things, large insects and small rodents alike, scurried for cover. The sight of miscellaneous vermin and tiny paws gave us pause, to say the least. After the initial shock subsided, we silently surveyed the depressing premises and considered our situation and limited options. One of my young compatriots, probably Sol, balked at the prospect of sleeping in an apartment that would have been too dreary for Robert De Niro's character in "Mean Streets." I was reminded of an "Odd Couple" episode when Oscar Madison had refurnished and a distraught Felix Unger commented, "*Even Ratso Rizzo had a cuter apartment.*"

Although I was still 5 years away from my law degree, I rationally argued that (a) we would not be spending much time in the place; (b) it was now only 15 minutes until shabbos; and (c) we had no plan B. Since such impeccable logic failed to sway Sol, I channeled the doomed Drew character in "Deliverance" and put my faith in the democratic process. I bravely asked, "*Who votes not to stay here tonight?*" Within a nanosecond, three hands shot up. Like Drew, I accepted defeat stoically, if not happily. I turned off the lights, tacitly relinquishing sovereignty over the abode back to the denizens of the insect and varmint worlds, and we left.

1974 was well before venues began charging for the privilege of parking at the venue, to ensure that you actually went inside to enjoy the event. So even though our tickets were for the following night, we were free to park at the sprawling outdoor lot at Roosevelt Stadium. We heard live music spilling out from inside the stadium; it was one of the supporting acts, either the ponderous southern boogie band, Grinderswitch, or the terrific country blues of the Marshall Tucker Band. We were parked quite a distance from the stadium and we walked closer so that we could better hear the show. At some point, I returned to retrieve something from the car; on my way back, I could see from a distance that my young cohorts were no longer a party of three. Steve, Sol and Shuch had already made a new friend. As I neared, I was horrified to see the four of them standing in a tight circle, passing around and swigging from an incredibly large, unlabeled bottle containing a disreputable looking purple drink. The new guy, a cheerful, stoner type, did not strike me as the kind of person who was into artisanal winemaking. The bottle was so large, spherical and unwieldy that they were having trouble lifting it up to their mouths. I jumped right into the circle, grabbed the bottle as best as I could, while yelling, *"Are you guys crazy, do you even have any idea what you're drinking?!"* The guys tried to explain to me that their new friend was "cool" – in fact, he had already renamed Schuch "Cool Breeze", owing to Schuch's uber mellow affect.

After I succeeded in extricating Steve, Sol and Cool Breeze, we moved on. It was a pleasant night and we hung out in the darkness listening to the Brothers. An old set list shows that the boys opened with "Wasted Words," the first cut from the most recent album, "Brothers and Sisters." Then, the band moved through six consecutive numbers featuring Gregg on vocals—something very unlikely to happen nowadays. Interestingly, they closed the show with three consecutive instrumentals, "Les Brers in A Minor," "Hot 'Lanta" and an extended "Mountain Jam" (as if they ever tried a non-extended version). After the show, Steve and I slept in the car. (As for Sol and Schuch, I assume they spread out their sleeping bags and slept on the hard blacktop beneath the stars, but frankly, I have no idea.) The night was peaceful except for one disturbance when a cop knocked on the window with his flashlight, rousing us. Luckily, all he did was shine the light into our car and move on.

Not surprisingly, we were up bright and early. Sol was the first to rise, because during the night, he was bitten on the lower lip by a nocturnal insect causing his lower jaw to swell to twice its normal size. (Sol never was the camping type.) With nothing better to do, we decided to line up close to the entrance, in order to ensure a good spot once the doors opened. Amazingly, many, many others had the exact same idea. Before long, the huddled masses were assembled by the thousands, at first leaning and then pressing against the shuttered front gates of the creaky old ballpark. At noon, after what seemed an interminable amount of time, the doors were finally flung open. There was a sudden rush of humanity; without any conscious effort of our own, we were carried through the gates by a wave of surging bodies, our feet off the ground. I'll admit, it was somewhat scary.

Once inside the decaying edifice, we dragged our blankets and cooler toward the middle of the field and claimed a vacant patch of dirt in what I would approximate as being right behind second base. Not too shabby. June 8, 1974—in my memory—was a sultry summer day with bright sun. By mid-afternoon, we had become quite uncomfortable in the stifling Jersey City humidity[1]. We were happy to have our trusty red cooler, which went everywhere with us in the pre 9/11 world. It was packed with drinks and with a couple of Mauzone southern fried chicken specials.

The crowd was friendly but the long day, the sun and substances were beginning to have an effect on the general demeanor. At about 3:00 p.m., two cute blonde girls came over to hang out, which was as good a way as any to break up the monotony. I talked to the girls for a while but my mind drifted as I surveyed the huge crowd that had by now packed the ballpark, all the way through the outfield and well into the stands. The fact of the matter is that I was never really a festival guy, what with the unruly crowds, poor conditions, sub-par sound, unavoidable traffic, port-a-potties, etc. At least there was a steady stream of good music playing that afternoon through the sound system. At one point they played The Band's second album in its entirety and Van's "Moondance" record as well. It was a good day for a daydream but when I returned to earth, the

---

[1] Weather records, however, tell a far different story. In fact, the temperature that day ranged from a brisk low of 61 degrees to a downright pleasant high of 77. In fairness to my beleaguered memory, it is possible that it felt much hotter within the packed stadium, on the overheated infield. (I recall when the Mets first visited the old Busch Stadium in St. Louis when it opened in 1966, and the local press asked Casey Stengel what he thought of the new stadium. The "Old Perfesser," trying to be diplomatic, said that it "seemed to hold in the heat real well").

two cute blonde girls were gone, as quickly as they had appeared. This was not unusual, as people were constantly coming and going, hanging out for a while then moving on. What was unusual was that our fried chicken had disappeared along with them. Oh well, we'd be home in another 10 or 12 hours anyway…

Roosevelt Stadium, waiting on 'The Brothers', photo ©jerseycityonline.com

At 5:00 p.m., it was finally time for some live music. The first band was Grinderswitch, a boring, southern boogie blues band that often toured with and opened for the Brothers. They never developed a following of their own and were undoubtedly the weak link in the stable of Capricorn Records acts who sprouted up around the Allman Brothers Band. But during the middle '70's, if you were seeing the Brothers, you had to assume that you'd be enduring an unmemorable opening set from Grinderswitch. Steve vividly recalls people in the crowd tossing bottles. Yes, the natives were getting a mite restless.

The Marshall Tucker Band must have gone on next, although I have no memory of hearing them (which can absolutely be chalked up to the passage of time rather than the ingestion of any illegal or legal substances). It is strange that I remember Grinderswitch but am drawing a blank on MTB, one of my favorite bands of that era, a band that always rose to the occasion when faced with the daunting task of playing in front of the Allman Brothers Band. MTB had the songs, the musicians, singers and presence to make it all happen. If the Brothers' take on southern rock was slanted towards the blues, the late Caldwell Brothers and other members of the Marshall Tucker Band leaned a little more towards the country side. Later that same year, we caught them at the Felt Forum (now the Theater at Madison Square Garden) in a classic triple-bill, along with the James Cotton Band and Charlie Daniels.

After another seemingly interminable break, it was time for the Allman Brothers Band. As of June 1974, they may have been the best band in the country—and the crowd was well past ready. By now, most of the audience had been waiting for many hours and the alcohol, grass and who knows what else had taken its toll. So, just after 10 p.m., when the band quietly shuffled onstage and assumed their positions behind their instruments, it was none too soon.

By now, Shabbos had ended, not with the traditional Ma'ariv (evening) service or with the candle-lit recitation of the Havdalah prayer but on its own terms, in a quiet, unnoticed manner. Certainly, we had not celebrated Shabbos as we normally would have and perhaps should have, with the traditional meals, synagogue services and a few words of rabbinic wisdom. But as teenagers, we managed to keep within certain admittedly wide boundaries of observance, as we arrived at the venue before Shabbos and remained there until afterwards, while we refrained from cooking, driving or using electrical devices. Throughout the ensuing decades, when I am on vacation and away from my community and synagogue during Shabbos, I have, on occasion, been tempted to stray. That is when I think back to my Shabbos with the Allman Brothers Band, which in a weird way, continues to serve as a signpost of my own personal outer limits for such occasions. (But I remain a firm believer that each person must make his or her own decision about such spiritual matters.)

The boys took their time tuning and settling in, while Gregg surveyed the scene of post-hippie sprawl. From behind his Hammond organ, he then leaned into the mike and slowly drawled, *"I see y'all got your campin' equipment, we might just play all night."* If anyone had been dragging just a bit, that served as a wake-up call. After soaking in the roar of approval from the tens of thousands, the band was off and running.

They kicked it off with "Don't Want You No More/It's Not My Cross to Bear." Gregg's voice was strong and pure. By now it was nearly three years since Duane's sudden passing, and Dickey Betts had matured into his role as the sole guitarist. In songs such as "Wasted Words" and "Jessica," his Gibson cut through the summer night. Betts was on fire, trading licks with pianist Chuck Leavell on a blistering "One Way Out." Betts' name is now (and has been for many years) included amongst the world's great guitarists. Lamar Williams had replaced Berry Oakley on bass and would excel until his untimely death from lung cancer caused by his exposure to Agent Orange, while serving in Vietnam. The band had recently brought in Leavell, and his freewheeling piano style brought a jazzier element into the mix, especially on some of the newer songs such as "Southbound." The two drummers, Jaimo and Butch Trucks, had been the constants, along with Gregg, throughout the long history of the ABB. This was the first time that I had the chance to see them do their polyrhythmic thing. I still recall the powerful, clear vocals by Gregg on "Midnight Rider" and on the T-Bone Walker standard, "Stormy Monday."

About three hours after it began, the band came out for an encore. Gregg had me going when he said something about playing an *"old Swedish love song"* and I wondered what that could be. But before I knew it, Williams' bass was rolling with the opening, portentous rumble of one of rock music's most reliable show-stoppers, "Whippin' Post."

After the elongated ending of "Whipping Post" had finally faded out (after about 15 minutes), we began to make our way out of Roosevelt Stadium, amid thousands of dazed, tired and blitzed fans. The vast majority were in far less than optimal condition. When I was halfway between the infield and the stadium exit at the center field wall, one stumbling, mumbling, bedraggled, incoherent fan, with matted, long, straggly blonde hair and a beer bottle in his hand, fell across my shoulder, nearly knocking me down. As I instinctively pulled away from him in semi-terror, he asked me, *"hey man, ya' doin' any mescaline?"* (I wasn't.) It had been a very, very long 32 hours and if I had not been ready to go home before that moment, I sure was now.

We tunneled our way from Jersey into Manhattan and then, somehow, I accidentally steered us up onto the Brooklyn Bridge. It was very late, and I was exhausted. I did not want to go to Brooklyn, so I pulled the move I had seen work well in The Godfather Part I—you know, when Michael Corleone was being driven to the sit-down at that nice, family restaurant in the Bronx, where Sal Tessio's people had connections and there was an old-style toilet with a box and chain… Screeching through the U-turn on the deserted bridge, we returned to Manhattan, then headed uptown to drop off the two city guys. Steve and I arrived safely home in Bayside shortly after 3:00 a.m. As we walked upstairs to our bedroom, I suddenly thought of my parents, grandma and youngest brother, all having gone to sleep hours ago. I thought to myself: it's nice to be back in a clean, quiet house where no one was throwing bottles, stealing fried chicken or doing any mescaline.

In the ensuing years, I saw the Allman Brothers Band many times. But they were never better than that first time. I can say the same thing about my first Dylan, Dead, Rolling Stones, Lou Reed and Springsteen concerts. That's probably because we have no idea how great these giants really are until we finally see them in the flesh, at which time they inevitably exceed our expectations. So the first time is always amazing and special, even if when the stars are past their prime.

In researching this essay, I discovered that the set-list for June 8, 1974 seems to have been lost to the mists of time, although one does exist for the show on June 7. By contrast, fans taking in the current Beacon run can leave each show with an authorized, sound-board recording of the concert—just one more revenue stream that bands probably did not even dare to dream about in 1974. (Then again, in 1974, they were making the kind of money selling records that today's bands can only dream about.) As for me, I could not have predicted in 1974 that forty years later, my pal Danny and I would be taking in one final Brothers show from our seat in the back of the Beacon's loge. I also could not have imagined that two of my sons, both home from college during spring break, would also be somewhere in the house with their friends. It was my youngest son Benjamin's first Allman Brothers show. Two years earlier, he played bass in a band whose repertoire included a faithful cover of "Southbound." My two older boys had already seen the ABB, and I was glad that Benjamin now had his opportunity before the band called it a day. We got together after the show and all agreed that it had been a real good one. Ray Glenn confirmed our reviews, saying it had been *"a night of great music, not greatest hits"*. Well said.

What exactly did my sons and I get to see and hear that night? Well, let's just say that it was not their father's Allman Brothers Band. The spiritual leader, Gregg had weathered the storms and had finally grown gracefully into his role as a supporting player. Still, from the opening lines of the Muddy Waters cover "Trouble No More," right through the "Southbound" encore, his bluesy vocals sounded remarkably undiminished by the ravages of time, trauma and illness. For years now, the ABB had been carried by the interplay and contrasting styles of two brilliant guitarists on loan from other bands: the slashing Warren Haynes and the slide genius Derek Trucks. We thoroughly enjoyed watching them do their thing on "One Way Out," with Robert Randolph sitting in on pedal steel, on "Stand Back" and on a joyous "Mountain Jam." The hefty price of admission suddenly seemed insignificant. As a bonus for us fans of The Band, Haynes sung a beautifully rendered version of "It Makes No Difference," with the Juke Horns lending soulful support.

The bottom line is that 45 years after the ABB first began its journey, it has remained true to its roots, right down to the bittersweet end. And despite the dearth of strong new material, The Brothers remained a killer live act, not a mere parody of its former self. Unfortunately, illness prevented Gregg from completing the Beacon run, with the band carrying on without him for a couple of shows, then postponing the final shows for about six months. When those last performances finally take place, I am certain that Ray Glenn will be in the house. As for me, I will always have June 8, 1974.

MUSKY FISHING ON THE
ST. LAWRENCE RIVER

"Three years sailing on bended knee,
We found no whales in the sea"
Pappalardi/Collins, "Nantucket Sleighride"©

Sometimes the most exciting part of fishing is the pursuit of a rare, difficult fish, which even if located, will in all likelihood, not even bite. Musky fishing is a prime example of this fishing paradox. When we went musky fishing, we fished by maintaining the boat at a mindlessly boring slow, steady troll, with the rods placed securely into rod holders attached to the sides of the boat. You don't hold the rods because on the odd chance that a musky does bite, it would not only pull the rod right out of your hand and into the river but would possibly dislodge your humerus from its socket, in the process. So, the act of trolling for muskies is usually a long, dull boat ride, sitting on the seat, doing hardly anything except waiting. Still, the very thought of a musky, a muskellunge, silently eyeing our lure deep beneath the surface, made the expedition as adventurous as we could have hoped.

Muskies are the undisputed king of the pike family and the largest and fiercest freshwater game fish. They can weigh close to 70 pounds, are difficult to hook and once hooked are prodigious fighters. Like all pike, their jaws are lined by rows and rows of tiny razor teeth. They are solitary stalkers, each patrolling a large area of a northern river or lake, searching for unwary fish or even the odd rodent unlucky enough to have tumbled into the water.

It is the summer of 1970: I am 15 and finally getting my shot at a musky. My brothers and I were raised on pickerel fishing, the musky's much smaller and more common cousin, but we had heard tales of this mysterious, scary predator, this freshwater barracuda. My folks have taken us along on their annual trek up to the St. Lawrence River, near Massena, NY, in search of northern pike, walleye, smallmouth bass and of course, musky. We had come along the previous summer but were deemed too young to accompany my father and his trusted Akwesasne Native American fishing guide, Tony Barnes, as they trolled in the deep churning currents alongside the Eisenhower Dam spanning the St. Lawrence. That previous summer, after several unsuccessful expeditions, my dad had finally caught his first musky, a 28-pounder. Our mom, who often accompanied dad and who managed to squeeze in some fishing amid her knitting and reading on the boat, had already landed muskies on two prior trips. So now, it is finally my turn. My first day out for musky is probably the most highly anticipated morning of my life, up to that point. Including my bar mitzvah.

We leave our rented trailer while it is still dark and quite cool. After loading the boat, Tony guns the big motor for about a half-hour run up the river, as we silently watch the sun rise. Even though it is August, I am shivering a bit. Because we will be trolling—that is, trailing lures along both sides of the boat as it slowly moves through the river—only two fishermen can fish at once, lest lines get tangled. So my brother Steve and I alternate on the 4 mornings of musky fishing, two days for each of us. Alas, my folks deem my 10 year-old brother David too young for musky. (Of course, he will eventually get his revenge by out-fishing us all, by a wide margin, throughout the ensuing years.)

We are using large, carved wooden plugs, about 9 inches in length, prehistoric in appearance, each armed with three sets of sharp treble hooks. These lures are designed to be trolled down deep, where muskies are more likely to be found during the hot summer. Truthfully, the dog days of August are probably the worst times to chase muskies, who, even during the best conditions, are notoriously unpredictable and finicky eaters.

Once the plugs are attached to the lines and the two spinning rods are placed into the rod holders on either side of the 16 foot boat, Tony puts the motor into a slow troll and the only sound that disturbs the silence is the steady chugga-chugga. So, basically, we troll and wait. You are not busying yourself by casting a lure (as they do in the Wisconsin musky lakes) or by moving a bait around or by changing flies to match a hatch or by wading downstream or by doing any of the myriad tasks that typically keep an angler occupied while waiting for the fish to (figuratively) wake up. Yet somehow, the mere anticipation of the ghost-like musky, a fish that will likely not show up at all, prevents this from becoming a mind-numbing exercise and instead, keeps everyone alert with all senses heightened.

Suddenly, the line in the rod-holder next to me starts to scream and peel out in rapid fashion. Now, in some forms of fishing, there is no doubt when a fish, especially a large one, strikes. While quietly drifting upon the flats down in the Florida Keys and a 100 pound tarpon grabs a baited hook or floating fly, the only question is whether you are hooked up with a tarpon or with a sub-aquatic runaway train. Or when a healthy rainbow trout grabs your dry-fly, goes air-borne and takes off upstream, there's no doubt as to what is going on and the only question is whether your technique and composure are up to the challenge. But when trolling a plug bearing 9 sharp hooks over thickly weeded waters from a moving boat, there is always a possibility that the sound of the screeching reel has been caused by the plug running aground while the boat continues to move on. So, Tony Barnes puts his cigarette into his mouth and lets it dangle there as he lifts the rod from its holder, holds it at a 45 degree angle while the line continues to spool out and contemplates what a life's worth of experience is communicating to him. I have no clue as to what he is sensing. He then hands the rod to me and tells me to strike "real hard" because there is a fish on.

I do as told, pulling up fast and hard and then he tells me do it again, in order to account for the particularly tough mouth of a musky. Now, I feel the fish. Sometimes, a large fish rockets to the surface and leaps in an effort to throw the hook. Many years later, in Labrador, I managed to lose a series of beautiful landlocked salmon, each one repeatedly hurtling into the air while shaking its head side-to-side, using the weight of the small lure to successfully dislodge it. But that is not the case with this fish. Instead, I feel a series of heavy, dull tugs each one pulling further down to the depths of the St. Lawrence. I have no recollection of my father's customary panicky shouts, warning me of everything that I was doing to surely lose the fish. I do recall Tony positioning the boat favorably, in order to afford me every possible chance to land it. After fighting a while, the fish finally lands safely on board and I have the bittersweet feeling of having caught what was up until that point the largest freshwater fish of my young life—but not a musky. It is a hefty 9-pound walleye, with beautiful, golden tones and it remains the largest walleye I have ever landed. It is the only fish we catch that morning, and two days later when I punch another ticket in the musky lottery, I once again come up empty.

The final day of musky fishing belongs to my brother Steve and my dad, while I remain behind with David and my mom. At about 11:00 a.m., I scamper down to the dock to await their return, because within minutes of their arrival, we will all be heading back out for bass and pike. I see Tony's boat zipping over the choppy surface, right in the middle of the wide river, coming from my left. While it is still in the middle of the St. Lawrence but directly opposite the dock and about several hundred yards away, it slows to a troll. I shake my head as I have seen this movie so many times before. It is time for the closing credits but my father can never resist one last cast, drift or in this case, troll right in front of the dock. They have fished Tony's favorite musky spot alongside the dam without so much as a single strike in four hours, but my dad always believes in that one last try, even if the odds are one in a million, because you just never know. My mind wanders as I begin to contemplate how the rest of the day's fishing might unfold. Then, I notice something happening on the boat. I cannot hear voices from this distance but I see people leaning over the side of the boat that is blocked from my line of vision, their backs to me. I see an indistinct object being lifted into the boat, with great effort. After what seems to be an eternity, my father and Tony notice me standing at the edge of the dock and Tony lifts a very large fish.

Later, we will learn that my Dad's big musky weighed in at a hefty 37 pounds, ultimately making it the second largest musky caught in the State of New York in 1970. My dad will have it mounted and it will spend many years on the wall in my parents'  basement until their art collection invades even that prized spot.

Decades later, at my folks' country place, there will be two photos of this fish: one of my dad, Tony and Steve, all holding the trophy fish, none of them smiling, as if it was all in a day's work. The other photo will be taken over 40 years later and will show Steve and me holding the mounted (but deteriorating) musky, just before taking it to the dump. Many years of proud and shared history will be etched into our smiles.

Photo courtesy of Florence & Seymour Eidman

Some 45 years have now passed since that fish was landed and I am still waiting for my first musky. Throughout the intervening decades, we have enjoyed several family fishing trips in search of everything from winter steelhead in the Niagara River to tarpon in the Florida Keys to native brook trout in Labrador. Sadly, especially for the Akwesasne, fishing pressure, pollution and a naturally occurring virus affected musky fishing up around Massena, NY, although a catch and release program has been successful in reversing the trend. Still, I've heard that Heyward, Wisconsin is now the musky capital, the guides there work pretty cheap and that the fall is the best time to get the big ones...

FM

"Everybody's restless and they've got no place to go,
Someone's always trying to tell them something they already know,
So their anger and resentment flow.
But don't it make you want to rock and roll, all night long,
Mohammed's Radio,
I heard somebody singing sweet and soulful, on the radio,
Mohammed's Radio."
Warren Zevon, "Mohammed's Radio"©

    I was 15 years old and we were inexplicably spending the first half of the long, hot summer in the city. And my mood was absolutely nothing like the Lovin' Spoonful's "Summer in the City." As much as our Mom tried to keep us busy, there was little action because all of our friends were away at summer camp. My brother Steve and I spent endless afternoons holed up in the room we shared, listening to all the hits on AM radio and to our tepid collection of albums and singles on whatever tinny equipment we then owned.

    As far as I knew, the music scene during the summer of 1970 was dominated by up-beat pop hits and heavier soul numbers. The former included Freda Payne's "Band of Gold," Vanity Fare's "Hitchin' a Ride," Blue Cheer's "Ride, Captain, Ride" and Three Dog Night's rollickin' cover of Randy Newman's "Mama Told Me Not to Come." The soul side offered up the Jackson 5 ("The Love You Save"), Stevie Wonder ("Signed, Sealed, Delivered"), Edwin Starr ("War") and the white soul of Eric Burdon and Rare Earth ("Spill the Wine" and "Get Ready"). The Temptations were right there, with their amazing, genre-crunching "Ball of Confusion," which resided on the pop charts somewhat uncomfortably alongside the unabashed schmaltz of The Carpenters ("Close to You") and every teenage girl's dream band, Bread ("Make it With You"). Finally, some old reliables were still charting, with Paul and The Beatles brooding down "The Long & Winding Road," while Elvis soldiered on with "The Wonder of You." I am intentionally ignoring the usual smorgasbord of one-hit wonders—and there were some big ones that summer. Okay, here's one you might have forgotten: "Which Way You Goin' Billy" by The Poppy Family.

At about that time, I acquired a new portable radio. For the life of me, I cannot recall its source, whether it was a gift, whether I had saved up for it or what. It was incapable of stereo reception but it pulled in the main FM stations without the static of the transistor radio that I had received two years earlier for my bar mitzvah, from State Senator Joe Zaretski. I took it out of the box on a sweltering summer afternoon and I absent-mindedly flipped the toggle switch from the AM position to FM, then slowly began to rotate the dial, from left to right.

Now, I had been addicted to pop music radio on the AM side since 1964 and was familiar with the AM jocks and each one's zany shtick, whether it was Cousin Brucie, Wolfman Jack or whoever. In fact, my friends and I prided ourselves on eschewing the ever-popular WABC in favor of the cooler alternative, independently-owned WMCA (570 on your dial) and its stable of "Good Guys" jocks. (My best friend Danny even managed to win a highly coveted "Good Guys" sweatshirt, but that's another story). The WMCA Good Guys included Harry Harrison, Jack Spector, Dino "On Your Radio" Valenti, and of course, "Dandy" Dan Daniels. My favorite was Gary Stevens and his inscrutable creature-partner, The Wooleyburger.

But as easily as I flipped the toggle switch on my new radio, I just as surely had fallen through an imaginary trap-door and into an alternate universe. As I slowly turned the FM dial, I heard beautiful classical music, free-form jazz and some musical genres that seemed to be from distant planets. I heard lively political debate and neo-revolutionary rantings. Eventually, the dial slid onto 102.7 and thanks to WNEW FM's strong signal, I finally heard something familiar. It was the unmistakable and gorgeous organ intro to "A Whiter Shade of Pale." I knew it instantly because it had been getting lots of AM radio play. I stopped turning the dial. After Gary Brooker's vocal finally faded out, something unexpected occurred. Instead of the mile-a-minute antics of a DJ or a string of bland commercials, another song came right on. This one did not ring a bell but its texture, tone and mood made it seem like the only song that should ever follow "A Whiter Shade of Pale." I wish I could remember what it was. I remember thinking it was strange that a rock music station was playing a song that was definitely not one of that week's top selling singles, according to the survey of local record sales.

Then things got even weirder: a third consecutive song came on and this one seemed to stretch out for a good seven or eight minutes. The Rolling Stones were then considered marathon men because their singles often pushed a bit past the three-minute mark, but this was crazy stuff. Finally, after about twenty minutes of non-stop music there was a five seconds pause and then, a velvety baritone voice broke through the radio silence, telling the listeners the name of the guitarist who had played the long solo on the last song, when it had been recorded and where, and even the label it was on. This voice was not yelling or trying to sell anything. Its owner managed to seem both casual and obsessive-compulsive, affecting the manner of someone who was pretty tired, maybe hung-over and just a trifle bored at having to explain the A, B, C's to a neophyte. He seemed anxious to get back to playing music and whatever else he had been doing. First, he had to "take care of a little business," which meant playing a couple of pre-recorded commercials. But even these were few in number, short in duration and blissfully absent in hype. Like I said, an alternate universe, a bizzarro world—but a good one! And unlike AM with its flat, mono signal, FM broadcasts were in glorious stereo (which of course meant that we now needed to upgrade the primitive sonic capabilities of our little bedroom). I was amazed, shocked and dumbfounded that this world existed right there in my parents' house in Bayside, Queens, right underneath my nose and I had known nothing about it. I don't think that I ever flipped that switch back to AM, unless it was to listen to a ballgame. Unfortunately, we were still several years away from having FM radio in our family car.

Let me digress to recall another story about the change in my listening tastes that occurred during the same summer in which I discovered FM radio (1970): Back then, we bought most of our records at the E.J. Korvette's discount department store in Douglaston, Queens, which had a very respectable records department, or we sent for them by mail from the Columbia House Music Club. One afternoon, my mom dropped me off in Korvette's while she shopped. I had my mind set on buying "The Fifth Dimension's Greatest Hits." Sad, but true. By dumb luck, or perhaps on the strength of "Aquarius/Let the Sunshine In," Korvette's was sold out of that classic album. Of course, my $3.50 was burning a hole in my pocket, so I searched the walls of record albums on display for a substitute (and not "Substitute," which I doubt I had heard of back then). The clock was ticking, as my mom was returning soon to pick me up.

Suddenly, my eyes were drawn to something completely different. The album cover was an old-fashioned, faded black and white photograph of guys in cowboy gear on a brown background. The background was not the usual flat cardboard;

it was a raised, corrugated, bumpy material or fabric. I did not recognize the men in the photograph and the names of the artist and album also drew a blank. It read: "Crosby Stills Nash & Young: Déjà Vu."

I bought it on a lark, took it home and spent that summer wearing out its grooves, even as my grandmother mumbled *"funeral music, funeral music,"* every time Neil Young's "Helpless" came around on my portable turntable. The following year, Crosby, Stills, Nash & Young all decided to take a break from each other and record solo albums. Of course, I found out about that from the jocks on the FM stations, either 102.7 or possibly its competitor over at WPLJ.

There is no need to explain the power, ubiquity and cultural sway of FM radio to members of my generation or of "My Generation." For them, it goes without saying. And it is nearly

Daily News, 1974, featuring WNEW FM's Allison Steele, the Nightbird

impossible to explain it to today's millennials, Generation Y or whatever they are. Perhaps a story will help. In 1972, on a scorching summer's day, a troubled man named John Wojtowicz and his cohort took hostages at a Chase Manhattan Bank branch in Brooklyn, in what would eventually become the infamous "Dog Day Afternoon" debacle (and famous movie, starring Al Pacino and John Cazale). The attempted robbery was motivated by Wojtowicz's desire to fund a sex-change operation for his pre-op transsexual wife. This was decades before the acronym "LGBT" would enter the lexicon. Events predictably spiraled out of control even as the thieves' demands were transmitted to New York's Finest. Wojtowicz, a devoted music fan, called in to Scott

Muni, the respected afternoon host at 102.7, known as "The Professor." Instead of pulling the plug, the station "bosses," such as they were, let things roll live on the air. The Professor, in his trademark gravel-tones, kept the mood light and cool, while he and Wojtowicz discussed Dylan history and spun Grateful Dead music. An eerie, surreal episode for sure, but this was what FM radio in NYC, circa 1972, was all about.

Now, you youngsters have to understand that not only was there no internet then, there were no cell phones, no cable TV, no VCRs or DVDs, no "on-demand," and definitely no iTunes or file-sharing. Not only was there no social media but Al Gore had not, as of yet, even coined the phrase "social media." Instead, there were 6 TV stations, heaps of vinyl records, different types of tapes and live entertainment. We had some excellent rock magazines such as Rolling Stone and Crawdaddy but mainstream newspapers were not much interested in whether Creedence would be breaking up or when the next Traffic album was coming out, if ever. So how did kids find out about important stuff back then? With rare exception, the soul sources of accurate information were the FM radio jocks. They told us when and where Rolling Stones tickets would be going on sale; then, we all started calling each other (on landlines!!) before heading down to MSG to wait on line all night. That was precisely how we scored front row tickets for the Stones' shows at the Garden in June 1975. You could count on the jocks to clue us in about everything, from where the next "Stop the War" demonstration would be taking place to who the next "new Dylan" would be. (Okay, they were never right about that one). As for the old Dylan, I remember setting my alarm for 7am on a non-school day during January 1975, so that I would be able to hear and tape the world debut of "Blood on the Tracks," on 102.7. I remember hearing "Idiot Wind" for the first time and just thinking, "Man!"

FM music was the background and backdrop to our lives. We woke up to it, did our homework to it and barely turned it down while talking on the phone—or to our parents. This was the era when the phrase "generation gap" came into vogue and the FM jocks often served as our surrogate parents, adults speaking to us about the things that we actually wanted to hear, whether it was politics, literature or in the case of the erudite Jonathan Schwartz, baseball. (Back then, there were no sports radio stations, either). We knew the personalities, moods and musical tastes of each jock as if they were family, whether it was the (now) classic rock leanings of Dennis Elsas, the country-rock preferences of Pete Fornatele or the spacey, midnight poetry of Alison Steele, "The Night Bird." Their on-air schedules became part of our collective Circadian rhythm and mutual subconscious, so that we knew which jock was in the studio at any given time without even thinking about it. These guys and gals became stars in their own rights, interviewing and hanging out with The Beatles, Dylan, the Rolling Stones, Duane Allman, Jimmy Page, etc. They MC'ed many of the best concerts and club dates and never had to worry about securing a prime table at The Bottom Line or any of the other clubs.

After the summer of 1976, I left New York City in order to attend law school in Boston. When I returned in 1979, something on the radio had changed. Certainly, shifts in the musical landscape had something to do with it, as the disco and punk eras had taken hold. Perhaps it had something to do with new ways of listening to music, e.g. the Walkman. Maybe we were all simply growing up and getting busier. But the FM glory days were over.

Here is what one of the legendary WNEW FM jocks wrote to me about his days on the job:

> *There are so many aspects to the job that were wonderful but, for me, what gave me the most satisfaction was the opportunity to turn people on to*

music and artists they might otherwise not know about.
To this day, the best compliment I can get is from
someone thanking me for turning them on to (name the
artist). Or when I'm told that most of the records they
have at home were first heard on my show. The fact that
in that "golden age" of FM rock radio those of us on the
air COMPLETELY programmed our own shows gave
us that opportunity of presenting music to our
listeners. I take great pride in having introduced
certain artists on my show like Ry Cooder, JJ Cale,
Garland Jeffreys, Peter Allan, Emmylou Harris, etc,
etc.

That, of course, hit the nail squarely on its head, reducing
the wonders of free-form FM radio to its most common,
wonderful denominator. Without it, sure, we still would have
had our Beatles, Doors and Stones albums. We listened to that
stuff before FM became our thing and most of us still love that
music today. Perhaps, if left to our own primitive devices we'd
even have moved on to Van Morrison, Dylan and Neil Young.
But where would we have heard Randy Newman singing "Sail
Away"? Or Eric Andersen singing "Is It Really Love At All" Or
Mountain's "Nantucket Sleighride"? Or Jesse Winchester's
"Yankee Lady"? Or the entire "Rock of Ages"? Or Ralph McTell
doing "The Streets of London"? Or anything by Joni Mitchell?
Or Fairport Convention? Or the New Riders? Or the Velvet
Underground? Or David Bromberg? The answer is we wouldn't
have. From what I gather, today's technology, which
emphasizes file-sharing, has cut out the middlemen, such as
record stores and disc jockeys. I hope that with all the sharing
and freedom, our kids have it one-tenth as good as we did.

FROM TURKA TO ENGLEWOOD

"Oh, we come on the ship they call the Mayflower
We come on the ship that sailed the moon.
We come in the age's most uncertain hour
And sing an American tune."
Paul Simon, "American Tune" ©

My brothers and I raised our kids together in Englewood, NJ. Up until fairly recently, all 18 people currently comprising the Eidman family, resided either in Englewood or in Queens, NY. Gradually, the cousins have left the collective Eidman family nest, although thankfully they still come and go. But there was a time, a century ago, when the Eidman family was substantially larger. Then, it was centered in the small town of Turka, situated at the confluence of two rivers, the Styri and the Yablunka, in the Carpathian Mountains at about 1,800 feet above sea level. Turka is located in what was then eastern Poland but is now western Ukraine, in the region of Eastern Europe known historically as Galicia. Before World War I, Turka belonged to Austrian Galicia but became part of the Second Polish Republic in 1918. In September 1939, following the invasion of Poland, Soviet forces occupied Turka but in 1941 it was captured by the Germans. After World War II, Turka, once again, became part of what was then Soviet Ukraine and its Polish community was expelled.

Before World War II, Turka was a hub of Jewish life. In 1921, amongst its 10,030 residents, were 4,201 Jews. By the time the Shoah [Holocaust] started, at least twenty of them were our Eidman ancestors, with other Eidmans residing in two of the neighboring villages. During the 1920's, Turka was home to a thriving branch of Hashomer Hatzair, the Socialist-Zionist youth movement that was founded in Galicia. Some of its members made Aliyah [moved to Israel] during the 1920's, predominantly to the Galilee. Of course, most of the Jews remained at home.

During World War II, the Nazis and local populous liquidated the entire Jewish population of Turka by murdering the Jews on the spot or by shipping them off to concentration and death camps (chiefly Auschwitz). After the war, a few survivors of the camps managed to flee to Israel and became part of a community established in Kiryat Motzkin, a suburb about 5 miles north of Haifa. In fact, the mayor of Haifa from 1951 to 1969 was Abba Chushai, one of the Hashomer Hatzair leaders, who had made Aliyah from Turka back in the 1920's. Some of my paternal grandparents' relatives (not named Eidman) settled in Haifa. I do not know whether they were survivors of the Shoah or if like Abba Chushai, they had departed Turka before the darkness had descended.

As for the approximately twenty known Eidman ancestors, records maintained by Yad Vashem [the Holocaust Museum in Israel] and other sources indicate that every Eidman residing in Turka during the War was murdered, either in Turka or at a death camp, most likely Auschwitz. Amongst the murdered were my paternal great grandparents, Moshe Michael Eidman (my namesake) and his wife, Tova Eidman. The records do not tell us whether my ancestors were killed in Turka or at a camp, only that they were "murdered." Other seemingly mundane records become portentous and ominous when understood in context. For example, the records for three water bills for three separate Eidman households in Turka suddenly went unpaid starting at the same time in 1942.

In any event, just as the baby Jor-El was shot forth from his doomed planet Krypton by his parents, one Eidman was sent forth into the world ahead of the hellfire that was soon to consume European Jewry. Circa 1927, Saul Eidman, the son of Moshe Michael and Tova, left his homeland, never to return. His destination was Cuba, where an arranged marriage to my eventual grandmother, Sylvia, awaited him. (Let's take a moment to try and imagine how different life was back then.) Saul was about 26 at the time, and had given up his opportunity to study medicine back home, so that his friend could take his spot. He was probably of modest skills and certainly with little or no language fluency that would be of use in his new life. I don't know much about Saul's life in Turka but I recall a striking photograph of him standing erect in his Polish Army uniform, with the omnipresent cigarette dangling from his fingertips. Decades later, when Grandpa Saul would stay with us up in the Catskill Mountains, he enjoyed the mountain air and views. I like to think he was reminded of the vistas, if not the life he had left behind in the Carpathian Mountains.

Shortly after arriving in Cuba, Saul Eidman and his new wife Sylvia came to the States. They settled in the Bronx and had three children: my father, Seymour, born in 1932, his brother Leslie in 1935, and the baby, Florence, in 1941. Despite the

Author, Grandpa Saul, Steve, Uncle Leslie, David.
Photo courtesy of Florence & Seymour Eidman.

deprivations of the Great Depression, my grandparents managed to provide a yeshiva [Jewish day school] education for the boys. This could not have been a simple decision, for a variety of reasons. For one thing, a yeshiva education was not nearly as common in the 1930's and 1940's as it is today. In fact, most immigrants believed that in order to assimilate into the American way of life, it was preferable to send the kids to the local public school. And even with yeshiva tuition being modest in those days, there was very little extra money to go around. My grandfather was raising three kids on a workingman's wages: he worked for a commercial bakery delivering to retail bakeries, first by horse and wagon and then by truck. Eventually he was able to start his own delivery business, delivering the same bakery products.

What makes the decision more interesting is that the household was not the typical "yeshiva family". My grandfather had little choice but to work 7 days a week, getting off for Rosh Hashanah and Yom Kippur plus a week's vacation during Pesach [Passover]. Although he was out working on Shabbos, my grandmother observed the day and kept the kids on track, making sure they never missed Shabbat services at the synagogue. She was a polio victim and was hobbled as a result of her disability but as photographs prove, remained a beautiful woman until her death, when I was not yet two. And despite my grandfather's schedule, the home was far from devoid of traditional Jewish values and culture. Yiddish was the first language at home and there was always Jewish music, in particular cantorial music. And of course, there was plenty of Jewish cooking. My father continued his yeshiva education through high school at MTA (Yeshiva University High School) and the religion took root in him a bit more deeply than in his siblings.

By becoming early adoptees of the American yeshiva system, my grandparents made a conscious decision not to fully assimilate and to protect their children's religion and culture from becoming indistinguishable within the American melting pot. This decision did not prevent their kids from eventually attaining advanced degrees and achieving professional fulfillment and success. In effect, the modern orthodox norm, as we now know it, of combining traditional Jewish values with secular achievement was already in place within the Eidman family—a full generation before it gained general acceptance in this country. This philosophy continued into my generation and beyond, as all of the Eidman cousins attended Jewish day schools, straight through high school. Most of those kids, now either grown or nearly grown, spent a year in Israel before college. Some of them even enjoy hearing a good "chazzan" (cantor) on the high holy days.

More significantly, the seemingly small decisions that Saul and Sylvia Eidman made to maintain and foster a Jewish home formed the foundation for the belief system and structure upon which many Eidman lives have been built. The particular style of Judaism and observance with which I was raised may strike some within the orthodox community as being lax, if not downright casual. But 'unorthodox' though it might be, it has certainly exerted a positive influence over the choices I have made throughout my life, including my choice of wife (or wives).

Now, some say that it is healthy to experiment with different religious philosophies or practices. Others go even further and say that as a result of all the social, political and economic upheaval in the world, the traditional practices have become outmoded and should be discarded. I would suggest that while modernizing tradition and observance may have its place, e.g. with respect to the role of women, over-liberalization is indeed a slippery slope and that without adherence to traditional religious practices and values, Judaism would, within a few short generations, cease to exist. And if I have admittedly, not done everything within my power to ensure its survival, I certainly do not wish to contribute to its demise. Without getting into the specifics of my own level of observance or belief, let me say that I have tried to stay true to the way in which I was raised, while enhancing or refining certain family traditions and observances just a bit. The jury is still out as to whether any of my children, nephews or nieces will similarly stay the course. I believe that after a certain point, it is no longer our job, and may even be counter-productive, to dictate lifestyle choices to our kids (with one or two critically important exceptions). I look forward to seeing how the next generation deals with this age-old question of religious tradition vs. secular modernization.

There are many reasons why I have tried to keep to the path. For one thing, it hasn't seemed all that difficult to me. That path, at least the way the Eidman family has constructed it, is a wide one, with plenty of latitude and space. For another, I believe that should I veer from it, I would have difficulty finding my way back. Or maybe it just comes down to the fact that I'm a creature of habit. (In fact, I almost titled this book "Creature of Habit," but I decided against using the cliché, true as it may be.) But more than anything, I am struck by the undeniable fact that our family's unique recipe — a blend of Ashkenazi Judaism, American liberalism, yeshiva education, popular culture, New York City street-smarts and suburban leisure — is tightly bound and connected to a single Eidman survivor of Turka. My grandparents would surely have derived great pleasure in knowing that we were doing our best to stay linked to the chain that Saul Eidman extended from Turka to New York.

Grandpa Saul may have passed away in 1990 but my memories of him and his taciturn ways remain forever burnt into my mind, as surely as his cigarettes, on occasion, burnt into the furniture. When I was still not out of my teens, he surprised me by telling me when to get married, that I should marry a "nice girl", and that I should name my son after him. The continuity of the chain was a concern of his. I was barely 19 when he directed me to name my son "Saul, S-A-U-L, don't change it." Many years later, we gave our son the Hebrew name 'Saul Jonah.' He would be pleased to know that thanks to his efforts and his resolute lifestyle choices, we are now some three generations further up the family tree. And while he would be pleased, I cannot really imagine him smiling. That was not his thing.

Grandson Steve's Memories:
Grandpa-Land: Where Cigarettes Have No Filters, All the Papers Are in Yiddish, and Jerry Koosman is a Good Jewish Boy.

"ALVIN CHARLES DAVIDOFF"

"He's a walking contradiction, partly truth and partly fiction.
Taking every wrong direction on his lonely way back home."
Kris Kristofferson, "Pilgrim Chapter 33" ©

One of the great ad campaigns of the last twenty years has been the series of TV ads for Dos Equis beer, featuring the "World's Most Interesting Man". While the narrator regales the audience with tales of the wondrous achievements of the nameless protagonist, the viewer is treated to silent film clips of often hilarious scenes showing our bearded hero's uncanny ability to dazzle men and women alike with feats of effortless strength, agility, wit or nobility. For example, the narrator might be saying, in a hushed tone, *"Even his enemies list him as their emergency contact... He can disarm you with his words or his hands, either one... He is the most interesting man in the world."* Meanwhile, we're watching our man in a montage of grainy clips: dropping from a helicopter onto a snowy peak dressed in a tuxedo; causing a queen to laugh hysterically; running through an African village carrying a lamb, with dozens of costumed villagers in hot pursuit. I particularly liked the one with our guy cooking up something wonderful in an industrial-sized kitchen, when a mountain lion suddenly leaps onto the table. With a single sweep of our mildly annoyed superman's arm and a stern look, the lion meekly jumps off the table, cowering with its tale between his legs. While this type of intrepid nonchalance may date back to Cary Grant or James Bond by way of Sean Connery, it is a trait we normally associate with works of fiction. In contrast to the "world's most interesting man", my real-life friend Alvin Charles Davidoff, as far as I know, never held sway over a full-grown cougar or "aced a Rorschach test." And as much as I love Al, or "ACD" as I call him, I would never refer to him as "dashing", even if he does exude a peculiar, old-school charm. But if there was such a thing as a "scale of interesting, from 1 to 10", Al would be way up there, like a solid 8 or even a 9. At least in my book. Except that his name is not "Al" or "Alvin Charles Davidoff"; this is the one of the few times in this book that in the interests of privacy, I am utilizing a fictitious name.

I met Al, or ACD, early in 1990. I had joined my uncle's law firm and moved into a beautiful, new full-floor suite on 6th Avenue. This space was shared with several lawyers, including Al. Al is a few years older than me, from the West Coast and was actually a real live 1960's Berkeley College radical. By the time I met him, Al was a strictly orthodox and 100% observant "frum" Jew, although I do not believe that he was raised as such. Come to think of it, I don't know anything about Al's parents or much about his roots, although some years ago, I did meet his sister who flew in from Texas, I believe, for the wedding of one of Al's kids. She seemed totally secular, if not unaffiliated, and very pleasant. Al, along with his lovely and ever-patient wife are well ensconced in the Breuers Community, which is a venerable German orthodox Jewish haven on the "good side", that is the west side of Broadway in Washington Heights. (Actually, that part of Manhattan is now going by the name "Hudson Heights", probably so as not to scare off the gentrifying yuppies who are slowly moving in). Suffice it to say that in Al's household there is no TV and no secular books or magazines. The kids, now grown, attended single-sex, "seminary-type" schools and the marriages were arranged. When we met, Al looked the part as well: dark navy or black suit, white shirt usually open at the neck, no tie except for court, black "kippah" (beneath black hat when outdoors), scraggly beard, and what we Jews like to refer to as a "cholent belly". (Cholent is the traditional Jewish stew that is usually cooked for at least 12 hours and eaten on the Sabbath.)

If Al's daily life and practices were governed by his adherence to "haredi" or devoutly Jewish principles, his worldview and freethinking philosophy never strayed all that far from the hallowed halls and green pastures of Berkeley. Going to Berkeley University in the 1960's is the stuff most of us only read about but Al lived the dream in a big way. Even today, tucked away inside a dog-eared folder in Al's office are copies of Al's FBI folder and a newspaper account, with photos, of when the fuzz tear-gassed a shaggy-maned Al out of his dorm. That was a time! In any event, there is little question that the Berkeley experience informed Al's suspicious views of authority and conformity. Not surprisingly, Al became a sole practitioner and once I got to know him, it was easy to see why he flew solo. Al is somewhere between a contrarian and an iconoclast, never accepting conventional points of view or behaviors. These are valuable traits for a litigator, if not for a normal, functioning member of society. Or of a law suite member, for that matter. For example, if we had a meeting of the eleven "suite partners", you could count on the same guy to be seated at the conference room table, jacket and tie in place, 5 minutes early. Soon, nine guys would straggle in right on time or within 10 minutes afterwards. Al, if he was to be bothered at all, would wander in 25 minutes late, tieless, white shirt untucked, tzitzis blowing in the wind, large black yarmulke askew. If he really wanted to get under the skin of the more up-tight suite-partners, he'd wear his slippers. Should his loyal and tough-as-nails secretary Samantha (also a fictitious name) buzz to say that Al was needed outside or if the direction (or lack thereof) of the meeting was not to his liking, he'd disappear and forget to re-appear. Not that it mattered, because if Al disagreed with the result, there was little guarantee that he would abide anyway. Al's individualistic approach to life was exemplified when the news broke about my friend, a legendary disc jockey's dramatic and steep fall from grace. Al simply remarked *"well, everyone makes mistakes"* and let it go at that.

Despite differences in our backgrounds, personalities and styles, it was clear from the start that Al and I had much in common. He, along with a couple of my other new suite-mates had just vacated space where the "personal injury maven" was my former and first law partner. Al was interested, almost fascinated about how I had managed to get myself mixed up with such a devious sort. After normal work hours, he would sometimes slide open his bottom desk drawer and take out a bottle of scotch and we would swap stories about the guy. For many of the years during which we shared space, I was the only one on the floor who could share a "d'var Torah", that is, words of Torah, with Al. Mind you, we never did this in a formalized "studying" way, but as an adjunct to whatever we were schmoozing about or sometimes just to hammer home a point.

I respect anyone who has managed to support a family through a one-person law practice, like Al did. His practice focuses primarily on commercial litigation, sometimes involving highly–charged and acrimonious disputes between individuals. Al litigates the same way he lives: in a bold style all his own, absorbing his adversary's best shot, not giving an inch, then hitting back twice as hard. He is the only lawyer I know who writes exactly as he speaks. When you argue with him, he may try to overwhelm you with a combination of hyperbole, high-drama, sarcasm and even volume. Likewise, his written arguments contain his trademark flourishes such as rhetorical questions, a great deal of bold print/underlining, liberal use of italics and more exclamation points on a single page than any attorney has a right to use in a lifetime. But every successful lawyer has his or her unique style and if I've learned a single thing along the way it is not to argue with success. Al's bravado style is the perfect cover for a keen intellect and his completely original arguments in which he has absolute faith and confidence. About a year ago, Al essentially made new law in the arcane area of default judgments when he convinced the New York State Court of Appeals, the highest court in the state, to reverse the judgment of the Appellate Division. Winning a case in front of the Court of Appeals is a crowning achievement in any attorney's career and I was very excited when I found out about it. To his credit, Al was so low-key about the whole thing, I nearly did not believe him. One thing about ACD, he is not one to be overwhelmed by the moment. I just wish I could have been there, watching Al field questions from the seven judges, with his ever-present mixture of nerves of steel, good humor and firm grasp of the issues. Or let me put it another way: I am positive Al did not win because of his cutting edge, GQ wardrobe.

If truth be told, Al's outspoken manner and his preference for swimming against the tide, rubbed some of our office colleagues the wrong way. Others were more willing to overlook stylistic differences, while valuing and respecting his tenacious tendencies. I always liked his long-time assistant, Samantha, but some found her no-nonsense, straightforward manner to be somewhat abrupt, if not downright prickly. I believe it says a great deal about both Al and Samantha that while staff and personnel in the law business come and go, they have lived together in near-harmony for many years. I always got a kick when, at the end of another day in the ACD maelstrom, Samantha would be on her way out the door and Al would bellow, *"Thank you so much for all your help today, Sammy"*. After regular business hours but before going home, it was time for Al to mellow out. With most of the staff and many of the lawyers already gone, Al would prove that his college years were not a total waste of time. After a scotch or two, he'd slide out an old acoustic guitar from behind his desk and show off some rusty blues and folk licks. I have to say, he was not bad.

How did Al transform from Berkeley radical to Washington Heights "frummie"? I can only speculate. It could be that in spite of his independent spirit, Al was one of those kids who was always looking for something, something different or hopefully better. Maybe the radical hippie thing wore thin on him around the same time it began to bore much of America. I don't know what the motivation was and I have never spoken to Al about it in any specific way. In fact, I am basing my timeline largely upon Al's collection of record albums.

The weight of the evidence suggests that is was during the early 1970's, that Al's life took a sharp turn to the right. It was at about that time that he got hooked up with Yeshiva Ohr Somayach (which translates to Academy of Joyous Light), based in Jerusalem. I recall a brutally stormy night in the late 1990's, when Al showed up unannounced at my home in Englewood with cardboard boxes containing his entire collection of vintage LPs which he asked me to *"hold for him"*. One of these records was the extremely rare and highly collectible Beatles' "butcher scene" original cover to the "Yesterday and Today" LP. Some of the boxes had *"Yeshiva Ohr Somayach"* written in magic marker across the top. The records, a fine, eclectic collection of folk, blues, country and rock, seemed to peter out about 1970. For example, Dylan was faithfully represented, right up to "Self-Portrait" (1970). No self-respecting Dylan fan stopped at "Self-Portrait", not with "Blood on the Tracks" still to come in 1974. Unless, just maybe, that fan just wasn't into this stuff anymore, or, maybe, was no longer playing popular music at home?

Al does not talk about his time at Ohr Somayach and I've gotten the impression that he prefers not to be asked about it. Yeshiva Ohr Somayach was founded in 1970 in Jerusalem and currently has branches in the US and in several other countries.

It caters primarily to college or post-college age men who are "baalei teshuvah." This is the term for Jews who lack traditional Jewish background but are seeking to "return" (literally translated from the Hebrew). They do so by catching up on the Torah study they have missed out on and by leading a life dedicated to adhering to strict observance of Jewish law. By any measure, the Ohr Somayach experience was undoubtedly a turning point in Al's life. He got turned onto the "frum", that is, very religious Jewish lifestyle in a very big way and I do not believe he has ever looked back in regret. I was going to simply say *"he never looked back"* but as you will see, that would be untrue. Much of Al's "old life" remains with him, even as he lives the life of a devout and strictly orthodox Jew. Al may have brought his old record albums to my house but that sure did not mean that he swore off the devil's music when he decided to become religious. He had gotten in way too deep during the 1960's to ever dig himself out. Or put another way, when the blues get deep inside of you, they don't ever leave. Al and I spent a lot of time, probably too much time, talking about music. Through these conversations, I confirmed what I already knew: I had gotten into the live music scene too late. Between 1973 and 1975, I saw the Dead, Dylan, the Stones, the Who, Traffic, The Band, Clapton, and many more. Of course they were all still great but they were also just a little bit past their primes. On the other hand, before 1970, Al saw The Doors, Hendrix, Joplin and every great west coast act, big or small. Oh yeah, he also saw that somewhat influential British quartet, you know, the one from Liverpool. So his musical tastes were finely cultivated. As recently as 2013, Al really freaked me out when he called, asking, *"McMike, did you catch that new Hendrix movie? No? Well, I'm in it."* And lo and behold, so he was. Apparently, thanks to the release by the Hendrix estate of previously unseen footage, a new documentary had just aired on PBS. Fortunately, Al's old college pal saw it and I was able to catch it later that week. Just over an hour or so into the film, there is a wild and wooly ACD, standing on the Berkeley campus circa 1968. He is compressing about 100 words into a 15-second interview, gesticulating grandly as he pontificates about the *"universal grooviness"* of Jimi's music. Watching this was a time warp experience and it really blew my mind.

When it comes to music, Al is even more opinionated than I am—and that's saying a great deal. Our discussions, debates and listening sessions would probably entertain obsessives and bore most everyone else to tears, so if you prefer to skip the rest of this paragraph, go right ahead, I won't be insulted. For the record, let it be said that Al's musical tastes reflect both his strident personality and his preference for the highly individualistic, idiosyncratic and sometimes just plain bizarre. Most of the time, there is an honesty, sincerity and unique quality to the artists he favors. I recall Al hanging out backstage with Ramblin' Jack Elliott at a couple of my shows, trading tall tales. In the office, Al had the annoying habit of setting his CD player on the "repeat track"

ACD, Ramblin' Jack Elliott, Author, 1996, backstage. Photo courtesy of the author.

mode and playing the same song over and over. Often, it would be a blues great, such as Blind Willie McTell. Or maybe some R&B from Rufus Thomas. Once in a while it would be something totally off-the-wall, such as Vanilla Fudge's hard rock cover of the Supremes' "You Keep Me Hanging On." In 2014 he called me to see if I could scare up some seats to catch the great Marcia Ball, who was playing on a Sunday evening at Mexicali Live. Afterwards, I took his photo with Marcia and his joy was palpable. Sometimes, Al's tastes were less discerning. For example, shortly after returning to me the brilliant "Clapton Live in 1974" CD, with a yellow stickie attached to it reading, *"not worth the plastic it is made on"*, he dragged me to a ZZ Top show at The Beacon. The show was formulaic and boring but I was entertained by watching Al make friends with everyone, including the band's former manager, now an entertainment lawyer with a major Manhattan firm. Al was also into rap, especially Snoop Dogg. I was never able to get him to do anything except denigrate the great Richard Thompson. Then one day, Al called me into his office to meet David Fricke, head music critic of Rolling Stone magazine. As I was leaving Al's office, I asked Mr. Fricke one question: *"Where would you rank Richard Thompson?"* He regarded the question in stony silence but slowly started raising his hand until it was way over his head. That finally got RT some overdue respect! (Come to think of it, I still don't know what that critic was doing in Al's office.)

Al didn't just keep up with the music—he never really could forget his California days. One day, he called me into his office to meet an "old friend, from the west coast". The friend was Elliott Landy, the great photographer who shot the covers to Dylan's "Nashville Skyline", the Band's classic second record and Van Morrison's "Moondance". He also photographed Woodstock (the festival), the Beatles, Janis and lots of other neat stuff. Despite the lapse of several decades, Elliott recalls ACD fondly, remembering *"that he was very kind to my partner and I and we knew we could depend on his integrity in our business dealings."* Thanks to ACD, Daphne and I visited Elliott's house in Woodstock, NY twice and Elliott's book of previously unpublished photographs of The Band currently graces our coffee table.

Fishing was another big part of Al's "old life" that he just could not bear to leave behind. I don't know how Al got into fishing but even after he embraced the baal teshuvah life, he continued to take annual expeditions to Alaska, in search of King Salmon and halibut. He would fish unfamiliar and dicey waters unguided, armed with a large caliber rifle. This would be available in an emergency—either to subdue a thrashing 200-pound halibut or as security against a grouchy bear. Like most dedicated anglers, Al revels in the photographic proof of his successful expeditions, especially of the photo of him holding a 45-pound King. Al opted not to share this "Grizzly Adams" side of his life with his sheltered kids. It was easier just to tell them that "Abba" ("father" in Hebrew) sometimes goes off to study at a distant yeshiva. (Some great yeshiva they have there in Sitka, Alaska!) I once paid a shiva call to Al's wife, and as it happened, Al was in court and not around. He had recently returned from an Alaskan adventure. I later found out that during the 40 minutes or so that I spent at the house, Al's poor wife was terrified that I would mention his recent excursion in front of the kids. I guess she did not know that I knew that the kids were not supposed to know.

As a matter of fact, Daphne and I have discussed the fact that Al was cloistering his kids from many of the world's gifts, including nature, music, film and literature. Al is well-schooled in all of these areas and they have continued to make Al's life just a little bit more rounded and enjoyable. As I mentioned, Al would occasionally take out his old guitar and display some bluesy, soulful chops. But he steadfastly refused to come and hear my sons play with their rock bands because he *"did not want to contribute to them falling off the 'derech' [proper path]."* Perhaps he was regretfully rueful of his own youth and I recalled something he had once written, during what must have been an intense period of reflection and self-analysis:

"His jerky motions and energy reminded you of a squirrel, firing brilliantly witty barbs in every direction at every target. His heart had been ripped open by childhood trauma, creating an aperture through which he radiated warmth to all beneficiaries of his affection.

He certainly knew what to say to make you feel good about yourself. In his early years, women were to him as wine to an alcoholic. And if champagne was not available, Thunderbird would do just fine, thank you."

If Al's past influenced his decidedly retro views on rearing children, he refused to let those opinions cramp his own style. Sometimes, these two sides of his persona were evident at the same time. One such incident occurred during the brief period of time when Al owned a speedboat, which he docked at a marina, close to our home. One summer evening, he stopped by, had some dinner at the house and we took my kids for an impromptu cruise down the Hudson. My son Jonah, then about 10 and always inquisitive, had his usual boatload of questions about the boat, its instruments, the river, navigation, the weather, etc., etc. After four, maybe five questions, Al told him that the best thing for a kid to do is to stop asking so many questions and to just pay attention. Not really my style of parenting. (In fairness, I got to know Al's eldest daughters who filled in at the office on occasion and he and his wife have every reason to be proud of how they turned out.) Many years later, my youngest son, Benjamin, worked for Al on several Sundays during a break between college semesters and Al, of course, treated him well. One of the perks was that Benjamin was afforded some unique insight into the world of ACD as one of his assignments consisted of scanning Al's old photos onto his computer. I'm thinking that Al might agree that my boys are turning out OK despite knowing how to play some Doors songs. Notwithstanding the evil influence of secular music, Al himself still goes to the clubs or even to some of my shows if there is something going on that he feels is worth checking out.

Over the years, Al's roots within the devoutly orthodox Jewish world have continued to spread. Some of his kids now reside in Israel and have married into prominent rabbinical dynasties. Yet, while these roots have taken hold, Al's wanderlust has grown in equal proportion. He has visited Mexico, the Dominican Republic, south-east Asia and who knows where else, on what I am guessing are low-budget but highly entertaining trips. He mingles well with the locals, taking photographs, making friends everywhere. On occasion, he will send me a photo, sometimes insisting on keeping me guessing as to the locale. Should I guess incorrectly, he refuses to give me the right answer and the mystery remains unsolved. His wife never accompanies him. He sometimes travels with an old friend but does not hesitate to go it alone. After a recent visit to the Dominican Republic, he told me that *"the Dominican is not a place for you."* When I asked him why that was the case, all he would allow was something along the lines of, *"Mike my man, I know you and it's not for you."* I don't have the vaguest idea why but I'm guessing that he is right.

These days, Al and I don't see much of one another. But it's sort of like the phenomenon of running into an old high school buddy. The bond of friendship forged during youth is very strong. Even after 20 or 30 years, you sort of pick up right where you left off. For whatever reason, many of us do not form such powerful friendships as adults. Perhaps it's on account of all the baggage that adults carry around, the roles that we unconsciously feel we need to play, the scar tissue that has formed over the years, the beliefs and opinions that at some point evolved into rigid doctrine. Who wants someone like that as a friend? Not many people do—usually only your old friends, the ones who knew you from before you got so heavy and depressed! For me, meeting ACD was an exception to that general rule. I wasn't a kid; in fact, I was 35 when we met, but we quickly became good friends. We worked in the same suite for seven years and then in the same building for another three or four. Many years later, we now see each other irregularly, maybe at a wedding or a bar mitzvah and we speak once in a while. And every so often, ACD might refer a client. Over the years, he has said some awfully nice things about me, on both a personal and professional level and I have enough of an ego to have appreciated that (but not so much of an ego that I will repeat here what he has said). I called Al before writing this essay, just to get his OK. We spoke for a long while and like always, it was without skipping a beat, just like those old childhood friends that we never were.

[Author's September 2016 update: Al continues to surprise me. Just last week, I attended the wedding of his youngest child and was informed by an old friend of Al from LA that Al's father, who passed away in 1987, was one of the world's most respected gastroenterologists. I did a bit of fact-checking and sure enough, even after 30 years, Al's dad remains one of the most influential physicians in his field. Al had never said a word to me about him.]

THE DAY MY FATHER TURNED 33

"Fifteen under zero when the day became a threat,
My clothes were wet and I was drenched to the bone.
Been out ice fishing, too much repetition
Make a man wanna leave the only home he's known."
J.R. Robertson, "Acadian Driftwood" ©

When I look back upon my childhood, there are a few days that stick out. By "stick out", I don't mean that they were important milestones although a few of them might have been. I mean that the details of these days remain vivid and clear despite the passage of even fifty years. February 21, 1965 was one of those days. In fact, if I was compiling a "top10" list instead of writing an essay, it would be at the top of the hit parade. (As things turned out, that might be a poor choice of words, as you will see). I certainly remember that day better than I recall the day of my bar mitzvah, which took place three years later. February 21, 1965 happened to be my father's 33rd birthday and he probably chose how we spent the day. Ironically, even though my mind has often wandered back to that day, I don't recall celebrating my dad's birthday and I did not realize the date's coincidence until I was writing this essay. (Sorry, Dad.) As things played out, his birthday turned out to be nothing more than a fluky footnote.

I was 10 years old and my brothers, ages 7 and 5, and we arose early on that Sunday morning. We did not own long underwear, but we needed to dress for the elements, so we piled layers of our warmest clothes on top of our pajamas. My folks would soon be loading the oversized trunk of our reliable old 1960 Oldsmobile '88 and we would be heading northwest from our apartment in Washington Heights up to Tennanah Lake in Roscoe, NY, for a little ice fishing. [As a logistical curiosity, it seems that despite the spatial limitations of apartment dwelling with multiple generations under one roof, we had sufficient closet or storage space to store ice fishing equipment. Not very common amongst the Washington Heights yeshiva crowd, but you have to have your priorities straight.]

Looking back, especially after having raised my own three boys, I must give my parents some credit. Or possibly question their sanity. It was roughly a two and half hour trip up to the lake. With Washington's Birthday falling on Monday, February 22 (there was no annual 3-day Presidents' Day weekend back then), the plan was to have a two-day ice fishing extravaganza and to spend Sunday night at a local motel of modest repute (reservations be damned!). Although it may appear or even seem obvious to some that this scheme had to have been connected to the celebration of my father's birthday, I assure you that it was not. Given our Mom's easy-going nature, the coincidence of my father's birthday was just a coincidence and she would have been (relatively) happy to go ice fishing even on her birthday. (Since her birthday is in early November, we thankfully never had to prove that). Put another way, if Dad wanted to get everyone up at the crack of dawn, prepare cream cheese and onion sandwiches and thermoses of hot liquids, then drive a couple of hours so that we can all freeze on a sheet of ice, well, Mom didn't need any special reason or occasion in order to join in. She was there. Of course, we couldn't restrict the fun to the nuclear family. Luckily, our Washington Heights cousins also thrilled at the thought of two windswept days on a frozen lake. My mom's cousin George Bart could never pass up a fishing trip, no matter how ridiculous or ill-conceived. George was 29 years old; he grew up in the building right next to ours and even as a grown-up engineer, he would come by to watch cartoons with us. I am unsure as to whether he was already married to his wife, Joanie ("Big Red"), at the time of this trip, but Super 8 film evidence proves that she came along for the ride. Rounding out the group were our twin cousins (and former baby-sitters), Diane and Susan, the daughters of our grandma's sister, Aunt Pearl. And so, the extended clan hit the road in two cars, ours and Georgie's.

My favorite fishing writer, John Gierach once quoted another respected writer who described ice fishing as *"that moronic sport,"* and frankly, there is something to that. Conditions range from cold to Arctic; you spend most of the time standing around, shifting uncomfortably and nervously from leg to leg on ever-shifting, cracking ice; and unless you are in Canada, Minnesota or Wisconsin, you rarely catch anything (except for the proverbial cold—or worse). As of 1965, we had not yet acquired an augur, which is simply a gigantic steel corkscrew, to manually bore holes through the 18 inches of rock-hard ice. (Much later, Dad would "invest" in a gas-powered augur.) All we had at our disposal on this trip was a homemade device fashioned by cousin George by pouring hot lead down into the long hollow shaft of a heavy steel chisel. Chopping each hole was a tedious, arm-wearying, gut-wrenching process. After managing to hack 5 to 10 holes through the stubborn ice, we would scoop the floating pieces of ice from each hole with what looked like a gigantic spoon with holes in it for the water to drip through. I think the big spoon was called a skimmer. Then we would bait our hooks, which were attached to a small spool of line at the bottom of a wooden contraption shaped like a cross called a "tip up." The tip up would sit on top of the hole, with the spool of line sitting beneath the surface feeding out line. When a fish pulled the bait at the end of the line, the spool would unwind, causing a long, thin, flexible piece of metal with a red flag at its top to spring upwards. So, when we saw a red flag in the air, it meant that a fish was on the line—unless, of course, the wind caused the tip-up to spring. Either way, any glimpse of a red flag would set off a mad, clumsy, slippery rush to whichever tip-up had been sprung. However, the real problem was that these exuberant dashes were few and far between.

We caught one pickerel that day. It was not very big. My father laid it down on the frozen surface and piled chopped ice on top of it. We would retrieve it from the deep freeze the next day, Monday, when we returned for round 2. When the red flags aren't flying, you do what you can to stay busy and warm. We saw a demented ice fisherman, as if there is any other type, drive a black sedan out onto the surface of the lake and proceed to do some skidding spins on the ice. That was fun to watch— although I would never recommend it. At some point, a small plane landed on the ice, which was truly a spectacle for us kids. It takes 8 inches of solid ice to support a car and only 3 or 4 inches to safely support a person. Tennanah Lake, by February, generally had 15 inches minimum, and usually 18. Every now and then, the ice would shift beneath our feet with a yawning crack, and it felt as if the tectonic plates of the earth were colliding. That would have been unnerving even on solid ground or if the depth of the ice was a full three feet, as it is in parts further north.

Old weather records show that it was actually a good day for ice fishing, if there is such a thing. Although the low for February 21, 1965 in nearby Liberty, NY was 7 degrees, the average temperature was close to 28 and it actually went into the 40s. Downright balmy. Probably in Roscoe and at the higher elevation of Tennanah Lake, it was a bit cooler. I got to hand it to my folks—what with all the fishing gear, extra clothing, food, wind and snow, they managed to shoot a bit of home movie footage while on the ice that day. Maybe 30 seconds or so, but just enough to give you a taste of the way it was. Steve, David and I were wearing ski masks as we slowly trudged along, carrying the tip-ups in our arms, across the ice. The twins were bundled up, waving at the camera. Joanie flaunted her big red hair and held the skimmer as Georgie began to vigorously chop

George Bart chopping away; Joanie waits with the skimmer.
Photo courtesy of Florence & Seymour Eidman home movies.

away at the ice. Then, I guess the old movie camera was turned off and safely packed away in its brown leather case for the duration of the trip.

Despite the relative warmth of the day and the thermoses of hot drinks, eventually the chill got to us and we repaired to the Tennanah Blake House, a small restaurant at the near end of the lake. Our mom had two nickels in her wallet, so my brother Steve and I were each allotted one and we headed straight to the jukebox. We inserted the first nickel and scanned the rows of possible selections. Most likely we were looking for Petula Clark singing "Downtown" or possibly, Gary Lewis & the Playboys doing "This Diamond Ring." (Even Nostradamus could not have predicted that 38 years later I would be a part-time concert promoter and that I would be roundly chastised by the composer of "This Diamond Ring", Al Kooper, when I jokingly suggested that he play it at one of our shows.) Mom only had the two nickels, which of course infuriated our little brother David. Before Steve and I were able to decide which songs to play, David randomly began to punch the buttons on the juke box. Before you knew it, the schmaltzy strings of "Auld Lang Syne" filled the air, much to the laughter of everyone in the restaurant. (Yes, there were people there!) David, not quite 5 years old, burst into tears and has had a fear of juke boxes ever since. Sadly, possibly owing to its lousy juke box, the Tennanah Blake House did not remain in business for long and was "repurposed" as a private home. [In an interesting post-script, about 40 years after David's juke box humiliation, his ex-wife Bonnie's older sister Allison ended up buying the place and to this day, our dad docks his boat there. Thank you, Allison!]

After everything got sorted away at the Blake House, we left to find some semi-suitable digs for the night. Unfortunately, every motel room from Roscoe down to Monticello seemed to have been booked. My folks told us that the motels had been booked up by skiers, but looking back, I've got to wonder, exactly where in that neck of the woods was everyone so busy skiing? Eventually, we gave up and, as hard as it was to leave behind our solo "pickerel on ice", we decided to scrap day 2 and head for home. My brothers and I were unhappy campers but at least there was no school the next day. We assumed the day's excitement had run its course and settled in for the drive back to Washington Heights.

My dad steered the Olds back towards civilization. It was about 6 pm when he turned on the radio in order to check on the traffic closer to the city. We suddenly heard the news that about three hours earlier, black civil rights leader Malcolm X had been gunned down while delivering a speech in Manhattan. The assassination occurred at the Audubon Ballroom, located on Broadway near West 168th Street, which was about 10 blocks south of where we would soon be exiting the George Washington Bridge and about a mile from where we lived.

The calm. AP Photo, used by permission

Malcolm's image, which remains controversial even in 2014, was infinitely more contentious in early 1965 than it is in its post-Denzel Washington days. His statements concerning white people in general and Jews in particular did more than merely rankle both, even as he galvanized significant segments of the black populous with his themes of black self-determination, superiority and separatism. His fiery speeches, which at times advocated for violent revolution, frightened many whites. This was an era when, thanks in no small measure to the illegal activities and disinformation campaign of J. Edgar Hoover's FBI, mainstream elements of the white establishment remained suspicious of even the Rev. Martin Luther King, Jr. By contrast, Malcolm X, with his *"white people are the devil"* rhetoric stirred up feelings of suspicion, fear and loathing amongst people of my parents' generation and background who were far to the left of Dr. King's critics. It mattered little that they were loyal Democrats and forcefully supported the civil rights movement. Phil Ochs may have mocked many of them when he sang *"love me, love me, love me, I'm a lib-e-ral"* but all that devil talk and violent revolution rhetoric, was a huge turn-off. And news of Malcolm's abandonment of Elijah Muhammad's Nation of Islam, his embrace of Sunni Islam and the moderation of many of his more radical views had not yet succeeded in changing his image in most middle-class Jewish homes.

When the news of Malcolm's shooting (right in our neighborhood!) shattered the silence of our drive home, I reacted by asking *"Who shot him?"* Someone immediately responded: *"I have no idea but whoever it was should be given a medal."* Now, I know that the person who said that was speaking metaphorically but given the context of the times, the comment remains understandable to me (again, as a metaphor and not in a literal sense). Even today it is extremely difficult and discomfiting to listen to some of Malcolm's hate-filled rants (which can be heard on YouTube), such as the one where he exhorted his followers not to *"shed crocodile tears over what happened to [the Jews] in Germany."* And much worse stuff, stuff that Spike Lee must have left on his cutting room floor. Considering that 1965 was a mere 18 years after the holocaust, it is not surprising that Malcolm's death resulted in few tears, crocodile or otherwise, within the mainstream Jewish community. As Garland Jeffreys sang, ©*"I was afraid of Malcolm, just like any white man..."* Bottom line is that although Malcolm had changed, without the internet and the round-the-clock news cycle, as of February 21, 1965, he was still viewed by many as the potentially violent purveyor of extremist racial hatred even if that may no longer have been true.

We slowly swung by the Audubon Ballroom but as they say, there was *"nothing to see here,"* just several police cars parked in front. By then, Malcolm X had already been declared dead at Presbyterian Hospital or as we locals used to call it, "Medical Center," just up the street.

We have a phrase in the law that comes up from time to

time, the *"totality of the circumstances,"* which is a lawyer's circumspect way of saying that the whole is greater than the sum of its parts. February 21, 1965 was composed of a lot of interesting and memorable moving parts and I guess that's why it remains so crystal clear in my mind's eye. There was the sense of adventure—picking up in the middle of a typically bleak Washington Heights winter, piling into the cars and going ice fishing. Think about it: trying to catch semi-dormant fish through holes in the ice that you dig yourself. What a way to cure a bad case of the old cabin fever! Leave it my parents, no one else went about it like that. Even though we did not get to stay overnight at some local dive motel, it was fun just knowing that we were planning on doing exactly that. In fact, I still prefer to go low-end when I fish, just as long as the sheets are clean. The long day ended when we shared in a bit of American history, as we drove right past the scene of an assassination that has continued to confound amateur investigators and sleuths (and with good reason). I think about my mom, helping to get us ready early that morning and my dad improvising an outdoor freezer for the solitary pickerel. I remember arriving home and wondering what would become of the pickerel we intended to retrieve but never did. I remember the twins, Diane and Susan joining us. They must have been about 20 at the time and up for anything, even ice fishing. It is hard to believe that we have fallen out of touch with them, although we recently shared with Susan photos of our grandkids on Facebook... And then there is George, a constant presence in our young lives but a distant relative after we grew up. Sadly, Georgie passed away, much too young, between the time of the first and final drafts of this essay.

February 21, 1965 had it all: adventure, history and family, rolled into one classic day of fun. With all of that, it's small wonder that Dad's 33rd birthday never had a chance to take center stage.

BOB DYLAN'S "ANOTHER SELF PORTRAIT"

"And there was no man around, who could track or chain him down.
He was never known to make a foolish move."
Bob Dylan, "John Wesley Harding" (1968) ©

"Oh, the lights were on the river, shining from outside.
I contemplated every move, or at least I tried."
Bob Dylan, deleted lyrics from demo version of
"Went to See the Gypsy" (1970) ©

When I heard that the next release in Bob Dylan's "Official Bootleg Series" was going to take us back to the misbegotten days of his 1970 double album, "Self Portrait," I recalled Greil Marcus' infamous 1970 review and I reacted by asking…"*What?* More of that sh-t?"

Now, I know that the original album has its admirers, including my brother Steve, but I believe that its negatives far outweighed the positives. The negatives included a distinct lack of focus, numerous overly orchestrated arrangements, cover versions that ranged from curious to embarrassing, and precious few new Bob Dylan songs. I did and still like Bob's singing on a few of the songs, notably the traditional "Days of '49" and Paul Clayton's "Gotta Travel On", but it seemed as if Columbia

Records managed to release four vinyl sides of weak material when they really had one fairly strong side to work with. As for the new project, it wasn't as if Bob's people needed to scrape the bottom of the outtake barrel in order to keep the Bootleg Series rolling merrily along. I am sure, or at least I am hopeful, that I am not the only person who periodically annoys Bob's manager (the keeper of the vault) with "brilliant" suggestions for the next release. For example, we are still awaiting the release of the acoustic Supper Club shows (NYC, 1993), which featured Dylan's finest singing in many a decade, before or since. Also, the highly underrated 1974 Dylan/Band tour has not been adequately documented, while the red hot gospel shows (1980-81) have not been officially documented at all.

So, it was with more than a smidgen of skepticism and with minimal enthusiasm that I approached the August 2013 release date of "Another Self Portrait". Perhaps I would not even bother to order it. But the Dylan modern marketing machine did its thing and in my "inbox", a fantastic 10 minute video magically appeared, featuring David Bromberg, Al Kooper and producer Bob Johnston, all reminiscing about how the original "Self Portrait" came to be. The film included some music, of course, and it sounded damn good; the video is well worth searching for on-line, maybe before you continue reading this essay. Soon after that, I received another video, this one having recently been made to accompany the release of "Pretty Saro," a traditional song that had been left in the vault back in 1970, omitted from the original "Self-Portrait." Bob was singing in his "Lay, Lady Lay" smooth tenor style and it may have been the most accomplished vocal he had ever put to vinyl. Having experienced similar belated discoveries of rejected gems such as "Farewell Angelina", "She's Your Lover Now", "Up to Me", "Blind Willie McTell" and "Series of Dreams", its omission from the original collection hardly shocked me. Finally, I received another e-mail with a healthy sampling of the 35 songs that were going to be included in the basic version of "Another Self Portrait" and they were all winners.

I barely managed to resist plunking down $100 or so for the expanded version that included Dylan & The Band's 1969 Isle of Wight concert (which I have on a bootleg) plus a re-mastered version of the original "Self Portrait" (which would only collect dust and take up space). Instead, I ordered the basic, 35-track 2-disk version. The first thing a schooled Dylan fan will notice, even before tearing the plastic from the cardboard, is that the title "Another Self Portrait" is somewhat misleading because the new release actually encompasses several tracks from "New Morning," which followed "Self Portrait" later in 1970, and even includes an unreleased "Basement Tapes" track from 1967. 1969's "Nashville Skyline" is also revisited here and samples of other sources are tapped, giving the collection a span of 1967 to 1971. But the emphasis is clearly a re-examination of the traditional songs that Dylan was recording for "Self-Portrait" in early March, 1970 plus the original material that he recorded three months later for "New Morning."

A theme throughout, which stands in contrast to the original "Self Portrait," is the stripped down sound, with Dylan's vocal brought right to the front of the room and surrounded sympathetically by just a couple of instruments, most often David Bromberg's acoustic guitar and Al Kooper's piano, but occasionally simply by Dylan's own lonely piano. In fact, Dylan's surprisingly engaging piano style on three songs, including the solo version of "Went to See the Gypsy" and a gorgeous violin by an unknown player in a slow, moody, alternate version of "If Not For You," are amongst the many pleasant surprises on "Another Self Portrait." (Naturally, one wonders how a classic session with possibly the world's most famous musician could include an "anonymous" violin player.) George Harrison, in the midst of his own "laid-back" period, lends some tasteful support as well. While listening to Dylan, supported by Bromberg and Kooper, deftly and confidently sing, pick and blow his way through the traditional "Railroad Bill," it is easy to forget that a few years earlier, he, along with The Band, was powering his way through the most explosive and controversial rock music the world had ever known. I can imagine Doc Watson tapping his foot and smiling to this simple, breezy track. All of this is in stark contrast to the cluttered sound that marred many of the tracks on the original Self Portrait, as Bob brought literally dozens of musicians, many of them great ones, into the crowded mix. And as Bromberg said on the video, Dylan may not have a great voice but *"he is a great singer...the man can put across a song like no one else can."* These quieter tracks highlight some of the greatest vocals of his career.

There also seems to be more of a thematic unity to "Another Self Portrait" than to its predecessor. Many of the songs deal with themes of reflection, meditation and the uncertainty of what lies ahead. Some have suggested that the mood of the album is autumnal, with the slow realization that changes are a-coming. During the heady days climaxing with "Blonde on Blonde" in 1966, Bob seemed to have all of the answers, even if the questions were not always clear. The 1968 comeback album, "John Wesley Harding" was a quiet collection of parables and fables but Dylan still remained the teacher, the guru, the man in full control. Now, for the first time since "Blowin' in the Wind," Bob seemed to be looking for some answers—or at least needing to take a step back to reflect.

That is certainly the case in "Went to See the Gypsy", which is thought to be based upon either a real or apocryphal encounter with Elvis. The new album includes two unreleased versions of this low-key ballad: a demo with Dylan and Bromberg on guitar and Dylan's solo piano version. Both are moodier and starker than the "New Morning" version, with the protagonist seeking out the mysterious gypsy but ultimately having to settle for the comfort of the familiar sunrise of his little hometown. There are some fine renditions of traditional songs about murderers, scoundrels and men hovering on the fringes. But the theme of quiet contemplation pervades the album. "Time Passes Slowly" recounts the pleasures of the quiet, country life while "Sign on the Window" finds the singer sadly bemoaning his loneliness while yearning for the simplest of pleasures. On this track, instead of scaling back, "Another Self Portrait" has restored Al Kooper and Charles Calello's majestic orchestral string arrangement that was written and recorded for this little-known Dylan masterwork. Similarly, Kooper and Calello's funky horn arrangement has been restored to "New Morning."

Every once in a while, either on record or in concert, Dylan covers a song that you suspect he wishes he had written. By 1966, when Eric Andersen wrote and recorded "Thirsty Boots," Bob Dylan had long since drifted away from the world and milieu that had spawned the civil rights marches that inspired Andersen's song. Perhaps, by 1970, Bob saw this classic as the flip side to his own "When the Ship Comes In," with Andersen's chorus, exhorting one to step away from the battles and to *stay for a while.*" Bob gives it a solid attempt on this album. However, where Bob's vast interpretive powers are truly brought to bear is on the stripped down version of Albert Beddoe's "Copper Kettle", where a moonshiner feels inclined to *"just lay there by the juniper"* and *"watch them jugs a-fillin' in the pale moonlight."* Bromberg's unobtrusive guitar and Kooper's quiet piano give Dylan all the room he needs to deliver one of his most affecting and haunting vocals.

Despite their common roots, the two albums could not sound any more different to my ears. While repeated listenings can make the original "Self Portrait" seem alienating, distant and superficial, its successor is increasingly inviting, familiar and deep. The Dylan of "Self Portrait" appears uncertain, halting and tentative. By contrast, he closes "Another Self Portrait" with his demo version of "When I Paint My Masterpiece," a title that declared his confidence in his ability to still produce the brilliant works that were in his future, even as his fans had come to doubt whether the spark was still lit. The title character in the Coen Brothers' "Inside Llewyn Davis" said, "*If it was never new and it never gets old, then it's a folk song.*" Someday, that definition will fit the entirety of the new release—traditionals, covers and even originals—like a glove.

By and large, the market and audience for "Self-Portrait" and "Another Self-Portrait" remain one and the same. The release of the two recordings was separated by half a lifetime, 43 years to be precise. During that time, this audience has experienced countless changes, as a demographic group and as individuals. In 1970, many of us thought that we knew it all and what we didn't know, we wanted Bob Dylan to tell us. Woodstock was over, its promise was already beginning to fade and a generation wanted to know what to do next. As early as 1966, Robbie Robertson was captured on film asking a silent Dylan, "*Where are you going to be taking it next?*" I guess that Robbie, like the rest of us, wanted to pretend that Bob had never warned us: "*Don't follow leaders, watch the parking meters.*" When the one guy who young people trusted, refused to provide any answers and instead, responded by releasing "Self Portrait," people were disappointed, confused and angry.

We now know that we know today much more than we did in 1970, but we also know that we still do not know all that much at all. We know now that Dylan never had all the answers and that we were foolish to think that he ever did. But we also know that during Bob's 50 odd years in the business, he has made an awful lot of great music, arguably more than anyone else has put out there. Most of the time, Dylan was miles ahead of the musical and cultural curves. Hell, he designed and built some of those curves. As we begin to look backwards over the arc of our own lives and reflect on the "what was", "what is" and "what might have been", perhaps it is comforting to sit back and listen to these simple original recordings. They were made at a time when Dylan, still in his twenties but wise beyond his years, was trying to do the same. He was trying to make sense of what had occurred, where he had been and where he was at that moment in time, not where he would be going next. There would be ample time for future masterpieces.

David Bromberg Remembers Recording "Self Portrait":

My memories of recording on Self Portrait are mostly of being alone in the studio with Bob. Al Kooper may or may not have been with us on some of the tracks. I don't remember him being there, but he says he was, so he must have been present for some of the sessions. I remember Bob calling me for the sessions. I wasn't sure that it was him on the phone at first. I thought someone might be putting me on, but I realized it was him fairly quickly. He told me that he was trying out a studio, and wanted to know if I'd come with him. That was how it started for me.

Author, David Bromberg, David Grisman, Jonah Eidman
May 2002 backstage at MDA Jam Benefit Concert, Englewood, NJ
Photo courtesy of the author

A YANKEE HATER'S VIEW OF DEREK JETER

"Three-two count with nobody on
He hit a high fly into the stand.
Rounding third he was headed for home
It was a brown eyed handsome man
That won the game; it was a brown eyed handsome man."
Chuck Berry, "Brown Eyed Handsome Man" ©

If any athlete has lived the dream, it has been the iconic Yankee shortstop, Derek Jeter. First round draft pick, Rookie of

This move was not helpful.
Photo courtesy of icon sportswire

the Year, the Core Four, the flip throw, the bloody face catch, the five rings, the patented jump throw, the super models, the MVP awards (alright, there were no MVP awards, but he came close a couple of times), the 3,000 hits, all those Yankee team records and pre-booked, confirmed reservations for both Monument Park in the Bronx and baseball's Hall of Fame in Cooperstown, NY. Perhaps the Captain's most remarkable achievement has been a 20 year run in the eye of world's media vortex with nary a hint of scandal. No small thing, especially considering his dating repertoire! And if Derek did not love his neighbor, fellow Yankee Alex Rodriguez, well, he had plenty of company. So, why do Yankee haters harbor an extra-special loathing for this Jeter guy, a decent sort of dude by any account, and the last Yankee to wear a uniform with a single digit on its back?

When I was in the 6th grade, my mom went to parent-teacher conferences and my Jewish studies teacher launched into a slow, mumbling recitation of my alleged deficiencies, of both intellect and character. After listening quietly for a bit, Mom told the rabbi that she was also a teacher and that no matter how awful a kid, she always began a conference by telling the parents something positive. So, before going on, Mom insisted that my teacher tell her something—anything—good about me. In that spirit, I feel obligated to begin this Jeter analysis with some positives. In fact, there was and is an awful lot to like about Jeter. Even detractors must admit that after the mythic Honus Wagner, Jeter is in the discussion for the second best shortstop in Major League Baseball history. Personally, I'd put him 4th, after Wagner, Arky Vaughn (whose great career was curtailed by WWII) and Cal Ripken, Jr. But let's face it, I never got see to Arky Vaughn play, let alone the Flying Dutchman (although that must have been something to see), so I can't argue all that convincingly in their favor. And if someone wants to put Jeter ahead of Ripken, well, that's really a matter of taste, with my preference for Ripken's power and defense winning out over Jeter's steady offense and speed. And I'm not even going to penalize Jeter for his blank slate, bland personality. Let's face it, Cal Ripken wasn't exactly Mr. Dynamic either.

As a member of Red Sox Nation, when the game was on the line, I never, ever wanted to see Jeter at the plate, especially not the Jeter of his primo years. And that had little to do with his supposed innate "clutch" qualities, his legendary "intangibles" or other super human characteristics. Like few batters, Jeter was a purely instinctual hitter without a paralyzing "philosophical" approach to hitting, other than "see ball, hit ball." What he did have was a natural inside-out swing, allowing him to wait until the last nano-second so that he was not merely fighting off inside pitches but rather hitting them with authority and occasional power, usually to right-field. Meanwhile, he would simply punish outside pitches, lunging into them and slashing hits to all fields. Should the pitcher make a perfect pitch, Jeter, more often than not, would foul it off. There was simply no effective way to pitch to him. Because he never gave in to the pitcher or gave away at-bats, he accumulated more infield hits and reached first on more cheap dribblers and shallow bloops than just about any player. At least it sure seemed that way. What we know for certain is that as of this writing, Jeter's unorthodox batting style has resulted in 3,356 hits (and counting) plus another big season's worth of hits (206) during his fabled post-season career.

DEREK JETER: OFFENSIVE JUGGERNAUT

From the standpoint of traditional offensive statistics, Derek Jeter's career is roughly comparable to modern day infielders Paul Molitor, Peter Rose, Craig Biggio, Joe Morgan, Wade Boggs and to a slightly lesser extent, Cal Ripken, Jr. (I am including Ripken because he played SS for many years and the others all were similar "offensive" infielders.) Amongst this group of 7 elite modern infielders, Jeter is 2nd in runs scored, 4th in RBIs (although he might still move a up a notch or even two), 6th in doubles, 4th in triples, 4th in HRs, 4th in steals, 2nd in batting average, 3rd in OBA and 3rd in slugging. OPS+ measures on base plus slugging and adjusts it according to the player's home ballpark. Jeter's OPS+ was 5th amongst this group. Obviously, he fits easily within this group but in no way towers above it. To get a bit more sophisticated, we can look at WAR (Wins Against Replacement), which measures the number of wins that a player added to his team above what a "replacement level player" would have added. This stat also considers fielding, at least to some extent. That would explain Jeter's relatively poor showing, as he comes in with a career WAR of 71.9, which is the second lowest in the group, which is led by Morgan's 100, followed by Ripken's 95 and Boggs at 91. Even Arky Vaughn, with a much briefer career than Jeter, beat him by one game. (For the sake of perspective, Babe Ruth is the all-time leader at 183. For players who played after 1950 and were not obvious steroid abusers, Willie Mays leads with 156. Despite being better than two Derek Jeters, I don't recall any special TV ads celebrating the Say Hey Kid during his final go-round, in 1973).

Lou Whitaker and Alan Trammel handled the middle infield for the Tigers for 19 years, finishing up when Jeter was getting started. Each one wound up with about 1,000 hits fewer than Jeter would eventually accumulate, yet Whitaker accumulated a career WAR of 74.9 and Trammel's was 70.4. If either goes to the HOF, they'll have to pay their way in, just like you and me. The fact of the matter is that Jeter hit better than Trammel or Whitaker but they fielded much, much better than Jeter. With his many team records, his 5 rings and his stellar post-season play, how high does the Captain rank amongst the many greats to wear the Yankee pinstripes? I believe that any sane baseball fan with even a modest sense of history, can put The Captain no higher than fifth best in the pantheon of Yankee greats, after The Babe, The Iron Horse, The Mick and The Yankee Clipper. Whether #8 (Yogi Berra) or #2 (Jeter) gets to be considered fifth best, is not my fight. Actually, I got to go with Yogi because he played for the Mets for about a week in 1964 and managed them to a pennant in 1973.

The bottom line is that even without the 5 rings, the media glorification and fan adulation, Jeter's offensive prowess establishes him as a worthy first-ballot Hall of Fame candidate. But all the chatter about "the first unanimous choice" and "greatest Yankee of all time" is just silly. Admittedly, most of that nonsense comes from Yankee nut cases, who place Jeter just below G-d and slightly ahead of Moses, Jesus or the Prophet, depending upon their religion.

DEREK JETER: DEFENSIVE SIEVE

As any true Yankee hater knows, the real crux of the Derek Jeter controversy is his fielding or more accurately, the lack thereof. Somehow, Jeter managed to charm the writers, male and female alike, into awarding him five Gold Gloves, without any persuasive evidence that he is a great fielder. Or a good fielder. Or a competent fielder. To the contrary, all empirical evidence proves, beyond a shadow of a doubt, that Jeter has been the worst fielding shortstop of his era. How could it be that the key defensive position on the most famous baseball team was being handled atrociously, yet hardly anyone seemed to notice? To begin, we must understand the historical context.

Derek Jeter played during an era when the basis for the evaluation of baseball defense evolved from educated guesswork to near-scientific analysis. During the early days of baseball, when fields were unkempt and gloves were small, it made sense to judge fielders based upon the percentage of misplays they made on balls that were hit directly at them. Way back then, catching an "atom ball", that is, a ball hit "right at 'em", was hard enough, and fielders were not expected to move much in order to make a play. Hence, the concept of 'fielding percentage', or the percentage of times that a player successfully converts an "atom ball" into an out. But because of the improvement in the quality of ballfields, especially infields, and in the skill of players, as well as the increase in glove sizes, almost all modern fielders were converting at least 95% of the balls hit to them into outs. So, based strictly upon fielding percentage, all fielders looked pretty much alike.

I recall that following the 1978 season, Pete Rose left his hometown Cincinnati Reds for the big bucks of the Phillies. At that point, Rose, aka "Charlie Hustle", was a third-baseman and the Phillies already had a decent player at that spot. In fact, they had Mike Schmidt, who was almost certainly the greatest third-baseman of all time. People looked at the published fielding stats and wondered which future Hall of Famer (little did they know!) would man the hot corner for the Phillies in 1979. After all, the two greats had nearly identical fielding percentages (Schmidt .963, Rose .961) and had committed similar amounts of errors (Rose 15, Schmidt 16). What the Philly management realized, thankfully, was that Schmidt, in 139 games, had converted 78 more balls into outs than Rose did in 156 games. Thus, Schmidt saved his team 78 hits, as compared to Rose, with virtually the same fielding percentage. Rose, never known as a glove man at any position, had earned a .961 fielding percentage by catching nearly everything (roughly 96% of the balls) hit right at him. Schmidt scored a similar .963 pct. on the balls hit right at him but he also caught balls that were not hit right at him, including balls hit down the line, in the hole, some slow dribblers and swinging bunts, etc. Ironically, the father of modern baseball statistics, Henry Chadwick, wanted to judge fielders objectively (that is, by counting the number of successful plays they made) and not subjectively (by the number of errors they were deemed to have been "morally guilty" of committing by an anonymous "official scorer"). But it was not to be.

Traditionally, fielders were also judged by 'how they looked out there.' By that I mean two things. First, whereas batters were evaluated based upon traditional "counting" statistics, the evaluation of fielders usually went something like this: *"Well, I remember this one time when Joe Schmo was playing deep, came charging in, made this amazing, tumbling shoe-string catch, jumped up and doubled the runner off of first. He was the greatest...."* (If we judged batters like that, Richie Allen and

Frank Howard would be remembered as the greatest hitters of all time, the equals of Babe Ruth.) Secondly, to some extent, fielders were also judged by their physical appearance and how they handled themselves in the field.

Hence, the problems with Jeter. For starters, who has looked more like a great shortstop than Derek, in his sleek #2 pinstripes, with his coolly unflappable yet authoritative demeanor? Perhaps Ozzie, but no one else. Then, you have the fact that traditional, error-based evaluation of fielding has benefited no ballplayer as much as Derek Jeter. How often have we heard that Jeter can always be counted on to make the sure play? That is just another way of saying that he is very good at catching the easy balls that are hit directly at him, in his dependable, confident way. As Ben Lindbergh put it in an article that appeared in Grantland on August 27, 2013: *"Jeter gets outs on an above average percentage of the balls he gets to, which helps obscure the fact that he gets to so few."*

Finally, you have Jeter's signature, ESPN highlight plays. His prescient "flip play" in the 2001 playoffs, nailing Jason Giambi's non-sliding, untalented brother at the plate, will remain an ESPN classic forever. So will his hard-charging chase of a regular season foul pop into the second row of Yankee Stadium, during the 12th inning of a tie game, with Johnny Damon (then a Red Sock) on second base. (I must admit that in researching this essay, I watched Jeter's leap of faith and bloody face foul pop, multiple times. Brilliant plays, both of them although Boston did have the last laugh that wonderful season.) And then, there is Jeter's "patented" jump play and bounce throw from deep in the hole. Far from being a great play, this is nothing more than a desperate, compensatory adjustment for his poor range, awkward footwork and weak arm. A real MLB shortstop gets to those balls earlier, plants his back foot and fires across his body, on the fly, to first. But again, the jump and throw *look* good, at least to the ignorant or brainwashed.

Such "Jeteresque" moments have helped create the legend and have garnered Gold Glove votes, while hiding the much more important and damning truths about Jeter's defense and his stubborn refusal to budge from the shortstop position. Thanks to modern metrics, the cost of Jeter's shoddy defense can now be quantified, with some degree of certainty. The fact is that Jeter's defensive weakness and vanity have cost his team measurably and not insignificantly. His defense, while never adequate, declined during the mid-2000s, when the Yankee defense was by far and away the worst in baseball. During many of these seasons, the Yankees fell just short of victory and its porous defense was largely responsible, with its "Captain" as a prime offender.

The issue concerning Derek Jeter's defense started getting kicked around about 10 years ago. The first edition of John Dewan's superb book, "The Fielding Bible," published in the spring of 2006, when Jeter was 31, contained a masterly article by Bill James entitled "Jeter vs. Everett." Dewan, whose company, Baseball Information Solutions, counts most major league teams amongst its clients, gave James a DVD containing 80 defensive plays. The plays were Jeter's 20 best and 20 worst plays from 2005 along with the best and worst 20 of "good field/no hit" shortstop Adam Everett. Bill James described watching the video as, *"Sort of like watching Barbara Bush dancing at the White House and then watching Demi Moore dancing in Striptease."* He went on to describe the vast stylistic, positional and strategic differences between the players. Then, he went about studying the issue at some length. James examined Jeter's defense from four distinct and statistically independent points of view:

1. Baseball Information Solutions had watched every game, while recording information about each batted ball, including its location, its direction, its speed and its type. Then, they figured out the likelihood that a MLB shortstop

would turn a given batted ball into an out. This study concluded that, *"Derek Jeter was probably the least effective defensive player in the major leagues, at any position."* For the sake of brevity, I am omitting the actual numbers, except to say that the difference between the underachieving Jeter and the overachieving Everett was 66 plays.

2. There are four holes guarded by a shortstop: up the middle, between third and short, in short left-field and in the infield. In 2005, the average MLB team yielded 487 hits through or into these areas, with the Houston Everetts yielding a stingy 425. If you've listened to enough Yankee broadcasts, you've heard countless variations on the following theme: "There's a groundball up the middle...past-a-diving Jeter, and on into..." Well, in 2005, Yankee games featured an awful lot of 'pasta diving,' as 522 hits fell within shortstop territory.

3. Relative Range Factor ("RRF") does not rely on the actual observations of games, as does the Baseball Information Solutions method. It merely counts up plays made per 9 innings and adjusts for all the variables, such as strikeouts and groundball tendencies of pitching staffs, the ranges of surrounding fielders, left/right biases of pitching staffs, etc. The method has been shown to be more accurate over multiple years, as opposed to during any single year. In 2005, DJ's numbers were decent, but, as James points out, 2005 *"was only the second time in his career that his RRF hasn't been absolutely horrible."* James went on to say he would be amazed, just amazed if he were to find "any other shortstop in major league history whose RRFs are anywhere near as bad as Jeter's." In fact, since the Ozzie Smith era, *"while no other recognizable shortstop had even one season in which his team had 40 fewer assists by shortstops than expected, Jeter had season after season in that category."*

4. James also discusses the zone rating system, which uses similar data underlying to the Baseball Information Systems method. Under this system, Jeter fares similarly poorly.

The bottom line is that systems 1, 2 and 3 all studied the same question from entirely different points of view, yet arrived at the exact same conclusion.

What was the cost of Jeter's defensive shortcomings during the 2005 season, as compared to Adam Everett? The roughly 70-hit differential between the two was comprised almost entirely of singles, which translates to 30 or 35 runs. Despite the huge gap in defensive proficiency, Everett did not have a better year than Derek Jeter because on offense, Jeter created 101 runs to Everett's 61. As Bill James astutely pointed out, it stands to reason that the worst defenders would be great offensive players.

Of course, when it comes to the New York Yankee golden boy, proof beyond any reasonable doubt is never proof enough. Jeter continued to accumulate unearned Gold Glove awards even <u>after</u> the publication of "Jeter vs. Everett" in 2006, winning that same year and after that as well. But the issue did not go away.

It was revisited by John Dewan in his article entitled "Jeter vs. Ryan," which appeared in his Fielding Bible Volume III, published in 2012. During the intervening six years, fielding analytics had progressed significantly thanks in large part to the availability of even more data and a greater interest in understanding fielding. By 2011, Brendan Ryan had inherited from Adam Everett the Mark Belanger mantle of "good field/no hit" shortstop. That year, Ryan had a 33 defensive run advantage over Jeter, in that he saved his team 18 runs as compared to an average MLB shortstop, while Jeter cost the Yanks 15 runs.

How did Dewan arrive at this conclusion? Imagine there is a line drawn from the batter's box to the SS position. MLB shortstops, in 2011, turned 65% of the balls that were hit to the right side of this line into outs. Ryan and Jeter were both average on balls hit in that direction, with Ryan converting the league average of 65% and Jeter converting 64%. But with every 6 to 8 feet that we move to the left of the imaginary line, toward third-base, the qualitative differences between the two players become more pronounced. By the time we have moved into the third "6 to 8 feet" increment to the left of the imaginary line, MLB shortstops converted an average of 34% of the balls into outs, while Ryan converted 56% and Jeter converted 26%. Move an additional 6 to 8 feet away, and Ryan's ratio was 13% as compared to the MLB average of 8%. Derek Jeter failed to convert a single ball in that range into an out.

This spring (2014), Baseball-Reference.com tallied up the players who cost their teams the most runs on defense over their careers compared to an average defender at their position. Its all-time leader is Derek Sanderson Jeter with 236 runs. Gary Sheffield is a distant second at 196. Michael Humphreys' brilliant and comprehensive 2011 book, <u>Wizardry</u>, is dedicated to the scientific study of the "Holy Grail" that is defense in baseball, throughout the ages. Below are a few random, famous shortstops throughout the eras, followed by the number of runs they saved their teams over the years, as a result of their superior defense, according to Humphreys. When adjustments are made for the era, e.g., pre-1947, pre-Latin American influx, etc., the numbers change, sometimes considerably and those are also shown.

Joe Tinker: 283 (adjusted down to 177)

Honus Wagner: 81 (adjusted down, somewhere below 35)

Luke Appling: 141 (adjusted down to 72)

Joe Cronin: 99 (adjusted down somewhere below 35)

Phil Rizzuto: 98 (adjusted down to 39)

Mark Belanger: 197 (adjusted down to 167)

Ozzie Smith: 151 (adjusted down to 135)

Rey Sanchez: 141 (adjusted down to 138; in a very short career!)
Barry Larkin: 112 (adjusted down to 106)
Derek Jeter: -270 (through 2011 only)

According to Humphreys' data, no shortstop in MLB history has been responsible for giving away even half as many runs during the course of his career as the 270 runs that Derek Jeter has cost his team. Even the defensively befuddled and befuddling Manny Ramirez only cost his teams "only" 131 runs in leftfield. (Bonus tidbit for Mets fans: Keith Hernandez leads all first-basemen, having saved his teams 212 with his glove and mustache).

It's not as if the Yankee brain trust, such as it is, was totally blind to what was going on, what with all of the pasta-diving, all of the compensatory jump-throws, etc. Ben Lindbergh points out in his 2013 Grantland article that Yankee General Manager Brian Cashman sat down with Jeter after the 2007 season, when Derek was 33, for a defense heart-to-heart. Derek, being the good guy that he is, took it to heart and fielded better for a season before Father Time continued to push him ever more downhill. If you are going to read one "Jeter Can't Field" article besides this one, try tracking down the Lindbergh article, entitled "The Tragedy of Derek Jeter's Defense", which originally appeared in the now-defunct Grantland on-line magazine at espn.com

DEREK JETER: THE LAST 10%

Derek Jeter's role with the Yankees can be broken down into three components. The first and largest piece is his offensive role, to which I would (randomly and unscientifically) assign about 65% of the whole. Thus, I gladly admit that Derek Jeter has been a certified 65% superstar baseball player. Next, accounting for about 25% of the whole, is the defensive piece. Here, Jeter has been deficient and defective, handicapping his already defensively-challenged team for nearly two decades. The final 10% is composed of "everything else": base-running, leadership, career longevity, the so-called "intangibles," etc. While this is probably the most subjective area, it is also another area where the Yankee organization, its fans, and the media have given Derek Jeter a free pass. I believe that any dispassionate view of Derek Jeter must find him lacking, sometimes severely so, in many of the qualities that separate the greats from the all-time greats.

As a base stealer, Derek Jeter has been very good and reliable, though not world-class. All in all, he has swiped 349 bases while getting caught 95 times, giving him a fine success rate of 78.6%. Amongst the players we previously threw into Jeter's class, Morgan, Molitor and Biggio were better, while the others were worse. Amongst other contemporaries, Bobby Abreu was comparable and Carlos Beltran was better. Base-running (other than stealing), including going first-to-third on a single and second-to-home, was traditionally judged in a similar fashion to how fielding was judged: that is, by reputation and by the naked eye, without the benefit of empirical evidence. That has changed and we now know how often the average runner advances on base-hits, on wild-pitches, etc. I doubt that the system is perfect for any single season but given Jeter's long career, any perceived inequities have undoubtedly evened out. The numbers indicate that Derek Jeter has been a surprisingly indifferent base runner, given his speed and his purported superior instincts.

When adding up all bases taken not by steals and then subtracting "negative base-running events" (e.g., see former Met, Daniel Murphy) Derek Jeter, over the course of his long career, has been 27 bases better than average, or about a base and a half per season. Perhaps there are reasons why Jeter has been mostly a "station-to-station" base runner. Maybe it has something to do with the short right-field at Yankee Stadium. Maybe it has something to do with the power hitters lined up behind Jeter. Whatever it is, once he has reached a base and the ball has been put into play, Derek Jeter has been an average major league player. By contrast, Beltran has been plus 148, Granderson plus 106, Kinsler plus 108 and Utley plus 171 (despite the fact that Ryan Howard bats behind him). Jeter is demonstrably better on the bases than Robinson Cano, who is 56 bases worse than average.

Derek Jeter has reaped endless praise from fans and media for his alleged 'selfless dedication to winning.' He has come to symbolize "Yankee pride" (whatever that means, exactly) and has been the face of the franchise for many years. It has become a matter of faith that he would never do anything to his team's detriment, let alone for the sake of his own vanity or fame. At the press conference before the start of his final season, Derek was asked to pick his favorite career highlight. In typical Jeter non-speak, he replied, *"Every time the Yankees win."* That non-answer was consistent with Jeter's well-crafted and well-honed image as the selfless captain who seeks no personal glory and yearns for nothing other than the betterment of his troops. But a Yankee hater's view of the hard quantitative evidence paints a very different picture…

If all Jeter cared about were Yankee victories, wouldn't slick-fielding and strong-armed Alex Rodriguez have been the Yankee shortstop when he joined the team in 2004?

If all Jeter cared about were Yankee victories, wouldn't he have used his status as "Yankee Captain" to lead by example in fostering an atmosphere of security, warmth and support around the skilled but perpetually insecure Rodriguez instead of giving him the cold shoulder when he joined the team?

If all Jeter cared about were Yankee victories, wouldn't he have permitted the Yanks to shift him, on occasion, to less stressful positions around the diamond?

If all Jeter cared about were Yankee victories, wouldn't he have marched himself into Joe Girardi's office and suggested that the manager move him, along with his crippling .254/.312/.300 slash line, down in the lineup?

Derek Jeter's teammates and opponents express universal admiration for him, in large part because of the way that he has "conducted himself" throughout his long career in the Big Apple. He has stayed out of trouble. He has done charity work. But he has not always set the best example for his peers and the younger generation of players who felt privileged to wear the pinstripes and to share the field and locker room with the great Jeter. His non-sequitur dealings with the press have tacitly told every player that it is acceptable to hide behind a screen of bland responses to every conceivable question and to give nothing to the public, once the game has ended. Would it kill the guy to once, just one time, let people know what he really thinks about something? Instead, one of the highest profile athletes of our lifetime has chosen to talk in well-worn clichés and trite truisms.

Not that Derek does not play the media game, however disingenuously, when he perceives it to be to his advantage. Even after the death of legendary Yankee Stadium announcer Bob Sheppard at age 99, Jeter continued to use a tape of Sheppard announcing Jeter's majestic arrival at the batter's box. And Derek let people know of his admiration and respect for the man. Nevertheless, not a single Yankee player including the Yankee team captain, bothered to attend Sheppard's funeral mass in Baldwin, Long Island, which took place on a Yankee off-day during a home stand. Jeter was similarly disingenuous when he strongly intimated that when it was time, he would simply retire. Rather than simulating the dignified, quiet retirement of Mickey Mantle, who left the game during spring training, Jeter opted for a season-long retirement tour heavy on the gifts and accolades but lacking in Mariano's classy, time-sharing sit-downs with local fans and stadium workers throughout the major league cities.

Dylan once sang, *"The newspapers went along for the ride."* Well, the media, and in particular the mighty Yankee media machine, gladly coasted along on Jeter's coattails. In plugging a retirement tour event involving Derek's status as the all-time Yankee leader in base-hits, the Yanks were highlighting the fact that Jeter broke Lou Gehrig's record of 2,721 base-hits even though, to that point, Jeter had played 44 fewer games than the Iron Horse had played. (Wow, a whopping 44 games!). True enough. What the Yankee flack failed to say was that it took Jeter more than 500 additional at-bats, nearly a season's worth, in order get his 2,721 hits. But then, who needs to know that slight detail? (Not to mention that the mere suggestion that Jeter was "better" than Gehrig is preposterous, but I guess it was worth it to demean the memory of the sainted Gehrig for the purposes of further sanctifying the holier divinity of The Jeter.)

As Derek Jeter approaches his 40th birthday, the sad but undeniable fact is that, aside from a series of pre-game parties, he has had nothing to show so far this season. His hustle was gone by the home opener when he went into a premature home run trot on a long fly ball which struck the fence and went for a single. He assumed a ball that bounced off a sliding Brett Gardner's glove was foul, when in fact, it was fair. Thankfully, Jeter stopped just a smidgen short of flipping the ball to a fan in the stands. Instead, his mental lapse merely permitted the batter to stretch a single into a "triple", costing the Yanks a key run.

As I finish writing this draft, the Yanks are at an even .500, 31-31, during this final campaign (2014) in The Captain's long career. Perhaps Jeter will turn his season around and the Yanks will follow suit. I would not put it past him. Didn't he hit a homer for his 3,000th hit, en route to going 5 for 5? I mean, the man can pull it together and rise to almost any occasion. People often remember a doddering, falling Willie Mays, stumbling around centerfield, but that actually occurred when Mays was 42. When Willie was 40, his slash line for the season was .271/.425/.482 with 18 home runs, 82 runs scored and 61 RBIs in only 417 at-bats. That Mays could no longer handle the fastball was proven by the uncharacteristic 123 K's; that Willie knew the strike zone better than the umpires who seemed reluctant to punch him out, was evidenced by the 112 BB's. That Mays was still Mays was best demonstrated by the 23 stolen bases in 26 attempts, at age 40. Let's see if Jeter can finish his "age 40" season by still being Jeter, by finishing with a flourish.

The bottom line is that Derek Jeter is not and has never been in the class of ballplayer that Willie Mays belonged to. Or Henry Aaron, for that matter. But he is the equal of many great offensive-oriented infielders, whose plaques proudly hang in Cooperstown. Jeter should have followed the career path of Robin Yount, another similar player, who after playing shortstop for 10 years and winning a MVP at the position, transitioned to the outfield, ultimately winning a second MVP as a centerfielder, en route to over 3,100 hits. (Yount also accumulated some 100 more extra base hits than Jeter did, but as a small-market guy, no one was falling all over themselves when he retired or even when he played, for that matter). It is clear that a change in position would have maximized Jeter's talents, minimized his deficiencies and probably enhanced his prodigious offensive game.

Derek Jeter has achieved more than enough to warrant entry into baseball's Hall of Fame on the first ballot. But there is simply no evidence to support the argument that he has been the greatest player of his generation, the greatest Yankee, or the greatest anything.

Gabriel Klausner: A Yankee Lover's View of Derek Jeter
Playing on the most hated team in sports through an era marred by
steroids and overpaid, underachieving peers who made more headlines
off the field than on it, Derek Jeter stood alone. He reminded nostalgic
grandfathers of the Hall of Fame ballplayers of yesteryear and inspired
an entire generation of young boys to dream of becoming the New York
Yankees' shortstop. It will be a long time, if ever, before baseball is
graced with another gentlemanly leader and humble champion such as
Derek Jeter.

REFLECTIONS ON DEATH AND DYING

"Death don't have no mercy in this land
Death don't have no mercy in this land
He'll come to your house and he won't stay long
You'll look in the bed and somebody will be gone
Death don't have no mercy in this land"
Rev. Gary Davis, "Death Don't Have No Mercy" ©

Town cemetery, Lew Beach, NY. Photo courtesy of author

A couple of weeks ago, Jews all over the world recited Yizkor, the traditional Jewish memorial prayer read on four significant holidays each year. By and large, the most important Jewish holidays are no literal or figurative day at the beach, as we incorporate the remembrance of our dearly departed into the already lengthy synagogue service. Yizkor is said by those who have suffered the loss of a parent, child, spouse or sibling, and in most synagogues, you can exit the sanctuary if you don't fall into that category. (Many synagogues have also added a communal paragraph in memory of Holocaust victims, fallen IDF soldiers and terror victims.) As kids, we didn't mind Yizkor because we were happy to escape the rigors of "davening" [praying] for even a few minutes. We would play outside while our less fortunate and more world-weary parents, remained inside as the chazzan [the cantor] led the congregation through this mysterious prayer.

A couple of weeks ago, on the second and final day of Shavuot, some of us, thank G-d, once again made our way into the shul lobby while Yizkor was being recited. One of my friends said aloud what the rest of us were thinking: with each passing year (in fact, with each passing Yizkor service), there were fewer and fewer of us out in the lobby, while more and more remained in shul. A sad observation to be sure, but nothing more than a rueful note about the natural order of the universe. People get old, they die, and the next generation pauses for a moment in order to pay proper respect. Often, it happens too soon, but at least when it happens *in the right order,* we take solace in that natural fact.

Next year, our community's assistant Rabbi and his wife will begin saying Yizkor for the baby daughter they recently lost. She died at only 2½ after fighting an intractable neuroblastoma for a year and a half. I do not know what this horrific experience was like for the Rabbi and his family. I do know that for the community which watched the ordeal so vigilantly and so helplessly, it was gut-wrenching. We learned a few details, even as we stood outside the gates, trying to keep a respectful distance. Mostly, we learned about a family's dignity in the face of unspeakable tragedy and of a community's ability to, for once, put aside petty grievances.

Alas, as for the age-old mysteries of life and death, of reward and punishment, of pleasure and suffering—we drew no closer to the answers. These are questions that have bedeviled men ever since Moses stood on the mountain and pleaded with G-d for the insight needed to share in the ultimate enlightenment. If Moses was left unfulfilled, should we be any different? If the murders of 6 million produced not a single definitive answer, should the death of one small child entitle us to uncover any hidden truths? Did our collective grief merit just a shred of inside information that we did not have before? When you daven week after week in the same spot, within the same shul, with the same people, year after year...but then on this one day, they slowly wheel a tiny coffin through the main aisle right to the front of the packed shul...that was exactly what everyone wanted. Just a hint of insight, a smidgen of understanding, just a wee small glimpse of clarity.

Of course, there was no such epiphany. All we were left with were the words of our shul's head Rabbi, who asked us to try to use this moment of unification as an inspiration, a reminder, maybe a spiritual springboard. He encouraged us to resist allowing our trivial squabbles to fester into sources of bitter divisiveness and enmity. This was a message we had all heard before but perhaps this singular moment of incalculable sadness would serve as the key to unlock our hearts to the message. I certainly hope so.

When that little girl left this world, I felt as if the face of death could not be any more cruel or dark. But then, even before we had an opportunity to catch our collective breath and regain our emotional footing, our community again stood as one in tragedy. This time we stood with the entire Jewish world, as three families in Israel embarked upon the grim task of burying three teenage sons, all murdered after being kidnapped in the West Bank. And finally, as if to complete the terrible trifecta, I was hit with the news that my client's husband, a young NYC Fire Department lieutenant, became the first NYC fireman to die in a fire in over two years. Weeks earlier, he had been honored for saving the life of a Hasidic child in Williamsburg. As usual, I kept hearing Bob Dylan in my head. This time he was strumming a lonesome acoustic guitar and singing: *"Everything went from bad to worse, money never changed a thing; death kept following, tracking us down, at least I heard your bluebird sing..."* Only there was no bluebird singing to anyone.

So if I've been thinking about death, dwelling upon its suddenness, randomness and cruelty, I've come by it honestly, as my grandmother might have said. Of course, death need not be sudden or even inexplicable in order to cause us to pause for a second and reassess our own lives. During the past year, my close friend Danny's brother-in-law, Howie Weinreich, succumbed after a courageous, five-year battle with cancer, at age 58. I met Howie when we were 16, toiling together as camp waiters. During the past two years, cancer also claimed the lives of three stellar legal colleagues of mine, all between the ages of 56 and 61. In my mind's eye, I see each of them as the very picture of health, each possessing the smarts and guts to go the distance in the courtroom. Trial lawyers are tough creatures and each fought hard, right to the end, eking out whatever little time he had left.

These tragedies naturally had me reflecting on The Big C. The sad, frustrating truth is that despite all the research, funding, advertising and public awareness campaigns, we are simply not winning the "war against cancer." Yes, we have made progress extending life expectancy after diagnosis and we can better treat certain cancers, especially childhood cancers. But roughly the same amount of people will die in the US from cancer as died ten years ago. Whether this is the result of what we've been putting into our food, our consumer products, our environment...I have no idea. But no matter what the doctors, researchers and scientists tell us, the numbers make it clear that we are not even gaining much ground in this battle.

Now that I've mentioned a few recent horrible, tragic deaths and some premature ones, I guess it is time to circle back to the "normal" cycle of life and death. Under the best of circumstances, our loved ones—the people who raised us and guided us throughout our lives—eventually get old, usually get sick, suffer for an indeterminate length of time and finally die. Before very long, almost none of my generation will be outside schmoozing during Yizkor. But do we even need to project that far ahead in order to summon up a sense of dread and fear about what might be? King Solomon, in Ecclesiastes, recounts how he pities the living more than the dead, because the living must deal with all of the natural evil that exists in the world. I can only imagine what Solomon would say about today's world. Perhaps the wisest of men knew where society would be headed long after his time on earth would end.

Death at an advanced age is less tragic than dying prematurely, but nonetheless foreboding in its own right. When a young person gets sick, I completely understand the urge to take advantage of the little time left—perhaps putting one's affairs in order, or getting right with one's faith, or trying to get a few undone things done, maybe even correcting wrongs from the past. On the other hand, I believe that late in life, it is better to depart this world quickly, without all the pain, drama and plain boredom. Modern medical advances have extended life but I am not sure that the quality of the extension has kept pace with the quantity. In so many cases, it does not seem worth the bother, let alone the expense. It's not that getting old scares me; it's that I'm pretty sure that I don't want to spend the last 10 or 15 years of my life, in a decrepit state, in chronic pain, mentally diminished if not enfeebled (or the other way around or both!), a burden to my family, marking time until the inevitable. That's not a distorted or desperately bleak picture, but rather a definite possibility, not just for me but for everyone.

I read an essay about Admiral Chester Nimitz, Jr., son of the famed leader of our Pacific fleet during World War II, and his wife Joan. They lived incredibly fulfilling and interesting lives, maintaining their health well into their 80s. They decided well in advance that should things begin to spiral downwards for one or both of them, they would depart the world together, at a time of their own choosing and by their own hands. One day, when that time had arrived and while it was still within their mental and physical powers to rationally ponder and effectuate such a drastic decision, they said their goodbyes and successfully enacted their plan. I encourage you to read the full story—it all made perfect sense to me. Just to be clear, I'm not advocating for any position on euthanasia, I'm simply stating that what the Nimitz's did does not seem irrational, cruel or even sad to me. Be your own judge: their story can be found on Slate.com, *"Deaths With Dignity."*

NOT YOUR AVERAGE SUMMER VACATION

"You know that goddamned road seemed like it went forever.
Exhaust fumes made our eyes turn red and swell,
With our clothes stuck to the seat and to our bodies
It was a stinkin' summer trip through southern hell."
David Bromberg, "The New Lee Highway Blues" ©

Yes, the 500 mile drive home along a choked New Jersey Turnpike on a steamy August Sunday did indeed seem like it went forever. But the rest of the cool summer trip through a beautiful and quiet part of the Confederate Nation was really terrific. As usual, I had procrastinated in agreeing to Daphne's idea for a family vacation. I put it off for the usual reasons, all of which were true and all of which were lame. Mostly, I feared being away from the office. Then, there was the fact that none of us could not agree on a destination, with our preferences falling anywhere along a continuum that begins with a cabin on a remote lake (me) and ends with a full-service resort (Benjamin). In May, Daphne had read about Virginia's Music Heritage Trail, known as the "Crooked Road" and was intrigued. It was now late June and my middle son, Jonah, would be leaving for college at the end of August, and I figured some family bonding time was in order. So before you could say "google maps," research was performed, hotels were booked and the tiny trunk of my hybrid car was packed to its gills.

The Crooked Road is a 333 mile network of roads and trails through southwest Virginia and the heart of Appalachia. It twists around the highlands of the Blue Ridge Mountains through several counties, winding along "Virginia's Music Heritage Trail," celebrating the region's deep roots of traditional music. Our 5-day trip took us through Carroll, Grayson and Floyd counties, covering just a small portion of the Crooked Road. Despite the State's best promotional efforts, this was not a "touristy" trip. But the opportunity to experience this fascinating part of the country, which lies a mere day's drive away from the bustle of Manhattan, more than compensated for the lack of glamour and creature comforts.

The theme of this trip was traditional American music, and right off the bat, the stars seemed to be perfectly aligned. Our destination was Hillsville, VA, which was about 500 miles away. Precisely at the mid-point, Bob Dylan was playing at the Merriweather Post Pavilion in Columbia, Maryland. So on a beautiful August night, we sat 5th row center and while eagerly anticipating the Great White Wonder, we sat through a sluggish performance by the legendary, but already aging, and now departed Leon Russell and a blistering set by the Drive-by Truckers. Then, the good karma continued as we luckily were treated to an awesome incarnation of the sainted latter-day Dylan, then in his 70th year. The trip was off to a good start.

On Wednesday, we completed the drive down to Hillsville, VA, population 2,700. Hillsville is the County seat of Carroll County but that night, the action was over in the county seat of neighboring Grayson County, in the even tinier town of Independence. The motto of Independence is "In God We Will Grow," but its growth seems to have topped out at about 950 hearty souls. At its center lies its historic Courthouse built in 1908, which every July 4th, hosts a celebration, featuring bluegrass, crafts and folk arts. On the other summer evenings, the gazebo and lawn outside the Courthouse are less festive but by no means dormant. As the sun begins to sink low, local musicians gather in a tight circle with their fiddles, mandolins and guitars. The players take turns calling out tunes, and the others jump right in. Meanwhile, townsfolk and a stray tourist or two, enjoy the show from benches and lawn chairs.

On this particular Wednesday evening, there were a dozen musicians crowded along the perimeter of the gazebo and about 40 people gathered on the lawn. We heard players young and old, of assorted skill levels, play a diverse and unpredictable series of tunes. I recall thinking that it is a rare treat to hear the hammered dulcimer take a solo on the old spiritual, "I'll Fly Away." This particular musician had talent and the clear, church-like tones of her instrument seemed a million miles away from the chaotic frenzy of Bob Dylan's "Cold Irons Bound", which we had heard the night before. But good music takes all forms and for two consecutive nights, we had gotten more than our fair share.

Local talent rules at the gazebo outside the Courthouse in Independence, VA. Photo courtesy of Daphne Eidman

The next morning, we set off for Grayson Highlands State Park, where the picturesque trails offer views of some of the state's 5,000 foot high peaks. The Park also offers access to the Appalachian Trail. We wound our way over mountains and through valleys, but couldn't seem to locate the entry point to the park. As they say, getting there is half the fun. Right smack in the middle of exactly nowhere, we drove past a gas station straight out of a 1930's movie. Naturally, there were two large, bored-looking good ol' boys, right out of central casting, sitting idly out front in rocking chairs, desperately in need of a visit from "Dentists Without Borders." Daphne and the boys thought it was a good idea to ask them for directions (something I, like most men, *love* to do). When I did, the larger of the old boys replied, *"Well, it's only the biggest damn park in the state..."* All kidding aside, they were actually friendly and helpful, informing us that we were just 5 minutes from the entrance to the park. They even offered me a free map of the area.

Maybe at this point, I should say something about the people we met in southwest Virginia. I don't believe that we encountered one person during our trip who wasn't friendly, engaging and warm. Each exuded a sense of honesty, decency and straightforwardness that is sometimes in short supply along our northeast corridor. (Of course, New York and New Jersey make up for that by serving the best versions of a local delicacy that seemed to be unavailable in the Old Dominion State: a tuna fish sandwich.)

Our hike that morning offered many beautiful vistas overlooking the deep valleys and the sugar maples that cover much of the Blue Ridge Mountains. That evening we headed to Galax, a town of about 7,000 in Carroll County, which bills itself as "The Gateway to the Blue Ridge Mountains." Unfortunately, we had just missed the Galax Old Fiddlers' Convention, which happens to be the oldest and largest old fiddlers' convention. (Let this serve as a cautionary tale: never book a trip at the last minute because you may wind up missing an old fiddlers' convention!) But we did check in at the classic, small town Rex Theater, where you can catch live music and a film, all for $5. That night they were showing the premier of a documentary entitled "Hillsville 1912: A Shooting in the Court," which was unfortunately sold out. Just as we were returning to our car, the box office usher headed our way at a brisk trot, through the pouring rain. He knocked on our car window and told us that a few of the evening's VIP's would not be showing up, so we would be able to buy tickets after all. Just another example of the good nature of the people who live in these parts. Before the film, there was a terrific band and they closed their set with a rip-roaring, gospel version of "I'll Fly Away" (apparently the theme song of our trip).

Then, it was time for the main event. The film told the amazingly convoluted story of the Allen clan, who during the early 20th Century, had resided and stirred up all sorts of trouble, in the very neck of the woods that we had been exploring. Two Allens wound up getting the electric chair on account of their roles in the deadly shooting of five people at the Carroll County Courthouse, including the judge, the sheriff and the state attorney. Although the film was exceedingly well made, it was apparent that we were not watching it at the Ziegfeld in Manhattan. For one thing, the people sitting next to us were descendants of the Allen clan and had their own perspective on these events, which they insisted that we hear all about, just for the sake of fairness and balance. For another, the movie projector broke in the middle of the presentation so we never actually saw the end of the film. (Had I been amongst a more devious populace, I might have suspected that this was a ploy to get us to purchase the DVD, which we did.)

On Friday morning en route to our next destination, Floyd, VA, we paid a visit to the Blue Ridge Music Center, which functions as a museum, information center and indoor/outdoor concert hall. We saw an informative exhibit which connected the surprisingly few dots between American old-time music and its European and West African antecedents. It was fascinating to trace the clear connection between a fiddle player living in a remote section of the Appalachian Mountains and an 18th century native of West Africa, who fashioned a rudimentary, single-string instrument out of materials native to the jungle. Of course there was some live music happening outside at the center, including a straight bluegrass version of "I'll Fly Away."

The tiny town of Floyd, VA, is yet another county seat, this one, of Floyd County. On Friday evenings, rain or shine, every street corner and storefront in downtown Floyd becomes an impromptu stage, as bluegrass and old-time bands take to the streets in a free festival of string music. Pedestrians stroll from

The scene in Floyd, VA.
Photos courtesy of Daphne Eidman & author

one corner to the next, from one band to the next, taking it all in. The ages of the players run the gamut, and they are joined by dancers, some of whom bring their own wooden squares to tap on. At the center of the frenzy is the Floyd Country Store. Aside from being crammed with the usual assortment of food, clothing, camping and hunting gear, in the rear was a full-blown stage and dance floor, along with seating for 100. The best local bands take turns on stage. On the dance floor, clogging rules the day: the dancers, ranging in age from teens to octogenarians, use the taps in the heels and toes of their boots to keep the rhythm. It was something to see.

Thankfully, the area is not inundated by all of the junk that typically bombards tourists on vacation. But while there were no national brand outlet stores, there was one memorably dusty store, which also doubled as a museum of the truly bizarre and the local historical society. And, as we drove around we could not help but notice the ubiquitous Waffle Houses, a food chain that carries a cultural iconic status throughout the south.[1]

---

[1] Parenthetically, a couple of years after this trip, I learned from Amanda Petrusich's excellent book entitled "Do Not Sell At Any Price" that this region is ground zero for the obsessive collecting of rare 78 rpm blues records that spent decades trapped in boxes or under beds. Lucky for

The bottom line is this is not a trip for everyone. If you're into glamour, thrills and spectacular sites, you might prefer Aspen or Telluride. And there are loads of major music festivals where, amidst traffic and crowds, you can hear one big-time touring band after another for three days straight. However, if you prefer to step into a fascinating, alternative and beautiful world and explore a neglected corner of the country where you can find live traditional American music every night of the week in a different small town, wind your way to the Crooked Road.

Benjamin Eidman remembers:

"The trip gave us an incredible glimpse into cultural facets of America that we had never seen before. From the music to the people to the food, this was an incredibly fun and culturally stimulating experience."

Ben Eidman, 2011. Grayson Highlands State Park, VA. Photo courtesy of Daphne Eidman

---

Daphne and the boys, I was unaware of this at the time of the trip, or I would have spent way too much time at flea markets in search of Blind Blake and Geeshie Wiley 78's on the Paramount label.

MY FRIEND LARRY

"I gotta shake myself and wonder,
Why she even bothers me,
If heartache were commercials,
We'd all be on TV.
Don't you know her when you see her,
She grew up in your backyard,
Come back to us Barbara Lewis Hare Krishna Beauregard."
John Prine, "Come Back To Us
Barbara Lewis Hare Krishna Beauregard" ©

Last week, I visited the Tel Aviv Museum for the first time in 40 years. As a callow 18 year-old, I had been impressed by its standing collection of old masters and impressionists. Now, as a hard-bitten cynic, a week away from the big 5-9, I saw the same paintings as the lesser efforts of the Van Goghs, Modiglianis, Cezzanes and Picassos of the art world. Thinking back, what I really remember about my maiden voyage to the museum in 1973 was that my friend Larry left his gold ring in the men's room there. (I never quite understood people who are so preternaturally clean that they must remove their rings in order to properly wash their hands, even while in a public restroom. But I know for a fact that Larry is not the only such neat freak out there.) Larry, three other friends and me had rented an apartment in Jerusalem during the first part of that summer. In between guided tours of the northern and southern parts of Israel, we were squeezing a day or two into Tel Aviv.

Soon, we were on an Egged bus, half-way back to Jerusalem, when Larry realized that he had left his ring behind. We disembarked in the middle of nowhere, waited in the broiling sun for a bus back to Tel Aviv, and returned to the museum while it was still open. And in this land of miracles, lo and behold, a museum janitor had found Larry's ring and order was restored to his neat and tidy world.

I met Larry two summers before that, when we waited tables together at our sleep-away camp in Livingston Manor, NY, where we were bunkmates. Technically, Larry and I had been classmates for three years (since 1968) at Yeshiva University High School, a decrepit castle of an institution in upper Manhattan, which was caught in a time warp somewhere between its allegiance to traditional Jewish values and its mission to prepare us for the future. The school's undisputed strength was its student body of about 500 boys, weighted heavily towards the brilliant, but ranging down to the really dumb (but very wealthy). In the interests of truth and not modesty, I can assure you that I fell squarely in the middle of the intellectual pack, whereas Larry was comfortably close to the top of that highly competitive pyramid. Larry and I did not meet at school because he was in the Talmud Division, known as "TA" and I was in the Hebrew Division, known as "TI" and if this is the first time that you are reading about the TA/TI dichotomy, then you have been skipping chapters in this book.

Larry made no pretense of rationalizing or coming to terms with the multitude of questions and contradictions inherent in our traditional Jewish background. Given our sheltered upbringings and cloistered surroundings, that was no small feat at age 16. With his religious agnosticism already well entrenched, Larry must have been an odd fit amongst the austere TA high-schoolers, who studied Talmud for 3.5 hours each morning, Sunday through Thursday (yes, including Sunday). Nevertheless, the rigors of Talmudic analysis probably suited Larry's steel-trap mind just fine. But like I said, I did not meet Larry at school and did not study with him, so I'm just deducing, based upon all of the available evidence. (I am reminded of an album that came out right about that time by a long-forgotten one-hit-wonder band called "The Jaggerz." The album, which featured the smash single "The Rapper", was entitled "We Went to Separate Schools Together" – well, Larry and I went to the same school separately.)

After our junior year, when we were 16, we both enlisted for a summer of pretty hard work as waiters at a camp in the Catskills. That was where we finally met. Larry was a Camp Raleigh veteran of several years' standing; in contrast, I was the new guy and was definitely treated as a rookie in this Jewish "Lord of the Flies" universe. Larry and I hit it off because for one thing, we were both small and wiry and got to tangle with each other in hotly contested basketball games. I liked him right off because of his easy, matter-of-fact brilliance and because he hazed me less than most of my waiter bunk-mates. Maybe I liked Larry because he was a little different than my innermost circle of friends. Unlike my other friends, we did not meet as young kids, but as 16 year-olds. He wasn't particularly invested in most of the pursuits that comprised my universe at that time. He was not a huge fan of spectator sports (although he did enjoy a well played Knicks game of that bygone era), did not attend rock concerts and made no particular effort to dress or act cool, but was nevertheless respected and included by the cool crowd. He even conspired with the only other 3 guys who I knew from before camp, to spend their days off together, leaving me, the rookie, to "enjoy" my precious six days off with 3 other misfits, all of whom were even more socially maladroit than I was. Despite not being a jock or an obnoxious self-promoter –or perhaps because of that— at summer's pinnacle, Larry was appointed as one of the two color war generals for the camp.

Camp Raleigh, a renowned jockocracy for the privileged, bestowed no greater honor upon its waiters.

Two years later, in 1973, Larry and I were preparing for our trip to Israel after completing our freshman year at college, me at Queens College and Larry at Columbia. I remember visiting him at his parents' modest apartment, over the Chock Full 'O Nuts on West 168th Street and Broadway. I discovered that while many of us were dug deep into the Kurt Vonnegut and Ken Kesey period of our literary lives, Larry was spending his spare time bridging the increasingly narrow gaps in his knowledge by reading encyclopedias from cover to cover, as in from Book "A" to Book "Z". I have since heard of others who used to do that, to read encyclopedias in the exact manner one would read a crime novel, but I had never before witnessed someone actually doing it. (I don't think people buy encyclopedias anymore and you can't really do that with the Internet.) No wonder Larry seemed to know a little bit and often a lot about everything.

In Israel, we were 5 guys in a 3-bedroom apartment and I drew the lucky straw, winning my own bedroom. My glory was short-lived because Larry, a Felix Unger neat-freak, was unable to abide the Oscar Madison habits of his designated roommate. After 3 days, he knocked on my bedroom door and announced that he was moving in with me. My own habits fell somewhere between Oscar and Felix but luckily, it all worked out fine. In fact, it was always entertaining to see what tricks Larry had up his sleeve. I remember learning that the extra suitcase that Larry had quietly dragged 6,000 miles from NYC was filled with aviator-style sunglasses that he had obtained on consignment from his father's optometry store to sell to fashion-deprived Israelis. This was 1973, long before the ubiquitous Tel Aviv discos, Bar Rafaeli and any notion of 'Israeli chic.' It was a semi-brilliant moneymaking scheme.

Larry's fastidiousness along with his own brand of precocious classiness was not news to me, though. It manifested in all sorts of situations. During the prior winter break, 6 of us squeezed into my parents' tank-like Buick Elektra to go skiing at Mt. Snow, Vermont. As teens, we were lucky to have saved enough money for cheapo trips using my parents' car, since no other parental support was likely to be forthcoming for such trivialities. Especially not for skiing, where, in my father's ever enlightened world-view, you were more likely to break several limbs than to return home unscathed. To cut costs, we all stayed in one dorm-style room at a half-decent lodge called The Smoke Rise Inn. (I vividly remember adjourning to the common room to watch the Miami Dolphins complete pro football's only undefeated season. Take that, Belichik!). Our dinners consisted of fried chicken from the kosher take-out place at home, with all the trimmings, which we kept in a cooler in the car and ate in the crowded dorm room. We juggled our chicken and beer while perched on the edges of our beds. Larry was a small guy but he loved to eat and was the perennial winner of the Camp Raleigh's cold-cut eating contest. After a hard day on the slopes, he understood that this was a meal to be savored and not devoured like savages. So Larry improvised his own little table by placing his suitcase across the top of a small litter basket, topped with a tablecloth he fashioned out of paper towels. Only then did he sit down on the edge of his bed and begin to slice away with his little plastic knife and fork. He always did have a touch of class.

Despite his keen mind and vast intellectual curiosity, Larry was a bit out of step with pop culture. When we were 20 years old, Larry decided that it was high time that we see our first "adult film," so we piled into my mom's car and off we went to a double feature of "Deep Throat" and "Debbie Does Dallas." Alas, being under 21, we were unable to get in, so we again piled into the car, heading off to see the much-publicized new Jack Nicholson film, "Five Easy Pieces". Larry was the only one in the car who had never heard of it. We explained to a suspicious but still hopeful Larry that it was a flick about a girls' high school basketball team. Then, in January 1974, Bob Dylan toured for the first time in some 8 years and it was a big deal. *A real big deal.* A friend of ours formerly known as "Bloomers" landed tickets for

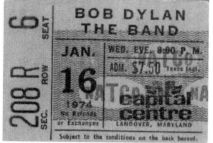

all of us in Landover, Maryland, near his college and Larry agreed to join, as he memorably put it, *"just to see what this Dylan guy is all about."* I hope that Larry appreciated the supreme greatness of what

When geniuses collide: Larry meets Dylan was Dylan/The Band in 1974.

Much later that night, after too many hours of drinking, laughing and general carousing, I remember Larry trying to doze off, while Danny Wohlfarth asked Neil Stein, *"Tell me about Maury (Geller), from Day 1."* I can still hear Larry mumbling from inside a sleeping bag, amidst a groggy haze, *"Oh no, Day 1…"*

Years began to pile up, as they have a way of doing, and soon careers, marriages, divorces and the like began to take the place of summer camp and teenage high-jinx. Sometime around 1991, Daphne and I were entertaining two newly-minted bachelors, during a Rosh Hashanah dinner at our apartment in Bayside: my youngest brother, David, had recently split with Bonnie, while Larry, by then a successful cardiac surgeon with seemingly limitless career potential, had seen his marriage to Judy, a similarly successful obstetrician, come to an end. Daphne and I watched from the periphery with bemused detachment as these two peripatetic and brilliant personalities discussed recent and future high-end vacations, including the best way to upgrade a hotel reservation while skiing in Gstaad. I thought ruefully about how things had changed since a decade earlier, when my own first marriage hit the rocks. Larry had taken me out to Moshe Peking for Chinese food and made every effort to get me to stop blaming myself and to get my head pointed towards the future. David too, along with my brother Steve, had been there for me around the clock. And with their help, I was able to move forward. I knew that life had so many good things still in store for Larry and David (and for Larry David). But right at that moment, watching them talk about how to spend money, I felt a little sad and helpless.

For reasons that were unclear, Larry dropped out of our lives not too long after that Rosh Hashanah dinner. (It could not have been because of the food, because as always, Daphne had put out an incredible feast). Larry had reviewed a couple of malpractice cases for me and one day, after settling a case, I realized that he had never billed me. When I was unable to reach Larry on the phone, I wrote him a check and decided to drop it off in person instead of mailing it. I walked over to his apartment building but the doorman told me that Larry had moved. As luck would have it, the mailman was there and said that Larry had put in a mail forwarding order. It was illegal for the mailman to give me Larry's new address so I gave him the envelope assuming that I would hear from Larry soon enough. I never heard from him again.

I heard rumors of a remarriage to his non-Jewish nurse and of several major geographical relocations. Maybe with his parents gone and just the one brother in Chicago, Larry did not have the ties to keep him in New York. After a while, maybe he figured that so much time had passed, so much water had flowed beneath so many bridges, that it would be awkward and pointless to catch up. Maybe he felt that certain things have happened in his life that would be hard to talk about. But it always seemed to me that if Larry wanted to be found, he would have left a trace.

One day very recently, my curiosity finally got the best of me and I hit the internet. One of the many unintended consequences of living in the modern world is that so much mystery has been removed from life. So many seemingly unknowable questions get answered, nearly as easily as striking the "enter" key. I am no computer whiz; if anything, I am closer to a Luddite. Nevertheless, it did not take me very long at all to figure out that Larry had, in fact, moved around a great deal. I also discovered that while he still practices a branch of cardiology, he is no longer performing heart surgeries.

I thought back to a day, so many years ago, when Larry told me that he was doing heart transplant surgeries. He had told me that the excitement of performing the actual surgery was over-rated—the best part was flying off to parts unknown in a private plane in order to speed the newly harvested heart to its recipient in good shape. Larry was more excited about aortic and mitral valve replacement surgery, which was becoming more and more sophisticated. I was positive that for someone like Larry, the sky was the limit. I just assumed that eventually he would become one of the nation's, if not the world's, greatest cardiac surgeons. To be honest, it came as quite a surprise to find out that things did not turn out that way for Larry. In the end, he ended up just like most of us who settle into our little professional niches but fell far short of setting the world on fire.

Although my research was not totally conclusive, I felt I had discovered a possible explanation for Larry's disappearance. Perhaps Larry prefers for us, who knew him back when, not to see him in his diminished, humbled state, after the world had scuffed him up a bit. It's tough to get knocked off of that pedestal and to come away unbruised and with dignity intact. If I could, I would relay to Larry that we still see him as the super-smart, cynically funny, fussy guy he always was, as the intermediate skier who loved to challenge the double-black diamond slopes, as the curious adventure-seeker who was up for anything. Now that I've internet-stalked him and succeeded in tracking him down, who knows, maybe one of these days, I'll even drop him a line.

ON LITTLE POND

"Sway to sounds of two guitars
Around the campfire bright,
Then mellow out like violins
In the morning light".
Van Morrison, "Gypsy"©

Since 1987, Daphne and I have spent practically every July 4th weekend (or sometimes the following weekend), camping with family and friends in the Catskill Mountains. The annual expedition had its genesis in a day trip that we took with my brother David and his (then) wife Bonnie to Little Pond State Campgrounds in the Beaverkill Valley region, during the summer of 1986. I had last checked out Little Pond some fifteen years earlier, when as a teenager I observed a sapphire jewel of a small mountain lake surrounded by spacious, wooded campsites. Unfortunately, this picturesque scene was overrun by noisy, splashy kids. I beat it out of there, on the double. But by 1986, I was 31, newly remarried, with a small child of my own; this time, I surveyed the scene through a different lens. We hiked around the deep, clear lake, encountered a fisherman who had caught a largemouth bass and checked out the eight "walk-in" remote campsites, located at the back of the lake, accessible only via boat or foot. It looked like a little slice of heaven and we vowed to return, with tents, sleeping bags and all our usual outdoor implements of destruction.

Photo courtesy of Daphne Eidman

The following summer found us rowing a long weekend's worth of gear, provisions, toys and firewood across the lake to one of the serene, inviting walk-in sites. My son Zack was then 4 ½ and we felt it was time to introduce him to camping. Also along on the maiden voyage was my brother Steve, his wife Diane and our friend, Phil "Fish" Goldwasser, who was always up for some good, clean, outdoorsy fun. That very first evening, while sitting around the fire, Steve freaked Zack out with his infamous, scary "Cropsey" stories. Later that night, Zack kept waking up in his sleeping bag, shrieking, *"Something touched meeeeeeeee!"* The next night, the men took the boat out on the lake to test our luck with the fish. As we silently trolled some worms in the moonlight beneath a star-filled sky, Fish attempted to read by flashlight. Despite the deep darkness, my angler's sixth sense told me that all was not calm at the business end of Fish's fishing rod. I called over, *"Hey Fish, is something going on there?"* He glanced up from his novel, and casually responded, *"There seems to be extreme tension on my cord."* With a desperate lunge, I managed to save the rod and reel which were well on their way to being pulled right out of the boat. Unfortunately, by the time I assumed control of the situation, the fish was long gone. And so, the Little Pond tradition was born.

For many years, we returned with an ever increasing, diverse and somewhat motley crew of camping characters. Of course, these included both of my brothers, their families, and our closest friends. But I also recall many far flung personalities from the periphery of our life, all of whom wanted to enjoy a few days of outdoor adventure and none of whom returned home disappointed. I remember the kids' sheer thrill at being there and the array of activities that kept all of them, of varying ages, busy. But

We even bring cigars. Photo courtesy of the author

mostly, I remember the small, funny moments. I think about my nephew Alex [now 30] at about 5 years old, walking into the lake fully clothed, wearing his only pair of dry shoes. When his beleaguered mother confronted him about his motivation, he pointed to 6 year-old Jason Fogel and explained, *"Because he told me to."* Or the time Erik Wohlfarth, a curious 6 year-old out fishing for the first time, demanded, in a low, conspiratorial, "Redrum-esque" (à la "The Shining") monotone, *"Show me the worms!"* [Erik is now a anesthesiology resident at Columbia Presbyterian Hospital, complaining about having to work with *"all these wires."*] And I remember when Neil Weiss, even back then prematurely bald, showed up with a scary mask and delighted in terrorizing the youngest amongst us. When we asked little Rachel Fogel to name her tormentor, she left little doubt as to the identity of the guilty party, exclaiming, *"I don't know his name; the one with hair on the sides."*

Sure, there was plenty of hiking, fishing, swimming, building fires, and all the usual camping stuff. But I think we enjoyed the lazy hanging out and the improvisational 'hanging in there', more than anything else. While hanging out, we mixed it up a bit (literally) when David, in his pre-health food days, cooked cholent in a Dutch oven buried into the ground (although it took him two trips to get his recipe to work). One year, my friends Myron and Danny brought guitars and led a late-night kumzits, which finally ended after the second stern visit from the park ranger, who stoically and memorably pointed out to us, *"It's a lot easier to pack up during the day than at night."* To this day, some twenty years later, Myron still insists that the other campers down the lake were actually enjoying our performance, especially our off-key "American Pie." And we hung in there when adversity struck, which was frequently and suddenly, whether it was due to the ever-present inclement weather, an injured kid or Erik Wohlfarth having eaten one too many Entenmann donuts. (Thanks to our many years in that neck of the woods, we were familiar with the laundromat in nearby Livingston Manor and with the fact that the machines there accommodated sleeping bags). The weather at Little Pond is always unpredictable: I remember hot summer nights with the bull frogs croaking at ridiculous decibels and an equal number of clear, cold Catskill evenings, when we sat, some of us wearing gloves, eating hot soup at midnight. There were a couple of occasions when we had to beat a very hasty retreat either by virtue of our own common sense or after a ranger forced our evacuation due to tornado warnings.

Of course, thanks to some of our guests, we also learned some valuable life lessons during these excursions, including the basic principle that it is never wise to try to wean your baby while camping. I recall being prevailed upon to walk to our friends' neighboring campsite in order to investigate the reason for their baby's hysterical, incessant howling. I discovered the mom rushing back and forth, in and out of the tent like a hyperactive mouse while the other campers on that site went about their business, pretending that this was all normal. Meanwhile, the baby's dad was sitting on a lounge chair, reading a book underneath a Coleman lantern suspended from a tree. When I asked him what was up, he informed me, *"The baby's crying,"* and went back to his book. Yes, those were good times.

In 2005, my brothers, some friends, and I all chipped in to purchase a large parcel of land and an unusable mountain along a quiet, scenic section of the Beaverkill River; we then stopped going to Little Pond and instead began camping on our own land. But last year, 2014, the women decided that it was time to return to Little Pond, where the showers are hot (and free) and the toilets work just fine. We enjoyed it so much that we went back again this year. The summer weather could not have been better and we did not even need to engage in the engineering adventure of setting up our dining canopy, which is just slightly less involved but more hands-on than an Amish barn-raising. Some of what we experienced these past two years was new. Most significantly and sadly, the kids, by now, have all flown the coop, so it was left to our friends, Danny and Jill and Myron and Debra, to join us on these reunions. When my kids read this, I hope they are not offended by my assurance that kids-free camping is not bad at all. In some ways, it was downright leisurely and stress-free—nearly too easy! (Of course, we are also comforted by the knowledge that our kids took to camping and have been very happy doing their own trips.)

One of the positive changes at Little Pond is a sensible on-line system that enables campers to book specific sites, nine months ahead of time. (No more rushing to the campsite at 6:00 a.m. in order to secure our favored site.) There were also two important structural changes. A well-maintained paved walking path now safely and easily connects the remote sites to the parking lot and swimming area. Hence, no more stumbling over gnarly tree roots while attempting to navigate to the bathroom in the dark. Also, steel (anti-)bear boxes were installed on most of the remote sites, which facilitate on-site food storage. But thankfully, in most ways, Little Pond has remained familiar and unchanged. There is no rec hall, public address system, laundromat, or store, as one might find in many commercial campsites (although ice and wood may be procured near the entrance). The campsites remain exactly as they were, large, wooded and basic, each equipped with just a picnic table and fire pit. And the State is still happy to rent boats for as many days as one requires.

This year, we once again paddled our gear across Little Pond, to our favored site, the one with the tiny brook running through it. For some reason, even though we were now schlepping for just the two of us, the effort seemed more strenuous than it used to be. But it was well worth it. The lake, a true gem of Catskill Mountain splendor, has remained clear and stocked with enough brown and rainbow trout to reward the patient angler's efforts (but not so many as to attract too many fishermen). Over the quiet weekend, we ate too much, drank too much and did much too little. Then, on Sunday, we packed and hauled everything back across the lake before promising each other that we will do it again next year. In fact, we have just made our reservations, nine months in advance.

THE BLIZZARD OF 1969

"I don't have no heavy hip-boots,
I don't have no furry hat,
I don't have no long-john underwear
Or layer of protective fat."
Jessie Winchester, "Snow" ©

In February 1969, I was in the second semester of my freshmen year at the Manhattan Talmudical Academy of Yeshiva University High School for Boys. Which is just another way of saying that I was a dumb freshie at MTA. Being picked on by upperclassmen and by a particularly sadistic algebra teacher was bad enough, but there were worse aspects to attending MTA. And I'm not referring to the fact that the school was for boys only, which in truth, wasn't that terrible. What I hated most of all was going to school on Sundays. OK, so we only had a "half-day" on Sundays, which meant that we got out at 3:40 pm instead of at 5:35 pm (although the students in the Talmud division schlepped on until 6:15 pm); and yes, we were off on Fridays. But that was poor compensation: neither made up for the fact that the Giants played football and the Mets played baseball on Sundays, and I consistently missed the games. It didn't help that my brothers, my non-MTA friends, my parents (and most Americans) were off on Sundays, and could enjoy the games (and life) without me. With my parents handling carpool duties for the return trip from Washington

Heights through various neighborhoods of northeast Queens, I would arrive home on Sundays no earlier than 4:30 pm, just in time to start on my homework before getting ready for school on Monday. It was traumatic. Naturally, by the second half of my senior year, I stopped showing up on Sundays altogether. When Rabbi Rapps called out my name for morning attendance, Abe Feld or some other wise-guy, I am told, would answer, "Gone fishing!"

February 10, 1969 was a Sunday. As usual, the night before, I watched "Get Smart," segueing into the Rangers game, with color commentary on Channel 9 by Win Elliott. Those were the glory days of the Rod Gilbert, Jean Ratelle, Vic Hadfield and Eddie Giacomin version of the Rangers, always exciting and always just short of a championship. My brother Steve's best friend, Howie Fogel, had been with us that shabbos and he stayed over Saturday night, as well. Steve and Howie were two years younger than me, happily enjoying the easy living of 7th grade at the Hebrew Academy of North Queens. By coincidence, Howie's older brother, Mark was in my MTA carpool, a junior and a bit of a hell raiser. (For instance, the following year, Mark would teach a few of us how to ride on top of the elevator at MTA.) The Fogel boys' father drove the Sunday morning carpool, as he worked (on Sundays!) in New Jersey, manufacturing ties.

The ringing of my alarm clock on Sunday morning was always the low point of the week. On the Sunday of February 10, 1969, I remember slowly sitting up in my bed, which abutted the 2nd story window looking down on a little courtyard out front. I opened the shutters, and saw nothing but white. I don't mean to imply that I saw snow on the ground; I mean to say that I looked up, down and all around and literally saw nothing but white everywhere I looked. I decided that even Mr. Fogel, as dedicated as he was to his silk tie business, would not be able to make it to his plant in Jersey. In that split second, the deep-seated dread transformed into elation. I trudged down the hall to my folks' bedroom, gave them the 'bad news' that school was certainly canceled, and was back asleep within about 60 seconds. In my euphoria, it would never have occurred to me that 14 people would die that Sunday as a result of the Blizzard of 1969.

By the time I rolled out of bed, it was apparent that New York City was in the midst of the biggest blizzard to hit the metropolitan region in quite some time. Records show that the City received 15.3 inches of snow, the largest storm it had seen in 8 years. Although in the years since, we received more inches of snow on 8 occasions, the impact of this one eclipsed most of the subsequent storms.

The snowfall began late on Saturday night and ended at some point on Sunday. When it did, we had to shovel our way out of our front door. Our small, 20 foot by 20 foot back yard resembled a box filled with cotton. We carefully slid open the back door and our two-year old Brittany Spaniel, Casey, did his

eager best to tunnel a path through the snow. By late in the day, the pangs of cabin fever were setting in and a few brave souls began to slowly venture outside to survey the situation. My parents' car was parked in the lot fronting

Casey, the canine snow plow.
Photo courtesy of Florence & Seymour Eidman

the parallel rows of condominium town houses, and this lot also served as our blacktop football field. Although my friends and I hated shoveling out the cars, we were known to gladly and hastily shovel the snow and chop the ice from the parking lot pavement so that we could play touch football. But as we trudged outside, it became obvious that there would be no football for a while.

By Monday afternoon, a gigantic plow had managed to push most of the snow into a large pile on the northern end of the parking lot, forming a steep white hill about 20 feet high. With my mother hocking us, we did our best to dig out our car, a white 1967 Oldsmobile 98. I'm not sure what good this did my folks because even after the car was shoveled out and the snowdrifts in the parking lot were reduced to a manageable 6-inch deep layer of frozen tundra, it was as if the blizzard had just ended on Corporal Kennedy Street. Tuesday and Wednesday passed without a single New York City Department of Sanitation snowplow arriving to clear our block. The street, normally a busy thoroughfare traversed by buses to and from Flushing, remained totally impassable. Schools throughout the City remained shuttered and kids everywhere built forts in the snow, dragged their sleds out of dusty basements, and had snowball fights.

Eddie Fierstein was a fun-loving, if overly rambunctious kid who lived in the row of houses perpendicular to ours. I remember Eddie and me standing in the middle of the plowed-out parking lot, scoping out the scene before us. It was a crystal-clear, sunny day. Along each side of the parking lot, between the parked cars and the houses, the hard snow was piled about 4 feet high in a long row, like a solid wall. On the other side of the snow wall, was the sidewalk running in front of the row of attached townhouses. Eddie and I were standing with our backs to my house while he was slowly flipping a good-sized snowball from one hand to the other, back and forth. On the sidewalk on the other side of the parking lot, that is, on the other side of the snow-wall, we saw one of the girls we hung out with, a pretty brunette, Michelle. She was walking towards her house, which was directly opposite mine. (Both my parents and Michelle's parents, the Ashkins, were original buyers of these Bayside Town House Condos, nearly 50 years ago. As kids, Michelle and I would wave to each other from our bedroom windows at night.) As Michelle walked towards her house on the other side of the snow fence, we only saw her from the shoulders up. The rest of her body was hidden by the snow fence. Her bobbing head, in a crocheted hat, moved from right to left, resembling nothing so much as a target in a shooting gallery. A moving target.

Without saying a word, Eddie fired his best high, hard one at the bull's-eye. Not surprisingly, Eddie's heavy snowball missed his startled target—Eddie was known for throwing hard, but struggling with his control—but continued on its unintended path right through the glass of the Ashkins' storm door. I can still hear the sickeningly slow "tinkle, tinkle" as the last few pieces of shattered glass, fell, one by one, from the door frame and onto the concrete landing. As bad luck or karma would have it, Eddie's taciturn dad was, at that very moment, walking along the same sidewalk, in the opposite direction towards Michelle. He could not have been more than 15 feet away and saw the whole thing. He did not raise his voice and barely batted an eyelash. I guess he had been down this road once or twice before. Eddie, or his even wilder younger brother Ira (who was eventually sent off to military school), had probably smashed the glass to the Fierstein storm door at some point, because Mr. Fierstein knew that it would take exactly $80 to repair the Ashkin door. Mr. Fierstein quietly told Eddie that he would front the money, which Eddie would then pay back out of his allowance. And that was that.

As the week passed, our Queens neighborhood and in fact the entire borough, remained covered in snow. That was OK by us, of course, because it meant no school. Still, we soon started to get bored with the snowball fights and with pulling our sleds around. At some point, we sought indoor entertainment. There wasn't much of anything on TV during the day. These were the primitive years of three network channels, three local stations, plus the "educational station." So we took to the imaginary fields of Strat-A-Matic Baseball, the real field of dreams. "Strat" is a brilliantly addictive game invented by Hal Richman in 1961, which combines realism and simplicity. With a combination of player cards, three dice, and a few ingeniously simple rules, we would "hit" and "pitch" to each other. To spice things up (and in order to compensate for the pitching-dominated 1960's, when hitting was so universally depressed that the rules were eventually changed), we would mix in the cards of Hall of Famers along with the current teams. It was cool to have, for example, Ty Cobb at his .420 peak batting average, in an enfeebled 1968 lineup. [One of my many regrets is that I did not get my kids into Strat. The game still carries on pretty strong today and they would have loved it. I guess you do the best you can for your kids but you can always do better.] That week, we played for countless hours in the Fiersteins' basement. After several days of being a good sport, a dazed and confused Howie Fogel, who had been stranded at our house since the storm hit, was overcome by boredom. He suddenly jumped up, screaming, *"All you guys do is play Strat-A-Matic all day and night, I can't take it anymore!"* The blizzard had clearly gotten the best of the poor kid.

Speaking of Howie Fogel, the snowbound prisoner of Corporal Kennedy Street... Howie lived less than three miles away, yet was marooned at our house from Sunday until Friday because no one bothered to send snow plows out to Queens for most of the week. In our heavy snow boots, we hiked down to the shopping center at Bay Terrace in order to haul some basic provisions back to the house, but most of the roads and virtually all of the side streets were not navigable. It would be decades before the term "SUV" entered the lexicon and the only people who drove 4-wheel-drive vehicles were the poor souls who were unable to avoid the draft.

At some imperceptible moment during the week, the mood of the common folk in Queens, and I suspect in all of the "outer boroughs" began to slide from a cheerful, *"What can you do? Gotta keep a stiff upper lip,"* to *"Can you believe this? Where the hell is Lindsay?!"*

Jon Vliet Lindsay was the mayor, born of an upwardly-mobile family and elected to the *"second toughest job in the country"* in 1965. He was a progressive Republican, which is a type of political animal that was still seen back then, in these parts, on occasion but eventually became extinct. On his first day in office, January 1, 1966, Mayor Lindsay was greeted by a bitter transit strike that crippled the City for twelve days. The next three years brought more labor strife including an acrimonious showdown with the powerful United Federation of Teachers. Lindsay struggled but managed to get Manhattan dug out from the worst of the blizzard; unfortunately, he appeared to forget that the City's limits extended somewhat eastward from Manhattan. When the Mayor finally trekked out to Rego Park, Queens, a full week after the storm, his limousine got stuck in the snow. He was greeted like a criminal throughout the neighborhoods of northern Queens; as he extended his hand to greet a woman in Fresh Meadows, she recoiled in horror, telling him to *"Get away, you bum!"* But instead of verbally venting their collective spleen, most New Yorkers extracted their revenge at the ballot box. In 1969, Lindsay lost the GOP primary to conservative Republican State Senator John Marchi. But New York politics was very different than it is today and the "Republican" Lindsay managed to win the endorsement of the state's Liberal Party. Running on the Liberal Party ticket, he had more success, and actually defeated a Democrat, City Comptroller Mario Procaccino. Lindsay eventually abandoned the GOP entirely, switching to the Democratic ticket in order to make a run at the 1972 Presidential nomination. Alas, he was unable to escape his past. During his singularly unsuccessful campaign, he was blamed for the spiraling problems of New York City, some of which were depicted in films such as "Taxi

Driver", "The Taking of Pelham 1, 2, 3" and the entire "Death Wish" franchise.

45 years may have passed but certain lessons remain clear. When the weatherman predicts snow, the powers-that-be make certain that the New York City Department of Sanitation remains at the ready, with its full complement of plows, trucks, salt-spreaders and what have you. Often, a "command center" is set up. I like to believe that our worthy leaders do this out of concern for their constituents' welfare and safety. But the cynic inside me remains 100% positive that the politicians are also acting out of a firm conviction that they do not want to become the next John V. Lindsay: a WWII veteran who dedicated his life to the public service, but is best remembered for forgetting to shovel the snow in Queens.

A MEMORABLE CLIENT

"He was a friend of mine.
He was a friend of mine.
Every time I think about him now
Lord, I just can't keep from cryin'
'Cause he was a friend of mine"
Traditional, "He Was a Friend of Mine" ©

My client Richard Silverman (fictitious name) passed away about three years ago at the age of seventy. I had met Richard back in 2000, when my former bookkeeper, Dan, asked me if I would speak to an old friend of his, who had lost his right leg in 1999. Soon, I met with Richard, a sixty year-old computer technician. Richard believed that malpractice by a physician led to the amputation of his leg. The physician was a Filipino vascular surgeon who had been working in Queens as a wound-care specialist. He treated Richard's diabetic wounds on his lower legs for about a year before the right leg required amputation and Richard was absolutely convinced that had the doctor treated his wounds properly, he would not have lost the leg.

Richard was a Type I diabetic, having been diagnosed at age 3. Type I diabetes is an autoimmune disease, where the immune system manufactures antibodies that, instead of attacking invading organisms, mistakenly attack cells in the pancreas that produce insulin. A Type I diabetic cannot produce insulin needed to regulate the glucose levels in the blood. If these levels remain too high over time, damage occurs to the small vessels, leading to micro-vascular disease and potentially blindness, kidney failure and nerve damage. Its onset is typically during childhood and in contrast to Type II diabetes, is unrelated to lifestyle choices. It is treated with insulin injections based upon the patient's self-monitoring of his or her blood glucose levels. By the time we met, Richard had been doing that for over 50 years. He considered himself somewhat of an expert on the endocrine system, the circulatory system, the nervous system and other body systems and organs adversely affected by the insidious progression of diabetes.

When Richard first came to the office, it was clear that he would not be the easiest client in the world. He was polite and respectful but if I had to describe his manner in a couple of words, I would say that he exuded a cantankerous charm. Richard was highly educated, extremely well-read and well-rounded. He rightfully did not view himself as intellectually inferior to any of his many physicians, let alone to some whipper-snapper lawyer.

Richard was born in the Bronx in 1940, got his degree in physics from CCNY and lived in New York City his entire life. He seemed to have a winning way with his jittery second wife Kathy, who worked in the publishing field. She devoted quite a few years to helping keep Richard relatively healthy, despite his proclivity for occasionally following his own counsel as opposed to that of the health-care professionals. Richard and Kathy shared many cultural interests including theater, opera and movies. They owned a modest house in a working class section of Queens. As I later learned, during healthier and headier times, Richard had lived in Greenwich Village during the Village's folkie heyday and we occasionally spoke at some length about our common love of folk music, baseball and the arcane minutiae of both pursuits. In fact, Richard had met my bookkeeper Dan during their Village days, when Dan hung out with Dave Van Ronk, John Hammond and a fidgety young newcomer from the Midwest, who told people that his name was Bob Dylan. Richard never had children of his own but after he married Kathy, he provided her two young boys with the exact same type of love and guidance that any biological father would be expected to provide. Richard worked in the computer field, eventually transitioning to consulting work, primarily to the perfume industry.

In medicine, 'comorbidity' is the presence of additional diseases or disorders that occur along with the primary disease. Any malpractice lawyer will tell you that a client's comorbidities will make a malpractice case much more challenging for a variety of reasons. Defense lawyers love to blame the patient's comorbidities for the unfortunate events that befell the ill-fated patient. They inevitably paint a picture of the heroic physician, bravely confronting the myriad of life-threatening diseases and treatment dilemmas and doing his or her all-out best to save the woebegone patient. For these defense lawyers, it is never the doctor's error that caused the horrible result but always the patient's pre-existing conditions or even the patient's own negligence.

Unfortunately, diabetics typically have several nasty comorbidities and Richard was no different. Chief amongst them was peripheral vascular disease (PVD), which restricted the normal flow of blood to his legs. Without adequate blood flow, wounds cannot heal, so diabetics, who wound more easily, remain particularly susceptible to infection. In fact, diabetics have an abnormal response to infection, causing wounds not to heal in a normal fashion. It's really a vicious cycle. Consequently, in 1989 and again in 1991, Richard underwent bypass surgery in his lower legs, in which a vein is attached above and below the blockage, to facilitate blood flow to the lower leg and foot. Those surgeries were performed by Gary

Gibbons, MD, a world-renowned vascular surgeon in Boston, who headed a famous diabetes center and who had pioneered the procedure. Thanks to the success of the bypasses, Richard could live, work and get about normally.

However, in 1997, Richard encountered a bad turn of events when he contracted an infection in his back, possibly from a non-healing wound. It quickly spread into his spine and, as is not uncommon with diabetics or patients with PVD, spread into his bones, causing a condition known as osteomyelitis. The disease attacked his nervous system, leaving him paralyzed below the waist and confined to a wheelchair. It is entirely possible that had Richard not insisted on being discharged from the hospital "AMA" (against medical advice), shortly after he was first admitted for severe back pain, the infection would not have progressed to osteomyelitis, leading to paraplegia. But there were many reasons Richard may have made this decision. For instance, as I would later explain to the jury in a different context, when someone has been a patient for virtually his entire life, he often feels that no one understands his medical condition or course of treatment better than he does. Or sometimes, he just gets tired of the endless, painful routine of day-to-day, hour-to-hour medical care. Perhaps this led Richard to make a decision that a "healthy" person might not have made.

Ultimately, after being readmitted, Richard was discharged from the hospital in a wheelchair and underwent rehab at the renowned Rusk Institute, with the goal of walking again someday. Almost immediately, as a result of his impaired blood flow and immobility, Richard began to develop diabetic wounds or pressure sores. So, in November 1998, Richard was referred to a wound care center, not far from his home in Queens, where he came under the care of Dr. Alfred (fictitious name), who began to treat Richard with a combination of creams and pressure wrappings. At that time, Richard had a single non-healing wound on the back of his right ankle. He began to see

Dr. Alfred several times each week but before long, he had multiple wounds on both lower legs. In August 1999, Dr. Alfred performed a 'debridement': using a scalpel, he removed the dead or infected tissue, which was directly over the area where Richard's right bypass graft terminated on the front of his lower right leg. However, the wound had already become infected and the infection had quickly spread right down to the graft. While poking with the scalpel, Dr. Alfred punctured the graft, compromising blood flow to Richard's lower right leg.

In September 1999, a mere ten months after he started seeing Dr. Alfred, Richard's right leg was amputated above the knee by Dr. Gibbons in Boston. Richard wanted to sue Dr. Alfred for failing to treat his diabetic wounds properly and for puncturing the graft that Dr. Gibbons had put into his leg, thus leading to the amputation.

A sad story to be sure, but as a medical malpractice case, these facts posed countless challenges that would work in favor of the defense. Amongst them were Richard's history of non-compliance, which included Richard's admitted refusal to see a vascular surgeon as per Dr. Alfred's referral. Then, you had the fact that Richard wanted to sue for loss of a leg that he had already lost use of two years earlier when the osteomyelitis had forced him into a wheelchair. Most significantly, the defense would argue that bypass grafts have a limited life and that the problems with the graft were due to the normal progression of the diabetes, which had afflicted Richard for over 60 years. As if to prove that very point, several years after Dr. Alfred's mistreatment of Richard's right leg and while our lawsuit was pending, Richard wound up losing his other leg (the left) as a result of the ultimate inability of the graft in that leg to stave off the long-term progression of diabetes. In other words, the defense eventually argued at trial that Richard lost both legs for the same reason, natural causes resulting from his diabetes, and there was never any question of medical malpractice. We needed to convince a jury that the situations with each leg were in fact very dissimilar. It was our burden to prove that with decent medical care, Richard would probably have kept the right leg and could have been fitted for a left-leg prosthesis. Not the easiest argument to sell.

These medical impediments scared away other, more experienced medical malpractice lawyers, including my most trusted and successful colleague. They also led a local vascular surgeon who reviewed the case on my behalf, to tell me that the case lacked merit. He believed that Dr. Alfred did not depart from the generally accepted standards of medical practice and that even if he did, his "departures" did not cause Richard to lose his leg. The bottom line was that Richard was a stubborn, 60 year-old man who had suffered from Type I diabetes for nearly all of his life. At this point, he had a longstanding history of peripheral vascular disease and bilateral grafts, he was already in a wheelchair, he sometimes permitted his glucose levels to jump to crazy levels (400!) and he was used to doing things his way. None of which bode well for this case. And, not to mention, we had no expert to support our argument.

But Richard was nothing if not persistent and persuasive. We ended up reaching an uneasy but reasonable meeting of the minds. Richard promised that he would do his level best to line up the erudite, accomplished and homespun Dr. Gibbons as his expert witness. I promised Richard that if Dr. Gibbons signed on, so would I. I had already probably gone further than I should have with this case but I liked Richard—I felt there was a sincerity and authenticity about the man. When I like someone, it does not guarantee that I will accept a case that I should otherwise reject but it can be a tie breaker. It's not out of any sense of nobility on my part, it's just a simple calculation: if I like the client, chances are, so will the jury. Once Richard got the estimable Dr. Gibbons on board, I climbed on as well, however reluctantly.

At this point, Richard and I were already two years into our relationship. Had I the prescience to know that seven years of tedious litigation and out-of-control case expenses were down the road, before we would have our day in court, perhaps I would have decided differently. I won't go into the many discovery issues that delayed the timely completion of this case, but at one point, the hospital where Dr. Alfred worked went bankrupt, effectively freezing our state court lawsuit for about two years. Once discovery got underway again, I traveled to Boston for the videotaped deposition of Dr. Gibbons. (This was actually an enjoyable trip because I was able to parlay it into a visit to Fenway Park. Feeling as if I deserved it, I splurged for a ticket right behind the Sox dugout.)

Medical malpractice defense firms usually work in teams, headed by the partner who will eventually try the case, assisted by an experienced associate or junior partner, then someone less experienced, then a paralegal, all the way down the line. Ed Gordon (fictitious name), a highly experienced medical malpractice defense trial lawyer from a firm that specialized in such cases, also made the trip to Boston, to depose Dr. Gibbons after I completed my questioning of the good doctor. I had focused my questions on Richard's long course of treatment and the medical errors committed by Dr. Alfred. Then, Mr. Gordon did a masterful job of leading Dr. Gibbons through the applicable medicine in a way that I could not do, since that would have constituted improper leading of my own witness. Ordinarily, he might not have done this at a deposition but he knew that it was unlikely that Dr. Gibbons would be appearing for trial in New York City and the deposition would be his only shot at him. Gordon's textbook examination eventually served as my template at trial for the case that I would lay out against Gordon's client. I would eventually utilize much of this "script" in my own cross-examination of Dr. Alfred.

Many people think that "medical malpractice" occurs when a patient has a poor outcome—but that's not it at all. In a medical malpractice case, the person who is suing must prove that the doctor or hospital committed "departures," that is, that the doctor or hospital departed or deviated from the generally accepted standards of medical care, causing an injury. In this case, we were claiming that Dr. Alfred had committed various departures from the generally accepted standards of wound care medicine, resulting in the loss of Richard's right leg. These departures included: Dr. Alfred's failure to consult with a vascular surgeon (in order ascertain the anatomical location of the graft in Richard's leg); his failure to treat what he referred to as a "point opening" on Richard's leg, over the graft, which quickly deteriorated into a full-blown diabetic ulcer, leading to infection of the graft; and his treating the wounds with compression bandages, thus further decreasing circulation to the wounds. We believed that each of these departures contributed—in a substantial way—to the loss of Richard's right leg.

Through all of the pre-trial delays and maneuvering, Richard remained strong, confident and steadfast. The defendant lawyers deposed him over the course of three physically difficult and taxing days, which were spread out over a month or two. Unlike so many clients, Richard made no attempt to disingenuously gild the lily by manufacturing the answers that he thought would be best for his case, but were not necessarily true. He had confidence in the jury's ability to deal with the truth and to understand the motivations behind decisions that he had made which, on the surface, could seem questionable. For example, many a client would have simply denied that he had canceled an appointment Dr. Alfred had scheduled for him with a vascular specialist. Richard, on the other hand, cogently explained his logic. Firstly, at the time, he was still in contact with vascular expert par excellence, Dr.

Gibbons. In addition, a recent Doppler test at Dr. Alfred's facility proved that Richard's grafts were open and functioning. Considering these circumstances, and the fact that Dr. Alfred failed to explain to him the need for this vascular consult, Richard deemed the consult unnecessary and canceled it. Coming from a thoughtful soul who had spent a lifetime dealing with physicians and hospitals, this explanation made sense and eventually carried weight.

Richard's pre-trial confidence in the system did not necessarily carry over to whatever confidence he may have had in his attorney. I worked closely with Richard on virtually every aspect of planning our trial strategy. He vigorously questioned all of it and even after long evenings on the phone, he remained skeptical of some of it. He would nudge me towards sophisticated medical positions that I was positive would be lost upon a jury of lay people. I tried to get him to understand that my "thing" is to simplify the complicated parts of the case. But Richard, with his brilliant physicist mind, found this frustrating. Late in the evening before the trial began, I pleaded, "Enough Richard, enough. Let's just try the case."

The day finally arrived when the judge who determines trial assignments for medical malpractice cases in Queens County, directed us to report to Justice Stone (fictitious name), for trial. My adversary, Ed Gordon, said that he needed to call his office and would meet me in the courtroom, just down the hall. I entered the spacious, wood-paneled court through the large doors at the rear, carrying my heavy trial bags. There was only one person in the room, a large, heavy-set black man in his early 50's standing in the middle of the courtroom. He had his back to the door and was posed with one leg on one of the chairs at the lawyers' table, hunched casually over the sports section of the New York Times. He was wearing black pants without a jacket and a deep blue shirt, open at the neck without a tie. He regarded me in icy silence and I told him that I had been *"assigned for trial to Justice Stone."* In hindsight, I should have suspected, but at the time I had no clue... The non-judicial figure poring over the major league box scores was, of course, the Honorable Calvin J. Stone. I also knew nothing of his history, of his having been censured twice for his lack of proper judicial temperament, or of his sensitivity, perhaps over-sensitivity to racial issues.

The trial lasted two and a half weeks, not especially long for a medical malpractice case. Before it even began, it felt like a courthouse version of the theater of the absurd. Before I had opened my briefcase (literally), Justice Stone threatened to dismiss the case based upon his twisted interpretation of a discovery rule, of which he decided I had run afoul. (To be honest, I was disheartened that my adversary, the experienced Ed Gordon just stood there and let this near-travesty occur but so be it. I guess he figured that an unearned victory was still a victory.) After a trip to the Administrative Judge got me past that minefield, Stone threatened to prevent me from using the videotaped deposition of Dr. Gibbons, because I could not explain why Dr. Gibbons was not in court. I patiently explained to Stone that even if Dr. Gibbons was literally in the building, New York law permits the use of a transcript or videotape of the doctor's deposition. Eventually, Stone and I stopped jousting just long enough for him to tell me to get ready to make my opening statement because he was calling in the jury.

At that point, it dawned on me that the man was nothing more than a common bully. For the rest of trial I treated him the way I treated bullies when I was a kid, which meant fighting back and holding nothing back even when I was getting the stuffing beaten out of me (which as a kid, was usually the case). Whenever Stone started up with me, I retaliated in kind, without fear of reprisal. I did this both outside and in the presence of the jury, whenever appropriate. And occasionally, when inappropriate. Outside the jury's presence, I read to Stone from e-mails I had received from sympathetic colleagues who had heard that I had been assigned to him. The kindest of the bunch read *"pray for rain."* In the presence of the jury, after yet another arbitrary, prejudicial and incorrect ruling, I asked the judge to turn around and look at what was hanging on the wall just behind him: the scales of justice. Stone did just that, then turned back to me saying, *"Unbelievable, just unbelievable. OK, go ahead and ask your two questions."* To which I replied, *"That's OK Judge, I don't even want to ask them anymore."*

The trial had more than its share of bizzarro moments. When the jury was not in the courtroom and we were off the record, Stone would sit on the bench, "holding court." During these breaks, he would pontificate to whomever was around (except to me, who he pointedly ignored) about all sorts of things that he (mistakenly) believed he knew a great deal about, including politics, medicine and baseball. Another memorably strange moment came late one afternoon, when a spectator inquired about the strikingly beautiful young woman who had been sitting in the courtroom, creating a minor stir. The hulking and balding jurist answered, *"Let's just say that she's someone who is very, very interested in me."*

As for Dr. Alfred, he was possibly the worst medical witness I had ever seen on the stand. Even Justice Stone thought so and told Ed Gordon as much. Perhaps Dr. Alfred just didn't understand exactly the way an American trial works. For example, I would lead him through the medical evidence, slowly asking questions about the endocrine systems, Type I diabetes, the circulatory system, etc. During this process, I would frequently ask medical questions suggesting an answer, such as: *"Isn't it true that diabetics often have diminished proprioception with respect to their feet, that is they don't know exactly where their feet are when they put them on the ground?"* In response, Dr. Alfred would look at me wide-eyed and reply, *"Why, that is correct Mr. Eidman!"* I would then follow-up with another (permissible) leading question, such as *"And because of that, they are prone to injuries to the feet?"* At which point, the doctor would literally spring from his seat in the witness box, point an index finger at me and, as if I was his prize medical student, exclaim, *"Excellent!"*

As the days passed, the trauma of the trial took its toll on Richard and his wife, Kathy. It physically taxed Richard, who was having difficulty making it through the day. Kathy was becoming more and more nervous as the case dragged on. What made it even harder for both was listening to half-truths and outright falsehoods from the defense side, which attributed Richard's loss of his right leg to his convoluted medical history and to his own acts, and which refused to acknowledge Dr. Alfred's departures. We did what we could to cheer Richard up. The presence and support of his stepchildren boosted his morale and spirits. In addition, my father, an experienced trial lawyer in his own right, attended virtually the entire trial and spent many hours with Richard, which kept Richard occupied and allowed me to focus on the case. Despite this help, as the number of remaining witnesses dwindled and we approached the end of the long and winding road, Richard's stout will seemed to have been broken.

One afternoon at about 4:00 p.m., as the day's session was wrapping up, Ed Gordon told me that he was authorized by Dr. Alfred's insurance company to offer Richard $75,000 to settle the case. That marked the first settlement offer ever made in this case. I believed that the offer was insultingly light, but I was ethically obligated to present it to my client. Unfortunately, Richard had left a bit early that day and I was unable to reach him until that night. When Richard met me at the courthouse the following morning, he told me that he was worn out and beaten down, that he wanted to accept the offer. I tried to talk him out of it, explaining that after case expenses and even with a reduced legal fee, Richard's share would end up in the hands of his creditors. Stubborn as ever, Richard was not to be dissuaded. To his credit, Richard seemed sincere in not wanting me to take any more of a financial bath on his case than I already had. When Ed Gordon arrived in court, I told him that my client had had it, and he was ready to call it a day and take the $75,000. Ed squinted at me through his glasses and said *"Mike, I'm so sorry, that was last night. Now, there's no longer any money on this case."* So that was that.

Before closing arguments, I was even more uptight than usual. A jury decides a case by answering a series of questions on what is called the Verdict Sheet. For example, the first question on the verdict sheet should have been *"Did the defendant depart from the generally standards of medical practice by failing to refer Mr. Silverman to a vascular surgeon?"* Judge Stone had twisted the language in the first question on the verdict sheet in such a way that I believed that even if the jury had answered that question in the affirmative, the verdict would not survive an appeal. Then Stone refused to give the jury the option of finding malpractice as a result of Dr. Alfred's failure to treat what he had called a "point opening" directly over the terminus of the graft, which became infected, leading to destruction of the graft. The judge did include a jury question concerning Dr. Alfred's dubious use of high-compression bandages over Richard's diabetic wounds, which we argued cut off the normal flow of blood through the graft.

We were waiting for the jury to be called in and I was in my own little world, trying to focus and to calmly "get into the zone." Ed Gordon had done a decent job during his summation but he didn't blow anyone away. He probably thought that he had the case in the bag. I had a lot to say and was concerned that I would have trouble getting it all done within my self-imposed one-hour time limit. By this point, I felt I knew this jury a bit but in truth, like all juries, they remained a bunch of strangers, a blank slate. I had no idea what they had been thinking. In fact, I believe that any trial lawyer who claims the ability to "read" a jury is lying. Most jurors see the black robe and quickly develop a "judge = god" complex. I assumed the jury took me for a loose cannon, fighting with Stone for two weeks solid.

I stood leaning against the rear wall of the courtroom, with my eyes closed, trying to rid myself of these harmful, negative thoughts. Suddenly, my meditative mood was broken by a familiar squeeze of my arm. It was my Dad and he was whispering in my ear, *"Remember, the key to your case is that Alfred never called up Dr. Gibbons!"* Now, over the years, my father had supported and assisted me through a number of trials and I don't believe he was ever truly satisfied with any of my closing arguments. So when I reached that part of the summation, I recalled his urging. I walked close to the jury box and said something along the lines of*: "Dr. Gibbons, up in Boston, he knew exactly where the grafts were in Richard's legs because he put them in and had the records. Dr. Alfred didn't have this crucial information. Fortunately, in today's world, there are so many ways to reach out to someone. All Dr. Alfred needed to do was to pick up a phone before he started to pick away at Richard's wounds with his scalpel. But he didn't do that. If he didn't want to phone Dr. Gibbons, why didn't he fax him? I'm sure they both had faxes. Or e-mail? Or a plain snail-mail letter? Not even a smoke signal?"* Or words to that effect. Afterwards, I asked my father whether I had adequately covered the issue and ever the critic, he told me that I had *"walked right up to it, circled all around it and let it get away."* Fathers and sons....

The night before, while planning my summation, I had grappled, once again, with the serious issue of how to convince a jury that the leg of a paralyzed man had real value. Fortunately, I was able to capitalize on a small mistake by my adversary. As the trial had droned on, Ed Gordon, as experienced as he was, was perhaps misled by the judge's antipathy to my case and by Richard's long and complicated medical history. In other words, perhaps he and his insurance carrier grew a bit over-confident. Near the end of the trial, I offered into evidence a record from the Rusk Institute, pre-dating the events in question and pertaining to Richard's rehabilitation from his initial lapse into paraplegia. But Ed Gordon barely glanced at the package, let alone questioned whether it had any relevance to the issues we were trying. He made no request to redact the record in order to remove materials that might be objectionable in one way or another.

That record, from years prior, contained an entry from a rehabilitation specialist, that said, *"I think he has a reasonably good potential to ambulate using crutches and bilateral AFO's (ankle foot*

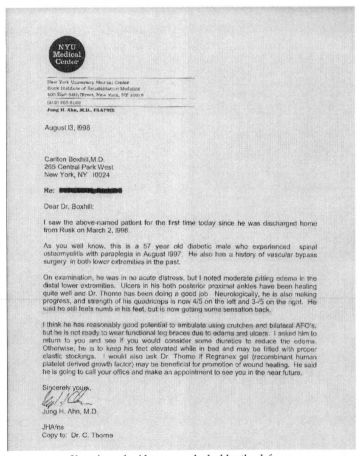

Key piece of evidence, overlooked by the defense.

orthoses), but he is not ready to wear functional leg braces due to edema and ulcers." During Richard's testimony, he had spoken about how he missed the comforting feel of the grass beneath his feet, as he walked through the park on a warm day. By letting in the record from Rusk, Ed Gordon handed me a wonderful theme on which to base my summation: the universal, life-affirming concept of hope. I spoke to the jury about the importance of hope, particularly to a perpetually ill person. I emphasized that Richard always maintained hope that he would walk again and feel the soft grass underfoot. Then I showed the jury an enlargement of the page from the Rusk record, which was already safely in evidence. Thanks to this record, I was able to say that in Richard's case, hope was not a pipe dream, not an amorphous, vague hope but something tangible, something real. In fact, it was right there in black and white, blown up to courtroom size. By losing his leg to a careless wound care doctor, Richard lost the one thing that had kept him going through all the dark times: he finally lost hope.

When word was sent to the courtroom that the jury had reached a verdict, it was late in the afternoon and Richard was not there. He and my father had already said their goodbyes, with a somewhat emotional Richard asking my father if they would ever see each other again. Dad, after a small pause, answered as honestly as he could with the single word, *"maybe."* In fact, when the verdict came in, the only ones around were Ed Gordon and me. After a few excruciating minutes, Justice Stone told the court officer to bring in the jury and he began to read from the verdict sheet. Stone began to read the initial questions that had been submitted to the jury, which required "yes" or "no" answers. Lo and behold, it became clear that we had won the case because the jury had found Dr. Alfred liable for the first departure and also found that this departure was a substantial cause of Richard's injuries. But halfway through, it also became clear that the verdict was inconsistent. On one hand, the jury found that Richard was not liable in any way for contributing to his own damage while on the other hand, the jury divided the responsibility for the damage 80% to Dr. Alfred and 20% to Richard, respectively. The jury's verdict was inconsistent. The judge sent the jury back to continue deliberating with the intention of correcting the inconsistency.

At that point, Justice Stone had not yet reached the questions in which the jury stated the amounts of money that it would award. As soon as the jury left the courtroom to resume deliberations, Ed Gordon and I ran to our phones. He came back with an offer that we quickly rejected. I countered with the number that Richard had suggested to me. It was not a huge number but it was fair considering that, more than anything, Richard wanted the case to be resolved and not to be the subject of a protracted appeal. The case settled for the number I proposed and the settlement was put on the record. (Later, I realized that I had made a mistake by not insisting that we first take the verdict and then settle the case only <u>after</u> the full verdict sheet had been read into the record by the judge.)

Justice Stone called the jury back in, told them that the case had been resolved and thanked them for their service. He made darn sure to hustle the jury out of court before we had an opportunity to speak with them, which we were now permitted to do. God forbid, we should have a chance to ask them about the rest of the verdict sheet, or about their impressions of the witnesses and the judge, or about anything that might help us to perform better in the future. Soon, Ed Gordon and I shook hands and said our goodbyes. Then, the court staff departed and it was just me and Justice Stone. He said something to the effect of, *"Now you're going to tell all your lawyer friends how I beat you up for two and a half weeks."* I lied and told him that no, all I was going to report was that we all worked hard and that the case got settled.

I was near the large doors in the back of the courtroom, struggling to open them, with my bag and my trial exhibits nearly tumbling from my arms, when I stopped. I turned back to the judge, who was still on the bench. I told him that I wanted to know what was on the rest of that verdict sheet. Stone slowly unfolded it, looked at it, folded it back up and said to me: *"Don't worry about it; you'd never have gotten out of Brooklyn with that number."* That was lawyer-speak for, *"This jury's verdict is so large that the Appellate Division [located in Brooklyn] would have overturned it on appeal."* About a year later, when I was in the Queens County courthouse, I punched the index number of Richard's case into the computer terminal in the clerk's office. I scrolled down the list of documents on file and saw this: "Verdict sheet: sealed." That was Stone's final indignity. In the end, I never found out how much the jury would have awarded Richard had the case not been settled. But ultimately, I knew this was a moot point. Even had we rolled the dice and taken the jury verdict instead of settling, I had no confidence that Justice Stone would have left the verdict undisturbed, regardless of what might await us down the road *"in Brooklyn."*

After the trial, Richard, a Chapter 7 debtor, remained patient while we worked with the United States Trustees' Office to petition the United States Bankruptcy Court to approve the settlement. Eventually, that court gave our work its seal of approval. From the settlement proceeds, my substantial case expenses were reimbursed, I received a fee, all of Richard's creditors who filed proofs of claim were fully repaid, the lawyer for the United States Trustee was paid and there was still a fair amount left over for Richard and his wife. Some nine years after he had hired me, he was very pleased to receive it. I hope he enjoyed spending some or all of it.

Shortly after that, I invited Richard and his wife to a small celebration I was hosting downtown, commemorating my 30th year of practicing law. Richard and his wife were music fans and we were having a great performer play that night. I was looking forward to seeing them but Richard called at the last minute to say that he just wasn't up to making the trip from Queens to Manhattan. I'm not certain if we ever had the opportunity to speak again.

About a year or so later, my bookkeeper Dan, who had originally referred Richard to me, phoned to say that Richard had died peacefully in his sleep. Richard had lived a life wrought with illness and physical strife; it was only fair that he was allowed to depart it without fuss or prolonged hassle. Unfortunately, I am relatively certain that he never had the opportunity to write the book that he had planned to write about the trial. In his staunch but naive optimism, Richard had hoped that he would eventually be able to interview Justice Stone and Ed Gordon. Knowing Richard, I'm sure his perspective would have differed drastically from my account, but I hope that mine would not have displeased him.

[Postscript: shortly before publication of this book, I learned that Justice Stone had suddenly passed away at age 62. In a weird way that I am not sure that I fully understand, I regretted not having had the opportunity to try another case with him.]

A BRIEF COMMENT ABOUT
RAP MUSIC AND FOLK MUSIC

"Banjo ringing, niggers all singing,
Uncle Tom is dead, get it through your head.
Hip Hop poetry, that's what's happening,
Blues is the bucket that I use for crapping in.
Wait a minute junior, you're talking kind of fast,
You 'bout to say something make me whup your ass.
You're talking out of your head, to you it's all a mystery.
Blues is your legacy, you don't know your history."
Guy Davis, "Uncle Tom Is Dead" ©

All of my kids listen to rap music, to one degree or another. My youngest, Benjamin is well versed not only in the music, but also in the history of hip-hop, its social significance and the biographies of its luminaries. Just the fact that I am using the terms "rap" and "hip-hop" interchangeably, speaks to my ignorance and admitted indifference, if not hostility, to this style of music, poetry, culture, what have you. (Apparently, and in the broadest terms, "hip-hop" refers to the culture and "rap" refers to the music which plays a major role within hip-hop culture. But if I am wrong about that, shoot me. Wait, maybe that's not the best choice of words when writing about rap music.). For the sake of simplicity, I'm going to use the term "rap" to include any music that is normally associated with that genre or with hip-hop culture.

241

For generations and going back long before my time, black artists held huge sway over various segments of black and white audiences alike. For many years, this was primarily true within the jazz and blues markets. By the time I began listening to music, stars who had evolved out of r & b, such as Chuck Berry, Little Richard, Ray Charles, and Jackie Wilson were already legends, past their primes. Sam Cooke was a dead superstar. Motown and Stax were titanic forces within the industry. There were so many black mega-stars that I cannot begin to list all of them here, but I'll mention just a few: The Supremes, The Four Tops, Otis Redding, James Brown, Aretha Franklin, Smokey Robinson, Gladys Knight, Ike & Tina, The Temptations and Wilson Pickett. And of course Jimi Hendrix hit like a ton of bricks. The blues giants were rediscovered, including Muddy, the Wolf and three separate Kings. Michael Jackson learned something from all of these. The undisputed greatness of each of these artists has been the subject of many books and is beyond the scope of this essay and the modest skills of this writer.

Pop music including rock 'n roll usually comes down to good lyrics matched to a catchy melody backed by a beat. That's how it's been since the early days of Tin Pan Alley. It's a formula that worked magic for Carole King, with and without Gerry Goffin, and it was the founding principle behind all of those Lennon/McCartney credits, as well. Let's face it, each of the names listed in the preceding paragraph added his or her own unique magic to classic tracks put down by world-class musicians, supporting brilliant melodies and heartfelt lyrics.

Black music and its market underwent a sea change when rap hit. I took an immediate dislike to it on every level. A visceral dislike, in fact. With rap music, I heard no melody at all, just an incessant drone, on top of a bass-heavy thump, lacking in variation or subtlety. At least that's what it sounded like to an (old) white dude like me, as it blasted from the oversize speakers of a passing muscle car. So when a rap artist actually released something melodic and memorable, such as Kanye West's "My Beautiful Dark Twisted Fantasy", my ears were already shut and it went right by me. As for the lyrics of rap, I always felt that the less said the better, as I lacked an abiding interest in the most non-redemptive aspects of modern urban life, including gunplay, the glamorization of the drug culture and the objectification of women. Thankfully, I found most of the lyrics indecipherable, as they were grunted by rappers with voices that in my estimation, should never have been allowed within shouting distance of a recording studio. (This was long before I saw the Broadway play "Hamilton" but in my opinion, the sheer brilliance of "Hamilton" was the proverbial exception that proved the rule).

Because of my deep appreciation of the black musical scene in the mid-twentieth century, there was something even worse, something more insidious and offensive about the whole rap music enterprise (and I'm not talking about the violent rivalries and real-life shootings). Although white people are certainly into rap (hello, Benjamin!), rap music was and is unquestionably the product of modern-day, black America. Traditionally, black performers, who were often schooled in the gospel tradition, were amongst the world's greatest and most evocative singers, whether it was in the jazz, blues or pop idioms. The show-stopping stagecraft and showmanship of black performers, whether it was Cab Calloway, Muddy Waters, Jackie Wilson, Chuck Berry, James Brown, Jimi Hendrix, Tina Turner or the Gloved One, fell between groundbreaking and otherworldly. It seemed to me that the black creators and proponents of rap music came along and blithely or even consciously threw the hallowed traditions of soulful singing and performance right into the gutter. Rap music can be "sung" by anyone brazen enough to grab hold of a microphone with one hand and his or her crotch with the other. As for "performance," if you can stalk and prowl up and down the stage, pointing your fingers downwards while you spout out the indecipherable but still recognizably pornographic lyric, then you too, my friend, can rap. And if rap music was and is the product of black America, young black America certainly bought the product, to the virtual exclusion of other musical genres, while large segments of young white America followed right along. So, with perhaps just a tad of condescension, I decided that black audiences threw away decades of musical brilliance, for what? So that P. Diddy could do whatever it is that he does?

There is a fine line between being secure or even strident in one's cultural tastes and being close-minded and elitist. Although I certainly failed to disguise my disdain for the rap genre, I tried, perhaps unsuccessfully, not to be totally dismissive or obnoxious when the subject came up with my kids. It had been hard to get my father to understand that I had musical tastes outside the scope of trad jazz. He was not particularly tolerant of our teenage Dylan worship (*"he sounds like he's singing through a pipe"*). As for our infatuation with Jim Morrison, we certainly didn't pick apart The Doors' lyrics around the dinner table. So having walked in my kids shoes, I

Ben & Author: some generation gaps are wider than others. Photo courtesy of Daphne.

tried to allow them their musical space, so to speak, without overtly criticizing their choices. I tried, but I am not sure that I always succeeded. And the span of the generation gap is something that with effort, can be narrowed—but never fully bridged. So inevitably, some of the discussions about rap music that I had with my kids, particularly Benjamin, had an eerily reminiscent ring to them. But this time, it was my kids on the receiving end of my own snide, old fogey comments. The more I reflected, it was, as Yogi Berra put it, *"déjà vu' all over again."*

Eventually I realized that not only was the context of my cynicism and my kids' exasperation familiar to me from a generation ago, but so was the substance of the arguments that my kids and I had been mustering in support of our respective positions. There was a powerful analogy to be made between the folk music I loved growing up and the rap music I was quick to hastily dismiss.

Dylan opened the door, for me, to the folk movement. Bob's music then led me backwards to Woody Guthrie, Jack Elliott, Pete Seeger, etc., and then forward to John Prine, Steve Goodman, the next Guthrie and all the "new Dylans". Not a single one of these acts was "musical" in any traditional sense, at least early on. In fact, when they started out, the great generation of Jewish songwriters that included Dylan, Ochs, Paul Simon and Leonard Cohen, subverted, if not out-rightly rejected the brilliant arranging powers and musical dynamics of the (also Jewish) generation that preceded them, which included Goffin/King, Weil/Mann, Pomus/Shuman, Leiber/Stoller and Neil Diamond. Some folkies, such as John Prine, even bragged about the fact that their songs were composed of the only three chords that they knew. And, what can you say about the voices—could a single one of them really sing, aside from the women? (Well, I guess Tim Buckley sure could, but how famous was he?) When Dylan hit, the great Bobby Womack told Sam Cooke that he didn't understand the fuss, that this guy could not sing at all. Cooke, arguably the greatest singer of his generation, gently explained to Womack that from now on, everything would be different. It would no longer matter how you sounded, it would only matter if you sounded as if you believed it, as if you were telling the truth. Dylan popularized a musical movement where you didn't need to play or sing well in order to get across. Does that sound a bit like rap music? Or exactly like rap music?

As for rap's rejection of traditional black showmanship: is there a musical genre with less stage presence than folk music? If you doubt me, check out some early Joan Baez videos. You might have trouble staying awake. In fact, one of the many qualities that distinguished the early Dylan from his dull as dishwater peers was his charisma and Chaplinesque stagecraft. For the most part, folk artists were subdued and unglamorous but deemed "authentic".

Which brings me to the content. Many of the early 1960'e songs that I care about were referred to as "topical" or as "protest" songs. Half a century after the passage of the Civil Right Acts of 1964 and the Voting Rights Acts of 1964 and 1965, black America continues to be pounded by racist attitudes, discriminatory policies in housing, employment and opportunity, gang warfare, drugs, the war on drugs and institutionalized poverty (and more), not to mention continued police brutality. Each of those scourges has contributed to the breakdown in the African-American family, which has, in turn, only exacerbated those problems. As Benjamin has pointed out to me many times, the harsh subject matter and language of many rap songs is nothing but a reflection of the everyday world populated by most rap artists. If '60's folk music often mirrored the protest of white, middle-class America, perhaps rap music is the protest music of modern day, urban, black America.

Finally, both genres played important, even critical roles in larger scenes. Nearly every Woody Guthrie song played a part in some larger movement, whether it was the labor movement, the New Deal, or anti-poverty reform. What Woody conceived during the depression and war years became a road map for the '60's. The '60's music scene did not merely give a voice to the anti-war movement; it also fueled the entire counterculture as it rebelled against traditional narratives in the areas of politics, sex, drugs, media and religion (to name just a few).

Similarly, rap music is a key component in the larger, youth-driven movement of hip-hop culture. Since the civil rights movement of the mid-'60's, African-Americans have been told that they will finally receive the same opportunities and access as do white Americans. Imagine the disappointment when they discovered that the effects of many decades of systemized discrimination and racism could not be erased through the stroke of a president or legislator's pen. Compared to the 1960's, we are now in an era where wealth and opportunity are even more concentrated in the hands of the few. This is a source of frustration and negativity for young people of all races. When you mix that with the continued challenge of being black in America, the frustration becomes combustible and converts into anger. Sometimes, the level of the anger rises past a simmer to a destructive boil. Artists, instead channel that frustration into various forms of cultural entertainment such as break-dancing, graffiti, beat-box and rap, which can all be contextualized as pieces in the much larger puzzle.

And if you think this analogy between 1960's folk music and current hip-hop is a stretch, go onto YouTube and check out the original video to Dylan's "Subterranean Homesick Blues". You will see Bob rapping in his early '60's monotone about the daunting street hassles of everyday life and of just trying to get by. Then, listen/read the lyrics to Kendrick Lamar, doing the same, circa 2012. Now, you tell me, who had it tougher? As the kids today might say, I'm just sayin'...

"DOWN ON THE CORNER, OUT ON THE STREET": BEFORE THE PARENTING POLICE STATE BANNED FREE RANGE KIDS

"The next thing I remember, I am walking down a street
I'm feeling alright, I'm with my boys and with my troops, yeah
Down along the avenue some guys are shootin' pool
And I heard the sound of acapella groups, yeah
Singin' late in the evening, and all the girls out on the stoops, yeah"
Paul Simon, "Late in the Evening" ©

I was reading an article in the Atlantic about a new chain of outdoor playgrounds in England where the kids play in unsupervised groups of mixed ages. Under the unobtrusive eyes of adults, kids play with fire, build their own toys with

Who needed helmets? Steven & David Eidman, circa 1962-63. Photo courtesy of Florence & Seymour Eidman home movies.

hammers, nails and saws and clamber atop all manner of shaky, makeshift structures cobbled together from assorted detritus, such as discarded furniture, old tires, and cinder blocks. This type of play is reminiscent of how baby boomers played on the streets or on the fringes of rural areas during their unstructured childhoods. Back then, our parents had no clue what we were doing from the time we left the house until we straggled back in at dinnertime or just before dark. Thanks mostly to a few well-publicized playground accidents and the tragic (but aberrational) disappearance of 6 year-old Etan Patz while walking to school, the era of unsupervised childhood came to a screeching halt about 30 years ago. Hence, the "new" playgrounds, replicating the old.

My family moved out of a rough and tumble section of Washington Heights in January 1967, shortly after my 12th birthday. Even when we were really little, my brothers and I were permitted to roam around, well out of sight of parents or grandparents, so long as we did not cross any streets. You'd be surprised at how much freedom that rule afforded us. We were able to hang out anywhere along the four sides of our block, including the alleys between the buildings and even in the hallways and corridors of the buildings themselves, none of which were ever locked or had doormen.

It is nearly impossible to describe how much less uptight parents were back then but here's one story that will demonstrate how loosey-goosey things were. After a hectic day of shopping, my mom and her friend found themselves on 181st Street, each saddled with a two-year old in a stroller and a cranky four year-old, namely me and my friend

Author (2nd from left) with his Washington Heights Posse. Photo courtesy of Florence & Seymour Eidman

Martin. We lived about a dozen blocks north, at the end of the bus line. The moms knew all the bus drivers so rather than lug us around to more stores, they put me and Martin under the care and supervision of a kindly bus driver who let us off at the last stop. We happily waited for our moms at the candy store next to the bus stop while they finished their shopping. Back then, it was all part of growing up and learning to take care of yourself. Today, not only would the moms get arrested but it would be front page news.

When I was about 8 years old, a few of us were playing in the alley around the corner from our apartment building. The alley abutted the storefront where my mom's hairdresser had his beauty parlor. (Possibly, one of us needed to "go" and when nature called, the alleys were our allies.) We noticed a discarded bed frame propped up on its side, leaning against the back of the one-story storefront. The bed frame, with coiled springs attached, formed a perfect ladder. First, we had fun scrambling up the bed frame and bouncing on the springs. From there, we climbed onto the roof, where we ran back and forth, making echoes by yelling down into the air shafts. Finally, my mother's hairdresser stormed up from the interior staircase and came after us. We "escaped," shrieking with laughter all the way.

We had an entire panoply of street games, all of which were designed to keep us 'on the block,' including 'Ringolevio', 'Johnny on the Pony' and 'Skully.' Even the main neighborhood sport, Chinese handball, or what we simply called 'Chinese,' was constructed so that we'd never have to leave the block, cross the street or step into the road. In 'Chinese,' the concrete sidewalk squares were used as each player's territory. As long as we were home for supper, we could spend hours 'on the block' without seeing or hearing from an adult.

Even when the weather kept us indoors, we kept busy by building model airplanes from kits or constructing mini-buildings with erector sets. When I was 11, "Batman" was a huge hit on TV, building upon the fan base which its comic book franchise had established, 12 cents at a time. My friend Danny and I created our own Batman "utility bags," armed with bat-decoders made from red cellophane taped onto bat-shaped cardboard cut-outs, and bat-razors, with the blades skillfully removed from old pencil sharpeners. As they say, "some assembly required" but no adults were required (or wanted).

Of course, the perimeter of our "roam zone" increased, little by little. At first, by about age 8, I was allowed to cross the street by myself, so long as my grandmother, who was usually home, watched from the window. Although I was only allowed to cross 192nd Street, this, in effect, doubled the area of my zone; it now included several stores that were previously inaccessible, including two candy stores that sold baseball cards. Before you knew it, certainly by age 9 or 10, we were allowed to go anywhere in the Heights, on foot or bus with our school bus passes, which cost $1.00 per month.

Even within walking distance, there was plenty to do. For example, we sometimes dug for "minerals" on the wooded hillside across from Marvin Kanal's apartment on Fort George Hill, using tools borrowed from my dad, a former geology major. [This was several years before Marvin turned a few household scraps into a gun capable of shooting from his apartment terrace into another wooded area about a quarter mile away. At about that same time, he devised "delayed reaction" fuses out of pieces of rope soaked in nail polish. I like to think that our childhood resourcefulness played some role in Marvin's future, where he successfully patented several less incendiary inventions.]

Meanwhile, the summers up at our bungalow colony in the Catskills held even greater opportunities for unsupervised adventure. Sure, there was a day camp, where we engaged in the typical activities, including calisthenics, kickball, volleyball, swimming, arts & farts, some Jewish study, etc., etc. But from when the camp day ended at 4pm until bedtime, we were on our own (except for a quick supper). We had the run of a 100-acre mountain, with its own pond and several old logging trails carved deeply into it. As long as were "around" by dusk, our parents gave little thought to where we were or what we were doing. We would interact with the adults only if we crossed the imaginary line that existed in the grey area—somewhere between *"good clean fun"* and *"what were you kids thinking?"* For the most part, we knew how to take care of ourselves and not to do anything too foolhardy or beyond our limits.

Only very rarely did the adults think we went too far. When I was about 10, I hiked up the mountain late one afternoon. I took my time coming down, mostly because I decided to descend by walking along the tops of the old stone fences that had once upon a time demarcated farmers' plots. By the time I returned to civilization, it was much closer to dark than to sunset. My angry mom was out there on the front lawn, stalking around looking for me. About two years after that, we spent weeks secretly building a monster in the back of an empty bungalow, using my pal Danny's bow for its arms and flashlights for its eyes. His cousin Kenny Auman (now a prominent Rabbi), had just gotten a small, portable tape recorder and we used it to record a scary monster voice. We knew "Little La" (David Metzger) would be an easy target. One evening, we had the monster tap with its "arm" on Little La's bedroom window just after his bedtime. He woke up in terror. In a flash, we were ambushed by the large but surprisingly agile Esther Metzger, who came after us with her big broom. But for the most part, our escapades involved harmless pranks such as Harold Gellis' concoction of "rotten egg odor" from some secret mixture of chemicals.

Back in the Heights, unfortunately, trouble began to find us even when we stayed within the lines. The neighborhood was turning tougher year by year, we were no longer "little kids" and thus were considered fair game by the emerging bands of local punks. When I was about 11, I went with my brothers and some friends to a James Bond double feature of "Dr. No" and "Goldfinger" on 178th Street. Since our bus passes were invalid on Sundays, our moms had given us each the 15¢ bus fare. But, instead of taking the bus home, we pocketed the fare and walked home. (After all, 15¢ was good for 3 packs of baseball cards!) Not far from the movie theater, we were set upon by a gang of 8 young muggers, who got in some good shots. They took our San Francisco Giants baseball caps, tossing them off of the elevated portion of Amsterdam Avenue and onto the top of a bus that was en route to the George Washington Bridge. This sort of thing must have been a common occurrence because we were not granted refuge in the local firehouse on 181st Street. We were saved only after our friend, the always nervous Richie Ainsberg escaped and returned with his 19 year-old brother in his car, armed with a Louisville Slugger.

Despite the growing danger, I never wanted to leave Washington Heights. I feared I would miss its streets, my friends and the action. But kids had no say back then… So just after my 12th birthday, my folks transplanted us, kicking and screaming, to the suburbs of Bayside, Queens. There, my brothers and I luckily were able to continue to spend most of our free time on our own or with friends, either from school or from our new neighborhood.

On the night before I left for summer camp when I was 13, I rode my bike several miles into Whitestone, where I met school friends who knew someone who knew someone there who sold fireworks. We got a little lost, negotiations dragged on and I returned home after dark. Yes, my mom was not pleased. As it turned out, I hardly used the firecrackers in camp and they lasted a long time. About a year or two later, Steve and I were wiling away our time, blithely lighting firecrackers and tossing them from the window of our second-floor bedroom. Unfortunately, one of the firecrackers had a short fuse and a split-second after it left my hand but before it left our room, it ignited with a BANG! You'd be surprised at how loud it is when a firecracker explodes indoors, especially in a small room. Steve and I were soon on our hands and knees picking up tiny pieces of shredded firecracker paper. It would be about two days before our ears finally stopped ringing. Illicit fireworks were an important part of the scene back then and when I was 15, a few of us spent a day off from high school, trekking down to Chinatown in search of explosives. Alas, our expedition yielded nothing except for new bruises: we were attacked once again and this time, a broom handle that was thrown at me while I was making my escape left a gash on my back.

Any "Honeymooners" fan can tell you that Ralph Kramden discovered that the chef of the future may not be all that he thought it would be. Similarly, shortly after we first moved to Queens, we received a glimpse of the childhood of the future. At the time, I was still silently fuming over the fact that my days of playing "Chinese" were over. My folks consoled me by signing Steve and me up to play little league baseball for the Flushing Jewish Center team. I had never worn a baseball uniform before, so that was cool, even if it was so big on me that the number 2 (future Derek Jeter??) was tucked well into my pants. I was excited to play in a real league, with real rules, real standings and a real pennant race.

I was twelve years old and had never before been exposed to the shady side of kids' sports or games. (Well, there was that one time when my dad had entered me in a kids' fishing contest and his friend David Glazer, found a dead trout in the bushes and snuck it onto my line, earning me a nice trophy). But getting back to Little League, aside from the fact that my family had no affiliation with the synagogue we were playing for, I quickly learned that when kids, adults and sports are mixed together, the results sometimes are inconsistent with the purposes of sports and all notions of fair play. For the first time, I felt incredible pressure not to strike out and for the first time in my life, I was habitually striking out. For the first time, we operated within a "star system," where the coach's star son got to do whatever he wanted. And for the first time, we saw how adults were willing to bend rules to help their kids win. The most flagrant example of this was during the playoffs, when out of the blue, we had a new player on our team. The new guy just happened to be a lanky pitcher, a pituitary freak with pinpoint control, who barely gave up a foul tip, let alone a hit. We ended up winning the championship behind the peerless pitching of our ace ringer. Even though we got to meet New York Met Ed Kranepool at the celebratory breakfast, something did not sit quite right with me about the whole experience.

Decades later, I had the privilege of coaching Little League baseball for about ten years. Although I was a good coach and enjoyed spending time with my kids and their friends, I was not always proud of my actions. Once, at a pre-season meeting, I allowed myself to get caught up in silly bickering over "fixed" rosters and I created a bit of a scene. Another time, I filed a formal protest, disputing the outcome of a championship game. Each time, I firmly believed that I was preventing some grave inequity from befalling innocent kids.

In fact, every one of the kids we were "coaching" would have been better off "choosing up sides" in a sandlot, without an adult in sight. The sad fact is that we have permitted kids to devolve into a state where they would not even know how to do that. So if the pendulum has begun to swing back towards less structure, less supervision and more independence—like in those English playgrounds—I am all for it. Perhaps, we will someday go so far as to allow kids to complete their own college applications.

SOME THOUGHTS ABOUT REPENTANCE, BEFORE THE HIGH HOLY DAYS

"I had a woman, down in Alabama.
She was a backwoods girl but she sure was realistic.
She said 'boy without a doubt,
Better stop your mess and straighten out.
You can die down here, just be another accident statistic.'."
Bob Dylan, "Slow Train" ©

"But repentance, prayer and charity, nullify the evil decree."
The High Holiday "Mussaf" Service

A good number of years ago, I met Rabbi Yisroel Mockin, a dynamic, young man, who ran a fledgling Chabad House at the Mt. Tremblant ski resort up in the Laurentian Mountains of Quebec. Chabad, also known as "Lubavitch," is the largest and best-known Hasidic Jewish sect. Unlike many of the more insular Hasidic groups, Chabad engages in extensive outreach efforts and worldwide charitable endeavors. In what was quite a memorable little scene, we met Rabbi Mockin during a Shabbat meal amongst friends, at an improvised table in the lobby of the resort. It was the middle of the summer and we could not help but notice a bearded young man in long black coat rushing by, but he suddenly stopped dead in his tracks, marveling at the unexpected spectacle of five or six couples enjoying Shabbat dinner in the lobby, amid the hustle and bustle of hotel guests and staff coming and going. Some of us wound up attending Shabbat services the next morning at the Chabad House and after Shabbat, I signed onto the Rabbi's e-mail list. That was a good ten years ago, maybe more. This year, before the recent Jewish High Holy Days of Rosh Hashanah and Yom Kippur, I received an e-mail from Rabbi Mockin that began with the following parable.

It seems that the Israeli Prime Minister was visiting the White House and wondered aloud about the bright white telephone that was kept in a glass cabinet, under lock and key in a corner of the Oval Office. The President told the Prime Minister that it was his personal hotline to G-d and he offered the skeptical Israeli an opportunity to place a call. After an intense and detailed private discussion with the Almighty, the appreciative Prime Minister offered to pay for the call but the President refused, insisting that the call was a gift from the USA to its trusted ally. But the Prime Minister was insistent, so the President checked the meter underneath the phone and said that the cost of the call was $100,000. The still-glowing Prime Minister whipped out his checkbook and cheerfully wrote the check. Six months later, the President visited Israel and was invited to meet with the Prime Minister at his home in Jerusalem. There, the President noticed a similar phone sitting under glass in a quiet corner of the Prime Minister's study. The President asked and the PM told him that it was his new hotline to G-d. Just then, the President recalled a matter of great urgency that he had neglected prior to leaving on his trip and the PM, with a big smile and sweeping gesture, urged the President to avail himself of the hotline. After a private 15 minute talk with G-d, the President thanked the PM profusely, and, as had occurred six months before, the appreciative leader of a nation insisted that his gracious host permit him to pay for the call. The PM eventually relented and checked the meter. He told the President that the charge was one shekel. The startled President asked *"Why so little? Why did this call only cost a single shekel?"*

The PM merely shrugged his shoulders and responded: *"Local call."*

I chuckled and assumed that the story was basically playing off of our belief that while in Jerusalem, one is nearer to G-d, etc., etc. But Rabbi Mockin tied the story to the Jewish High Holy days, the approaching Yomim Noraim, or Days of Awe. He remarked, *"On Rosh Hashanah, I think of G-d as within earshot's distance of my whispering lips. These thoughts help elicit a more authentic prayer from me."* In other words, the days preceding and during the High Holy Days of Rosh Hashanah and Yom Kippur comprise what one of my rabbis referred to as the *"t'shuvah season."* T'shuvah, literally means "return" or "response" but in Judaism, it refers to the process of repentance, as in a return to the proper path.

It is not an accident that in Judaism, the same word means "return" and "repentance." I believe, in fact, that this points to one of the most fundamental differences between Christianity and Judaism. Christian theology and teachings are largely based upon the concept of "original sin," that is, that the negative aspects of humanity's existence and people's natural inclination towards sin derive from the "original sin" of Adam and Eve, who ate the forbidden fruit in the Garden of Eden. In some fashion, Adam and Eve's original sin was genetically transmuted to their descendants, who remain collectively responsible for it. Conversely, Judaism views humanity not as the product of an original sin but as inherently decent and good. It is only when one's will weakens and yields to the evil inclination that is within us all, that one must do "t'shuvah," or return to the natural state of decency and rectitude. Hence, "t'shuvah" = "return."

The t'shuvah process itself is not easy or simple; again, as a matter of distinction with Catholicism and some other branches of Christianity, it involves much more than a secret confession to a man of the cloth and recitation of a prescribed formula. Our scholars, notably Moses Maimonides, describe in great detail a multi-part process of t'shuvah (but that is beyond the scope of this modest essay). Indisputably, one may perform meaningful and acceptable t'shuvah during any time of the year. The Talmud, in the Tractate Shabbos, page 153-a, teaches that the great Rabbi Eliezer ben Hyrkanos said: *"Repent one day before your death."* His disciples then asked him, *"Does one know on what day he will die?"* The Rabbi responded, *"All the more reason he should repent today, lest he die tomorrow."*

In that vein, my current teacher, Talmudic scholar Dennis Weiss, posed the following question: If one may perform t'shuvah at any time, why do we need a designated "t'shuvah season" or for that matter, the High Holy Days? What purpose do they serve when we can perform repentance and receive divine forgiveness on any day, right up to the time of death? For an answer to that question, Rabbi Weiss turned to the language of the "Ne'ilah" service, that is, the special teffilah or prayer that Jews recite near the close and culmination of Yom Kippur. Ne'ilah contains a paragraph that begins with the words, *"You (G-d) extend a hand to sinners..."* Rabbi Weiss explained that while, yes, we can and should avail ourselves of t'shuvah all throughout the year, the High Holy days remain a period when the process is uniquely accessible. That is because during those weeks, G-d reaches down and extends his hand to us. By so doing, He enables us to make, in Rabbis Weiss' words, a *"quantum leap"* and engage in the t'shuvah process more easily. Rabbi Weiss explained that during most of the year, a proper t'shuvah requires a thorough and probing examination of our ways, in order to discern what led us astray from the proper path. During these few days, however, we can expedite the process and obtain heavenly forgiveness without the same degree of introspection and self-analysis, provided that our prayers are heartfelt and sincere.

Before I go further, I should point out that the t'shuvah that I have been referring to applies to transgressions that a person committed against G-d. In contrast, if someone has sinned towards his or her fellow man/woman, entreaties to the Almighty, no matter when made or how sincere, do not expunge the sin. Absolution for such person-to-person sins requires direct solicitation of forgiveness from the aggrieved party. A story comes to mind on this subject...

Many years ago, an Orthodox Jewish shopkeeper embarrassed and insulted my friend Stan (fictitious name), by "dumping" him in order to wait, at great length, upon a later arriving customer who wanted to make a much larger purchase. Stan quietly pointed out the affront to the shopkeeper, who compounded his error by justifying his actions based upon the relative profit of the two transactions, since Stan wanted to purchase wicks for his Chanukah menorah while the other customer was shopping for a silver Menorah. The High Holy Days were nine or ten months away but Stan took a business card from his wallet and handed it to the confused shopkeeper. Stan calmly explained that the shopkeeper had engaged in the sin of embarrassing a fellow man in public, a particularly heinous transgression according to Jewish law. Stan told the shopkeeper that he expected the shopkeeper to call him at some point prior to the next High Holy Days and then, Stan would forgive him (as he would be required to do). The mortified and shaken shopkeeper immediately expressed great contrition, practically begging Stan to forgive him. Stan replied that no, he wanted a phone call, at which point Stan would forgive the man. [As an aside, should someone refuse to grant forgiveness, the sinner is required to make a total of three such attempts. Should forgiveness still be withheld, at that point, divine forgiveness is granted.]

Getting back to the topic of sins committed against G-d, I mentioned before that the Jewish way requires more than anonymous confession to an intermediary (which brings to mind another Christian-Jewish divergence, in that Jews believe in going directly to the source rather than through a middleman). In fact, G-d remains prepared to offer forgiveness even to the most lost souls, that is, the ones who society has written off. In that vein, I am reminded of a seemingly bizarre incident, when in 1991, Bob Dylan received a Lifetime Achievement Award at the Grammys. Never comfortable before an audience unless he is performing, Dylan stammered a bit in front of the star-studded crowd and then said only this:

> *"Well, my daddy, he didn't leave me much, you know he was a very simple man, but what he did tell me was this, he did say: 'Son,' he said... (long pause, plays with his hat) ...He say...He said so many things (audience laughter, another pause)... 'You know it's possible to become so defiled in this world that your own father and mother will abandon you. And if that happens, G-d will always believe in your ability to mend your ways.'"* (He then muttered a quick, generic "thank you", took his Grammy and departed the stage).

At the time, some thought that this was merely another case of "Dylan being Dylan," the enigmatic mysterioso. But one

dedicated Dylanologist realized that Bob had quoted verbatim from the siddur (prayer-book) of 19th Century Orthodox Jewish scholar and philosopher, Rabbi Shimshon Raphael Hirsch. In the 27th psalm, which is recited twice daily during the period surrounding the High Holy Days, King David stated, "*My father and mother have abandoned me but G-d will remember me.*" In his commentary to the

R' Shimshon Raphael Hirsch

psalm, Rabbi Hirsch explained that one can become so corrupted in this world, that even his own parents would not recognize him. Even then, G-d will remember the person's inner goodness and qualities, always leaving ajar the door for t'shuvah. Something in that idea must have appealed to Bob Dylan or rang familiar to a man whose path in this world must have been quite different from the one that his middle-class Jewish parents envisioned for him. As usually is the case, it is well worth noting Dylan's deliberate choice of words. He did not state that despite parental abandonment, G-d will always forgive our sins. Instead, he stated that the affirmative obligation is upon each of us, *"to mend our ways"* and that G-d believes in our ability to do so. When we accept that encouragement, go beyond making a simple confession and reward His faith in our ability to correct our ways, G-d will surely extend his hand in forgiveness.

Now, why did Dylan choose that moment, at the Grammys, before a worldwide TV audience, in order to quote Rabbi Shimshon Raphael Hirsch? Well, that can be chalked up to him being a mysterioso, I guess.

ON THE ROAD WITH THE GUYS

"Goin' places that I've never been,
Seein' things that I may never see again.
And I can't wait to get on the road again."
Willie Nelson, "On the Road Again" ©

To borrow a phrase from fishing writer John Gierach, I have always been "clobbered up" with some sort of significant "responsibility" or another, for the past forty years. Beginning just after my 21st birthday, here is what I did: began dating future wife #1, entered law school, marriage #1, finished law school, bar exam, job hunt, work, formation of law firm, marital issues, birth of son, breakup of marriage, work, breakup of law partnership, contentious divorce, work, dated future wife #2, more work, married wife #2, bought apartment #1, bought apartment #2, sold apartment #1, joined law firm, a lot more work, built country home, bought primary home, sold apartment #2, , birth of son #2, more work, birth of son #3, started concert company, breakup of law firm #2, more work, raised kids, psychotic tuition bills, sold country home, passed another state's bar exam, more work, even more work, even bigger tuition bills, ridiculous health insurance bills, more work. Before I knew it, I was on the wrong side of 60. So, if I look back wistfully at a few trips from my youth, in particular the ski trip just after my 21st birthday, when we spent late nights around the fireplace listening to the new Dylan album ("Desire"), well, I hope you sort of get why I look back at that time wistfully.

When we were 9 or 10, my friend Danny and I would talk about the wide-open future when we would have the freedom and means to travel to remote and exotic locales and catch blue marlin (on light tackle, of course). When I was 14, my parents began taking us fishing with them on the St. Lawrence River, along the New York-Canadian border. Exciting as this was (and it was!) it was still a family vacation to upstate New York, where we slept in a mobile home. However, my adventures and misadventures began in earnest when I got my driver's license (after only two tries) shortly after turning 17. That was my entrée into the wonderful and wacky world of road trips, usually in search of bigger fish, better skiing, cooler music or a critical ball game. And sure enough, the grass really was greener way across the fence.

It all began rather inauspiciously with a poorly conceived trip on a dreary, chilly June day in 1972, within mere weeks of when I obtained the holy license to drive. Four of us packed my mom's red Buick Skylark with the white vinyl top and headed to Shandalee Lake in Livingston Manor, for some early season pickerel fishing. The great blue marlin remained thousands of miles away and would have to wait. Perhaps a bit over-optimistically, we decided to ignore the forecast that called for a 100% chance of rain. We knew to distrust the forecasts because whenever snow was predicted for a school day, it rarely materialized. Much to our surprise, as it turned out, the weathermen confounded us yet again: it rained continuously, all day long, varying in intensity from a heavy mist to a steady pour, eventually drenching us through and through.

We caught next to nothing and Phil ("Fish") Goldwasser, of course, fell in the lake. This happened while I was rowing the small wooden "craft" that I had talked the proprietor of the local inn into renting to us. Phil had been sitting on the small corner seat in the front of the boat, with one leg folded beneath his butt.

Just as I was executing a tight turn, Phil shifted his position and all of a sudden, he was no longer in the boat. What made the scene all the more comical was the fact that Phil was unable to see from beneath the hood of his heavy parka, which was quickly filling with water as he flailed his arms up and down, much in the manner of astronaut Gus Grissom after he prematurely blew the door to the hatch off of his Mercury capsule after splashdown and had to evacuate. With each flop of an arm, Phil became more and more submerged. Thankfully, like all fish, Fish was a strong swimmer—or shall I say, flopper. If it had been me, I likely would have drowned. One would think that the absurdity of this ridiculous expedition had now reached its apex but one would be wrong.

After finally admitting defeat and calling it a day, I rowed into shore, guiding the front end of the boat onto the bank, while the drenched Dr. Fish jumped out. Then, we needed to drag the rest of the boat onto land. My brother's friend, Steve Heller, was seated in the back of the boat. The rest of us got out and yanked the front of the boat onto the land with such force that Heller did a backwards somersault with near-perfect form, flying over the back of the boat, while executing a rarely-seen reverse-cannon-ball into the shallows of the lake. My final memory of that trip is all of us sitting in the car in stony silence, with the heat on full blast.

The following spring, my pals Danny, Myron and I decided to inaugurate opening day of trout season with a quick trip up to the Willowemoc. That year, opening day (April 1) coincided with the day before Passover. That day was also fishless and otherwise forgettable, save for when I locked the car keys in the trunk of the same red Skylark. A crafty local mechanic easily jimmied open the door, then brilliantly removed the car's rear seat, enabling him to reach his outstretched arm through a small opening between the rear seat and the trunk, grabbing my jacket which held the keys in its pocket. Visions of a Livingston Manor Passover Seder at the Willowemoc Motel finally faded.

Gradually, we got our act together and the trips improved, both in terms of destination and execution. We began to hit the road for some major musical events, the first being Bob Dylan's triumphant comeback tour with The Band in January 1974. My buddy Mike Blumenthal was attending George Washington University and he managed to score a bunch of tickets for the Baltimore shows. So Danny, Aaron Stein, Neil Stein, our friend Larry, Mike and I had all the fun that you can squeeze into 48 hours, as we emptied the GWU Hillel House of every ounce of its Manischewitz Cream Concord White Wine before and after the Dylan shows. 40 years on and perhaps 50 shows later, I am convinced that Bob has never again approached the power, stage presence and audience connection that he had on that tour. Aside from the Dylan shows and a lot of drinking and story-telling, we also did the usual touristy stuff. I remember posing with arms aloft, Nixon-style in front of the Watergate Hotel and at the nearly deserted National Wax Museum, with my arms around President Lincoln's generals,

11/4/75: en route to Providence for Dylan's Rolling Thunder Revue

after I had clambered into one of the exhibits. Five months later, we spent a lost weekend in Jersey City with the Allman Brothers. Then, in late 1975, during my senior year in college, it was time to follow Dylan's then semi-secret and now legendary Rolling Thunder Revue tour to several dates in the northeast. Looking back, it occurs to me that I was always the one supplying the wheels, or should I say, my parents' wheels…Thanks, Mom and Dad!

On that note, I'm reminded of another series of road trips made possible by my parents' land-yacht, also known as a 1970 Buick Elektra. I used this reliable and spacious car to transport a bunch of us to Mt. Snow, Vermont, the place I learned to ski, for several college winter break vacations. My senior year in 1976, about 9 or 10 of us squeezed into a yellow mini-bus (the Buick finally taking a rest), and drove to a big, rented house on a hilltop in Mt. Snow, for a week's worth of wintry shenanigans. On the first ski run of the morning, I crash-landed at the top of an icy hill and I received stitches underneath my eye. I was back at the top of the very same mountain by lunchtime, ready for more (skiing, not suturing). This is more than I can say for the ski pants belonging to the owner of the house that our friend Julian "borrowed" (without asking), and proceeded to shred during our alcohol-assisted suicidal midnight toboggan runs.

I will always look back upon that trip with just a touch of sadness because, it was the last time in my life that I was truly free, as in *"freedom's just another word for nothin' left to lose,"* as the song goes. Since then, I have always had something to lose. I had just turned 21 at that time. Within a couple of weeks of arriving back home, I met and started dating the girl who would become my first wife. Within months of that, I was in law school. And so it goes. Yet despite still being on the figurative treadmill, I have no major complaints. I've shared my life with great people, plenty of good fortune has fallen my way and while full of a fair amount of responsibility and pressure, my life is a good one. And unlike my kids, I never did have a "gap year". Instead, I had my road trips.

[In case anyone was wondering, I've been writing these essays in dribs and drabs, in bits and pieces, in fitful starts and sudden stops. (In fact, the beginning of this essay was written about two years after this part, which explains why I was 61 "then" and 59 "now".) It has been a week since I left off writing about my missing gap year and I was intending to move on down the time and space continuum, probably to Idaho (1990) or Labrador (1992). Unfortunately, I still need to linger for just a moment in Vermont (1976) because this morning (January 31, 2014), I returned from the funeral of Howie Weinreich, who was one of the guys on that trip. All of a sudden, Vermont 1976 seems to have taken place several lifetimes ago. I met Howie in 1971, when we waited tables together at Camp Raleigh. By Vermont, he was already dating Danny's sister, Gaby, who would become Howie's wife a couple of years later. Although we may never have been part of each other's inner circle, I like to think that we were part of each's outer circle for more than 42 years. Howie had been dealt a pretty bad hand, genetically speaking. He had already lost two siblings to cancer at young ages. Sadly, Howie was not spared this fate and after a truly courageous fight spanning five years, he succumbed yesterday at age 58. I will miss his cheerful presence at our concerts and at our home on Purim night.]

So even if I did not get a gap year, I'll say it again, I've had it pretty good. I've been pretty darn lucky, despite having gotten myself all "clobbered up" with family responsibilities and all the collateral pressures that those responsibilities bring on. As a matter of plain fact, it is only because of those family responsibilities that I have had a good and somewhat meaningful life...

Which brings me back to what I wanted to write about. In 1990, my brother David booked an early June rafting trip down the middle fork of the Salmon River in Idaho. The 40 minute flight from Boise into Stanley, Idaho in a tiny, noisy prop plane, took an hour and 40 minutes as we bounced along treacherously while circling around the nasty weather, just barely above the tops of the Douglas Firs and Ponderosa Pines. All the while, our weather-beaten bush pilot cracked corny jokes about his 747 being in the shop (after Phil had questioned whether the plane's fluttering left-wing was suffering from metal fatigue). Neil Weiss showed up with no clothes or equipment at all other than the T-shirt and cut-off shorts he was wearing plus a case of beer under each arm. Despite the late hour, we convinced a local outfitter, the only shopkeeper in Stanley, to reopen, just so that Neil could buy some proper river wear, since it was darn cold. Then, we were refused service at the K(it) K(at) K(lub) bar. And all this excitement happened before the rafting trip even began. The next morning, when we finally got our first glance at the raging river, swollen with the spring melt, I would have gladly returned home had that been even remotely possible. So, I swallowed hard, said a silent, mental equivalent of "Teffilat Haderech" (Traveler's Prayer) and put my trust and fate into the hands of both the good Lord and the capable guides of Echo River Trips. There were quite a few memorable moments, but one in particular comes to mind. On the third day, just as our raft rounded the final bend towards camp, Phil ("Fish") Goldwasser, of course, got swept overboard by a series of rogue rapids and into the icy waters of the Middle Fork. Once again, he was retrieved, none the worse for wear. After 100 miles and 5 days of world-class excitement, Rocky Mountain splendor and backwoods adventure, we safely disembarked to the lovely mountain town of Salmon, Idaho.

One of the best aspects of these trips is that the guys, unimpeded by the restrictive covenants of normal society, get a rare opportunity to exist in their most uninhibited and natural states. In other words, it is alright for the boys to be boys. They can fish all day, eat junk, drink, forget to shave for multiple days, tell off-color jokes without apologizing and it's all fine. The more, the merrier, in fact. And when my dad comes along, those rules apply to him, maybe even more so.

L to R standing: Selwyn & Seymour; sitting: Phil, David, Jeff, author, Norman & Neil. Photo courtesy of author.

In 1992, he accompanied 7 of us on a week-long trip to a remote fishing lodge in a G-d forsaken but mosquito-remembered section of Labrador. Everyone complained about something on that trip: whether it was David bemoaning the lack of world-class fly-fishing at our earthy lodge; or Neil citing the plagues and "pestilence" visited upon us by the incessant hordes of biting insects; or Jeff Bernstein complaining that we were not davening three times a day; or Selwyn carping that we were not spending enough time in the pike beds. My dad, in his 60th year, complained about nothing. He was just thrilled to be catching large lake trout, landlocked salmon, speckled trout and northern pike in a beautiful and remote locale. In fact, he was almost as happy as he would have been catching perch, pickerel and sunfish ("what a beaut!") some 2 hours northwest of Bayside, NY. He even commandeered the kitchen one night and prepared his specialty: fried fish with his patented raspberry sauce.

Needless to say, this expedition was not without a few close calls. One, in particular, was not even a near-miss because it was actually a direct hit. David, Neil and Norman the Silent Electrician got banged up but lived to tell about it. Their oblivious guide decided that the perfect time to roll a cigarette was while he was gunning the boat, full-throttle in a river pock-marked by enormous, semi-submerged boulders. These boulders were so large that you could not help but see them. That is, unless your attention happened to be focused on something that requires total concentration, such as threading a needle, playing chess against a grandmaster or rolling a cigarette on a bouncing speedboat. Luckily, aside from bumps, bruises and one possible class-2 concussion, there was only one tragic victim: sadly, Norman's beautiful new Sage fly-rod did not make it. And two days later, of course, Phil once more fell into the river when our guide, Denis, sped away from the dock while Phil was still in the act of getting into the boat. I recall being entertained by the sight of Phil with his legs outside the boat and his arms draped over its side, body-surfing or hydroplaning along the top of the water, as the boat sped merrily along. I can

L to R: Author, David Eidman, Seymour Eidman, Steven Eidman. Photo courtesy of author

still hear Denis yelling at us in his French-Canadian accent, *"Sal, Mike, git heem, git heem!"*

Skip ahead ten years... In 2002, the San Francisco Giants made it to the World Series, trying (unsuccessfully as it turned out) to be the first S.F. Giants team to win it all (an omission that was roundly corrected in 2010. And 2012. And 2014.) But in 2002, Dad, my brothers and I embarked upon a whirlwind 36 hour cross-country trip, in order to take in two games of the Series between the Giants and Angels. At 70 years old, Dad took full charge of making our Giant-sized banner, which *read "Bayside, NY and Englewood, NJ love the Giants."* Thanks to that banner, we did not have to buy a single beer as the surrounding fans were battling over who would have the honor of buying us the next round. Dad was in such good spirits that he had us almost convinced that we were fortunate to be staying at a sketchy hotel close to the ballpark, where instead of a lobby with a concierge, desk and chairs, there was a man behind a wire ticket-booth window. As dad said, *"who wants to waste time walking through a lobby?"* As for the creepy, all-night donut place across the street from the hotel, Dad kept telling me that it was *"his kind of place."*

Road trips have also allowed me to spend some special time with my sons, in a way that transcends the typical dynamic that usually pervades full-on family vacations. One April, my eldest son Zack and I found ourselves tussling with 100 pound tarpon off of Islamorada, in the Florida Keys, in the middle of the night. We were back at the dock by 6:30 a.m. and then slept past noon, before making like Jimmy Buffett and tooling around Key West all afternoon. .) It doesn't get much better than that. (Speaking of the devil, we actually saw Jimmy, driving his cream colored Rolls Royce convertible, roof down, along the main drag).

The following year, in January 2012, Jonah, Benjamin and I stood up to the nastiest, meanest and toughest football fans in the world, while Eli Manning hung in there against the nastiest, meanest and toughest defense, as the Giants beat the 49ers in the cold mist at Candlestick Park, en route to the Super Bowl. Two weeks later, in Indianapolis, my nephew Alex and I watched from behind the end zone as Eli's long sideline pass floated down impossibly into the tiny space between the New England defender and the sideline. The ball made a soft landing, down onto the soft, outstretched palms of Mario Manningham, who somehow managed to keep both feet in-bounds, as the Giants, for the second time, took out Belichik and Brady's Evil Patriot Empire. That was some run, and some trip.

But when all is said and done, the size of the fish, the importance of the game, or the height of the mountain are not that important. The secret to any successful road trip is the right mix of people and the overall vibe. In 2012, eight of us celebrated my dad's 80th birthday in Islamorada. We saw nary a tarpon, bonefish, permit or snook, and our guides were undependable at best. Nonetheless, we enjoyed ourselves immensely. The weather was great, the mood was as relaxed as could be and we managed to catch over 20 species of lesser game-fish. (I was positive that some of the names of these fish were being randomly assigned to them by our jokester guide, right on the spot, such as the "Blue Runner".) We ate the fish that we had caught each day and greatly enjoyed the meals, along with what Dad claimed was the best coleslaw he had ever eaten-quite a compliment, coming from the expert. We even let dad "suggest" that we have drinks at the classily named "Hog Heaven" three or four nights in a row, on the peaceful bay side, where the tourists did not flock to photograph the sunset on the ocean side. The friendly staff there allowed us to spread out and linger as long as we liked, while we fed the fish swimming beneath the dock on which we were drinking. Dad debated the young, hardcore Pittsburgh Pirates fan behind the bar as to the respective merits of the throwing arms of Willie Mays and Roberto Clemente. The NBA playoffs and 6 different baseball games were playing on the various TV sets. Hog Heaven, indeed.

It is true, as they say, that the catching is sometimes good, sometimes bad, but the fishing is always good. Not a bad life there, in the Keys, but we all had things that needed our attention back home and we had to get back. As we returned home and said our goodbyes at Newark Airport, we agreed that we ought to do it again someday. And three years later, we did.

Fellow Roadie Sam Rosmarin on the Next Islamorada Trip (2015):
Please allow me to join the chorus of voices singing the praises of the Islamorada trip. It was for me a joyous week in all respects, particularly the time I got to spend with each of you.
I know how lucky I am to have been on two boats that landed tarpon and I was also fortunate enough to know while we were experiencing these things that the trouble finding bait, the long hours motoring to find fish, the not so good weather at the end, were all part of the whole experience; in fact they were part of what makes catching prized fish so enjoyable. The long quiet stretches with no bites and all the other not so pleasant aspects are the entry fee for the big one sweepstakes. Mike and Neil have been fishing forever yet they still displayed little boy excitement when they were anticipating the possibility of fighting (let alone landing) a tarpon and they both glowed (if how I feel is an indication, likely forever) after they succeeded at the very thing they'd been dreaming of. We all felt that little boy thrill of anticipation when each day dawned full of piscatorial promise. Tarpon or not, everyone caught fish, including 6 Mahi Mahi caught by 6 of us at exactly the same time, and then we enjoyed eating those fish in the good company we provided each other.
It was a treat for me to witness the dynamics of this group and to have had the pleasure of connecting with everyone. Half of us were Eidman men. I already knew and deeply liked and respected Sy and Mike. I told David in an earlier message that the enjoyment I experienced fishing on Tanana with them, when I said it was an honor and a pleasure spending a day with the Eidman boys, was doubled after spending the week with Dave and Steve. As I told him, in my estimation, the Eidmans are uniquely joyful, intelligent and extraordinary men. Watching them display encyclopedic knowledge of things that give me pleasure (baseball, boxing, The Honeymooners, etc.) made me feel privileged to be in their midst. In that regard, my trip takeaways will

include spending a few minutes with Sy in the Amara Cay parking lot watching a video of Jack Carter singing, dancing and telling jokes on the Judy Garland show, talking about my parents with Steve, and responding to the hip-hoppers at Hog Heaven by commandeering the juke box , having Mike commend me for the message song I played (Bob Seger's "I like that old time rock and roll") and having Dave request Grateful Dead without knowing and immediately before Friend of the Devil was the next song.

I also felt privileged and took great pleasure in spending time with Ehud, Larry and Neil. I wisely took the time to speak to each of you and greatly enjoyed the time I spent doing that. It is very satisfying, in this self-evaluating, post-parent world I suddenly find myself, to know that little Sammy from Brooklyn can get along so well (at least in my mind) with such smart, decent, fun-loving men.

Thanks again to David for everything he did to ensure a good time was had by all. Thank you all for allowing me to spend the week with you and for giving me some lifetime memories. May you all continue to enjoy good fishing, good health and good times together and may we all have more moments of little boy joy.

Sam's first tarpon, following a 25 minute battle. Photo courtesy of author.

A ROOMFUL OF ELEPHANTS

Photo courtesy of Daphne Eidman

*"Odds and ends, odds and ends,
Lost time is not found again."*
Bob Dylan, "Odds and Ends" ©

Part One: Elephants & Gorillas

On what was to be his final album, John Lennon included a song that he wrote for his son, Sean. It contained the line *"Life is what happens to you while you're busy making other plans."* That line had previously appeared, more or less verbatim in a 1957 Reader's Digest magazine. People often quote it because they believe that John Lennon imagined it (he didn't) and because it distills a universal truth into a few simple words (it does). By way of example, the book that you have been reading was written while I was busy making plans to write an entirely different book.

I began writing these essays in early 2013. It had been a long, cold, lonely winter and I was probably suffering from some form of seasonal affective disorder, more appropriately known by its acronym, SAD. Vague notions of mortality and legacy, which for some time had already been inhabiting the attics of my life, were soon sneaking into the kitchen, chewing up small bites of my attention span. I was then less than two years away from the big 6-0 and all of a sudden, it seemed as if the road that I was looking at through the windshield was far shorter than the long ribbon of highway in the rear-view mirror. Three of my legal contemporaries, all stalwarts of the plaintiffs' bar, had given up the ghost within about a year of each other, and although I did not talk about it much, it weighed upon me. Their deaths were unavoidable reminders that life is fleeting, fragile, tenuous. Reflecting on this really darkened my mood because I couldn't help but realize that when all is said and done, much will certainly remain unsaid and undone. It was so much easier to look back than to dwell on what might be. I needed a new project to sink my teeth into, preferably something that would help me to connect the convoluted but immutable past with the impending and uncertain future.

Writing seemed to be a way of doing that. By forcing me to dig into my past for material, it allowed for reflection, analysis and maybe even some catharsis. It definitely took my mind off of the dreary winter days and I soon began to believe that maybe, just maybe someone else might actually want to read some of this stuff. Or maybe not. Either way, I figured that writing was as good a way as any to keep my mind occupied. All the better, writing was something I could do on my own, in my own way, during the quiet hours at the end of the workday.

I had no problems coming up with source material. For some people, looking back is like looking through the wrong end of a telescope, where even nearby objects appear far away. For me, it was just the opposite and it was more like gazing through a good pair of binoculars or glancing at the passenger side-view mirror of a car, where everything appears much closer than it actually was. A half-century may have passed but it seemed as if it was only yesterday that I was a happy child in Washington Heights, cavorting amid five sets of relatives, all residing within mere blocks of one another. I began to mentally reminisce about those carefree, joyful days.

I thought a lot about my maternal grandmother who played such a big role in my upbringing and of my paternal grandfather, with his grim demeanor and devotion to the New York Mets and his imagined all-Jewish lineup (except for Cleon Jones and Tommy Agee). My grandma and grandpa both survived well into my adulthood and held such high hopes for me. I still see them clearly in my mind's eye, but I see them as old people nearing the end of difficult lives. I truly regret not having taken enough time to learn about their youth, their Wonder Years, their glory days. Did they have happy days during their youths, as I had? How did they spend their youthful years? As for their ancestors, the generation that either brought or sent my grandparents to America, of them I know next to nothing. Even now, I cling to my childhood memories, such as when my great-grandmother, "Bubby" would bring home a live carp from the local fish store, before the holidays. With a mixture of wonder and dread, I would lean with my elbows on our bathtub, watching the heavily-scaled creature swim mini-laps, while it unknowingly awaited its inevitable fate. (King Solomon, in "Ecclesiastes", compared fish caught in the net and birds ensnared in a trap, to people, who are prone to unpredictable disasters; perhaps we are more like that carp, going in circles until an ignominious end). In any event, I safeguard those childhood memories. But, in the ordinary course of human affairs, once I am gone, the memories will die with me. And even my memories only go so far. The details and the nitty gritty of my ancestors' lives in Europe, were long ago lost to the foggy ruins of time. For instance, even my great-grandfather and namesake Moshe Michael Eidman of Turka, Poland (now Ukraine) is a mystery man, just a name on a record in the Yad Vashem archives. We recently discovered a brief letter written in 1941 to my grandfather, Saul Eidman, in the Bronx, from his brother in Turka (both were sons of Moshe Michael Eidman). The mundane details, so sadly banal in retrospect, only whetted my appetite for more, much more.

Nowadays, we will leave a larger historical footprint, if not a bigger impression. We have recorded stacks of unwatched home videos and have projected megabytes of social media into 'the cloud'. Nevertheless, I am convinced that our descendants will be nearly as clueless about us as we are about our antecedents. I imagine that roughly fifty or so years after we pass on, the details of each of our lives will be reduced to little more than a random leaf in a family tree or a digitized entry in an online directory of family lineage. Sad, but natural. So, when I first got serious about this book, the high concept was to produce something interesting and mildly entertaining about my life and times. I decided that while Moshe Michael Eidman may remain a mystery man, a historical cipher, his great-grandson and namesake would not.

One quiet evening, I sat before the computer, shook off the mental cobwebs and began to type. I thought it would take me about six months to get this done and boy, was I off. (In my defense, I was envisioning a much briefer tome but as often happens, one thing led to another. Also, I had no clue that "post-production" would take much longer than writing the first draft.) I started with the essay about my favorite childhood record store. Soon enough, I was writing about my great-grandmother, deeply enjoying leaning back in my chair, closing my eyes and conjuring up her image. When the material kept flowing, I realized that I needed to get organized. I composed a list of possible essay topics but I did not stick to it; I actually ended up with more topics than I could fit in this volume. (And the order in which the essays appear in this book was not the order in which I wrote them). But unless demand unexpectedly outstrips my modest expectations, I am not promising a Volume II. But should a sequel ever materialize, I already have two potential titles for it, maybe three. Just in case. I mean, my Mom always told me to *"never say never"*.

I was pleasantly surprised that writing this book came easily to me. It was a peaceful, solitary and cathartic way to exorcise a few demons. I assumed that getting started would prove daunting; after all, I still remember learning in fourth grade a Hebrew idiom that translates to *"All beginnings are difficult."* Ironically, I encountered practically no difficulty in getting

"The Dominican Dandy"

underway— but in true Grateful Dead spirit, I experienced tremendous problems trying to arrive at the end of the jam. What began as a series of six essays eventually, little by little, morphed into a 28 essay megillah, culminating with this one. (In the end, I ended up with 30 essays; I am not sure how that happened). But I struggled mightily with this essay, and I considered typing "The End" after #27, in honor of my favorite pitcher, Juan

Marichal. More than once, I nearly scrapped this essay altogether but I felt a weird, emotional attachment to the title. So for better or worse, I put it through, to quote T.S. Eliot, *"a hundred visions and revisions."* More importantly, had I cut back to 27, I would have ignored the elephant in the room, which is the undisputed truth that even after 27 chapters, I had failed to fulfill my mission, which was to write a coherent and readable story about my life.

The evidence is right there in the table of contents. Run your finger down the list of essays and you will see a mostly random list of incidents, tangential people and off-hand topics that, for the most part, filled in the margins and edges of my life. By contrast, I made a series of conscious and subconscious decisions not to write about the topics that matter most to me and which have taken center stage during my first 60 years. (Well, by now, it's past 61, getting on towards 62). When I began, I expected to be writing about: my parents, my significant and insignificant others, my brothers, my sisters-in- law, my divorce, my kids, the Eidman cousins, our family in Israel, the state of Israel, "Solo Monotheism" (my imaginary, perfect religion), my love/hate relationship with the practice of law, places I have lived, my fixation with the Catskill Mountains, my favorite books and films, the best concerts I have attended, the ones I am sorry to have missed, my music promotion business, why, where and with whom I have fished, where I have not fished but still want to, people who I like, don't like or who have influenced me, pop culture, why I cannot swim, left-of- center politics, memorable teachers including the good, the bad and the ugly, the things I love to do and the things I hate to eat. And so forth. Just as Bob Dylan said that each line of "A Hard Rain's A Gonna Fall" was originally intended to be a separate song, each of those items was supposed to be a distinct chapter. I realize that I touched a bit upon some or many of those subjects but not in any deep or insightful way. So, instead of writing that book, I wrote a different one, about an old record shop, a friend who dropped out of my life, an ice fishing trip and the caretaker from our bungalow colony. In other words, a book about nothing. Or to be more generous, about trivialities. The sort of book that George Costanza could relate to. Perhaps, I am being a bit hard on myself —after all, I set out to write a book in my spare time and I did. But still.......

Why didn't I write a more revealing, personal and focused

book? For starters, I was hamstrung by my stubborn refusal to write a traditional, linear memoir. That would have been relatively easy and severely boring. Also, I did not want to compromise and to split the difference between my preference to speak my mind without inhibition and my desire to let sleeping dogs lie and to not to rock too many boats (and to avoid using too many clichés). In writing their excellent autobiographies, Keith Richards chose the former style (just ask Mick) while Neil Young opted for the latter (ask Steve Stills). Both styles worked but I think you need to choose one or the other and neither one seemed to be a good fit for me. Simply put, I have too much Jewish guilt to be Keith and harbor too many old grudges to be Neil. Last, believe it or not, writing about all of the important stuff is really hard.

I believe that's what separates a transcendent genius like Leonard Cohen, z"l (of blessed memory), from a talented entertainer like Steve Goodman. Steve wrote quirky, insightful and funny songs about hotel rooms, late-night TV ads and Monte Hall while LC wrote abstract and ambiguous dirges about salvation, redemption, religion, love, lust and betrayal. Thirty years after Steve's demise, I continue to miss him dearly, but let's not pretend that what he was doing was as difficult as what Leonard did. Steve would have been the first to tell you that and to make his point, he probably would have omitted the fact that LC or no LC, it was Steve who wrote the greatest train song ever written. But I digress.

The bottom line is that it is difficult to tackle the important subjects and it takes a real writer's chops to do so with clarity, incisiveness and gusto. I know because this essay has been murder to write and in my heart of hearts, I don't feel at all satisfied with it. Let's just keep the clichés rolling along and say that it was a heckuva lot easier to sweep all the proverbial dirt beneath the proverbial rug, while ignoring the elephant in the room. In fact, when I compare the quirky table of contents to the list of meaty topics that I failed to tackle, I realize that I've been ignoring a whole roomful of elephants. And a few 800 pound gorillas, as well. Since I don't know if I'll ever get around to writing <u>that</u> book, here are a few thoughts about some of the elephants that are sitting conspicuously in my room...

Part Two: Mom & Dad

"My mother and father watched over me
And made sure I never really got hurt,
Made sure I was never stifled or bound
That's what everybody needs in their background.
That's the rock you build your mountain on
And it can never never fall down"
Graham Parker, "Blue Horizon" ©

Mom & Dad, circa 1986

Do I really need to expand on that heartfelt lyric? (If you've been skipping over all the song lyrics, go back and read this one). Bob Dylan once explained his own famous reticence by saying *"The songs are my lexicon."* Graham Parker's few lines tell you more about what my parents did for me than I ever could. Graham, a sweet man who built his reputation by writing acerbic and bitter songs (and who I had the privilege of promoting twice in concert), apparently never forgot his roots or believed that the debt he owed to his folks had been repaid. I could say *"ditto"* and leave it at that but let me throw a bit of detail and color onto Graham's broad but heartfelt brushstrokes. My parents, Florence Eidman (nee Teller) and Seymour Eidman were born in New York City during the depression and dedicated themselves to building better lives for my two brothers and me, first in the hardscrabble streets of Washington Heights and then in the suburb of Bayside, Queens. As octogenarians, they continue to live full and fulfilling lives. My Mom retired from teaching years ago but never stopped setting an example for all of us when it came to the right way to go about everything, especially that frustrating subject known as "mothering." But she went further and obtained an advanced degree in grand- mothering. Recently, she has been working towards her Ph.D. in great-grand-mothering and as usual, she has been getting straight A's. Through all of this, she has never neglected her primary area of concentration, which is parenting 101 and remains one of the few people whose advice I fully trust and once in a while, even seek out before it is offered.

My Dad is an autodidactic pseudo-renaissance man, who ought to be the subject of a book or mini-series, because no mere essay will ever do him justice. He is a retired trial lawyer who enjoyed more than his rightful share of success in the rough and tumble worlds of both criminal law (trying capital cases when New York still had the death penalty) and medical malpractice. During the pre-internet days, I marveled at his abilities to teach himself the intricacies of medicine and to skillfully negotiate settlements for twice what each case was worth. The mini-series about him would contain whole episodes devoted to his mastery of topics as diverse and wide-ranging as Cambrian-period fossils, cantorial music and arrangements, late 19th and early 20th century American art, swing-era jazz, fresh and salt-water fishing (separate installments), pre-World War II baseball (including the Negro leagues), Jewish mobsters and a host of other subjects of increasingly diminishing general interest.

Part Three: On Getting Unmarried

"The moral of this story, the moral of this song,
Is simply that one should never be where one does not belong.
So if you see your neighbor carrying something, help him with his load.
And don't go mistaking paradise for that home across the road."
Bob Dylan, "The Ballad of Frankie Lee & Judas Priest" ©

Chico & Harpo 'editing' the Captain's mustache.

Do you remember the Marx Brothers shtick in their classic film "Monkey Business", where Chico and Harpo Marx start to trim a dozing customer's big mustache, repeatedly giving him "a little *snoop* here", trying to make both sides perfectly even? After all the "snooping" and snipping and before you knew it, pretty much the entire mustache was gone, except for a tiny "Hitler" patch. Well, that's exactly what happened with this section of the essay. I originally wrote a whole bunch of things about mental instant replays, abject failure, blame, guilt and confusion. Then, I began to "snoop" away at what I wrote until before I knew it, the page was blank.

Part Four: My Three Sons (& A Daughter-In-Law)

"You who are on the road
Must have a code that you can live by
And so become yourself
Because the past is just a goodbye."
Graham Nash, "Teach your Children" ©

Parenting is a high-wire mental gymnastics act where you are constantly negotiating a balance between telling your kids which end is up and letting them figure that out for themselves, consequences be damned. My three sons are still works in progress but at this point, at ages 34, 25 and 22, much of the work is now in their hands. I have tried to be neither the distant, absentee father nor the control freaking, helicopter dad. I am positive that in some respects I have failed miserably but have succeeded in others. In truth, it is not always easy to figure out exactly where you could have done better, but in my humble opinion, my kids have turned out pretty darn well, so I am thankful for that. Also, I have just enough self-awareness not to claim too much credit for my kids' successes because it would be foolish for me to believe that I have influenced them more than their mother(s) did.

My eldest son, Zachary, was a product of my first marriage, to Pamela. He married a terrific girl, Dina and they are the parents of my first and only grandchild (so far!), a funny, non-stop dynamo of activity, named Cooper Pierre Eidman, who at 4 and 1/2, wants to know why I got a haircut with a big empty spot right on top of my head. Zack's training is in website design and programming but he has been working in the whirlwind world of life insurance, where he is on a management track for one of the major life companies. Unlike his dad, he has a strong creative side; I believe that it is probably just a matter of time until his fertile imagination produces an invention or innovation that will shake up the world just a bit. His wife Dina has fit into our family dynamic seamlessly. She is a CPA, working in human resources for a major financial institution.

Benjamin, Dina, Zachary, Jonah & Cooper, 2016. Photo courtesy of author

My wife Daphne and I have two sons. Jonah graduated from college last year, with a degree in mechanical engineering. He is working very hard for a start-up company in the area of home energy efficiencies, having revamped the company's analytics right off the bat. He is at the stage of his life where he is old enough to play guitar with my friends but young enough for me to get a kick out of that. Our youngest is Benjamin and he has completed three extremely successful years of college, majoring in public health. I truly believe that the progressive wing of the Democratic Party needs his passion, vision and smarts and I would love to see him go in that direction, possibly with a law degree on his resume. (Oops, there goes the control freak side of me…..).

Part Five: Friends (not the overrated TV show)

"But my heart is not weary, it's light and it's free
I've got nothin' but affection for all those who've sailed with me."
Bob Dylan, "Mississippi" ©

Author, Myron & Danny, 1966
Photo courtesy of Ernie Wohlfarth, A"H.

Author, Danny & Myron, 2015
Photo courtesy of Daphne Eidman

The Talmudic Tractate of Avot, which deals exclusively with moral standards and ethics, directs us to *"acquire a friend"* (in the singular). To get slightly more low-brow, I recall a TV ad for a high-end tequila, in which actor Michael Imperioli from "The Sopranos" asks *"Whatever happened to best buddies? Today, everyone has 850 virtual friends."* (Which, of course, is far too many to share that primo tequila with.) Well, I hear you, bro. And I hear John Lennon, who once said that, *"Being honest will not get you many friends but it will always get you the right ones."* I have tried to follow those principles in cultivating my friendships. Life is not a popularity contest, although many people behave as if it were. When it comes to friendships, I believe that less (or fewer) is more, provided that one chooses wisely. I wouldn't trade my small circle of long-time (in some cases, life-long) friendships for anyone's social media network, on- line directory or cyber-space group. And even though it's not a long list, I am not naming names. (Get over yourselves, you know who you are).

Part Six: A Criminally Brief Note Concerning Daphne

"Sara, Sara, it's all so clear I can never forget.
Sara, Sara, loving you is the one thing I'll never regret."
Bob Dylan, "Sara" ©

Daphne with her parents, Gabrielle & Sam.
Photo courtesy of Daphne's sister Monica Mechtinger

After some 30 years of marriage, I believe that I can safely say that thankfully, things are working out better for Daphne and me than they did for Sara and Bob. My best friend, Danny once told me that the smartest decision he ever made was in the woman he married. But Danny could have made the exact same statement about me. No one would have disagreed, especially not me. Until Daphne came along, I held a strong intention not to remarry as I believed that I wasn't suited for marriage. I could have written a detailed account of my state of mind way back when we met and how it all played out in my head. But instead of focusing on my neuroses, let me attest (with the permanency of print) that for the past thirty years, Daphne has enhanced each and every one of the important areas of my life — at home, at leisure and at work. One of her many qualities is a powerful aversion to the spotlight, so I will take this opportunity to highlight a single, seemingly humdrum, yet integral area of our life together.

In part due to her modesty, people believe that Daphne *"helps out"* in my law practice, shuffling some papers, answering phone calls, churning out a few letters. Nothing could be further from the truth. In reality, Daphne does much of the initial investigation of complex cases, drafts most of our court papers, handles a great deal of the client contact, has spearheaded all of our marketing efforts, from our website to our promotional materials, and has totally revamped our bookkeeping system. Along the way, she has naturally learned her fair share of law. She has established warm relationships with many of my clients and they feel comfortable calling when I am not around because they have such confidence in Daphne, who often takes care of the situation before I even hear about it. I have a reliable network of legal-eagle colleagues and I do not hesitate to call upon them for advice; however, when it comes down to making a sensible decision about whether or not to take the case, or the best strategy to employ, or whether to accept a settlement offer, Daphne has earned my absolute trust and respect. Thanks to her work in the office, we have been able to take things to an entirely different qualitative level.

Working together for seventeen years and counting is an impressive accomplishment, and I honestly cannot envision what the practice would be like without her. As for our concert promotion business, she is the strong and steely woman who stands steadfast right behind the quirky genius. (If there was a way to do this, I would put one of those smiley icons right here).

Part Seven: A Quick Look in the Mirror

"It's time to go inward, time to be still,
If I don't do it now I don't believe I ever will....
It's time to go inward, I hope I have the nerve
To take an inventory of the causes that I serve."
Rodney Crowell, "Time to Go Inward" ©

A long time ago, when he was still a very young man, John Sebastian sang: ©*"And now, a quarter of my life has almost passed, I think I've come to see myself at last."* It's taken me quite a bit longer but after 62 years, I believe that I do know myself reasonably well. I see the good, which is the side that I try to show most people, most of the time. But I also see the other side, the side that I keep hidden like the dark side of the moon. That side is inhabited by some misanthropy, aloofness, anger, impatience, fear, suspicion, distrust, cowardice, narcissism, stubbornness, narrow-mindedness, laziness and some depression. All of those are in me somewhere, some in smaller percentages than others, and thankfully none in crippling doses.

Mirrored Self Portrait, Sausalito, 2015. Photo courtesy of author

Due to my intestinal fortitude and other positive traits such as loyalty, a sense of humor and some smarts, the negative traits have not impeded me from living my life in the way I want (for the most part) and doing the things that I need to do. I have generally been able to deal with my dark side, on my own terms, with reasonable, if not universal success. I do not believe that I possess more unfavorable characteristics than the typical person. We are hard-wired to have both sides and human nature involves the ongoing tug of war between the two. I have worked through this on my own, wisely or unwisely without the help or guidance of therapists, counselors or Svengalis, in order to be neither overwhelmed by the negatives, nor oblivious to my dark side. As Van the Man has said, *"no guru, no method, no teacher"* (except for Dylan, now and then). And like Van, I wish to acknowledge and even appreciate the struggle within.

One negative trait that I believe has had an adverse impact upon my enjoyment of life is the fear factor. I have not been able to conquer certain fears; unfortunately, my inability or more often, my unwillingness to do so, has all too frequently held me back. For example, even though I feel happiest and most at ease on a lake, stream, river or ocean, I never bothered to learn to swim properly, which of course, would have required me to tackle my fear of drowning. True, my early introduction to the sport had been ill-advised and counter-productive and even later, I survived a terrifying experience or two.

Nevertheless, when it comes to outdoor excitement, I was always an adventurous soul, whether I was climbing the highest tree, canyoneering down the side of a ravine or skiing on trails more advanced than my actual skill level. No doubt, had I learned to swim with even a modicum of proficiency, I could have taken up scuba diving, gliding above the coral, on the prowl for moray eels, channeling my inner Lloyd Bridges from "Sea Hunt". People have often told me that 'it's never too late.' In fact, I had an elderly client who learned to swim when she was about 70 and it became part of her daily routine. The problem, to once again quote T.S. Eliot (from the same poem), is that *"in short, I was afraid."* And I am just as afraid of the water today as I was when I was a small child.

When it came to finances and my law practice, I have been

overly and perhaps neurotically risk-averse and conservative. I have always been terrified at the thought of burdening my small law practice with debt, even if certain investments (in larger space, advertising and additional staff, for example) would have proven beneficial towards the growth of my practice. With the many uncertainties and vagaries of a law practice built wholly upon contingent fees, parsimonious insurance companies and the whims of juries, I was and remain terrified of the risks. I now understand that had I overcome my fears, my practice would likely have grown well beyond where it is today. Had I bitten a few bullets and taken a few plunges (mixed metaphors be damned!), I would almost certainly have brought my family a higher level of comfort and security. But I was never able to get myself to pull the trigger. To be fair, I have won and settled my share of interesting cases and have earned the respect of my clients, colleagues and adversaries alike. Still, after all these years (currently just past 37 and counting), I have never taken my practice to that next level, that rarified and lofty plateau where one doesn't lose sleep over when the next new client will walk through the door.

Like I said: at this juncture, I know who I am and who I am not. I am a smart and personable guy, skilled as a plaintiff's trial lawyer in and out of the courtroom. But like the cowardly lion en route to the Emerald City, I could have used some courage.

Part Eight: Ecclesiastes, Bob Dylan and Modern Times
(the times, not the Dylan album,
although I mention the album once)

"Some people say the world's a strange and evil place
And all the shadows fall across your face
Because the world's a strange and evil place.
Then others say because the sun shines every day,
That we should live life come what may
Because the sun shines every day."
Alejandro Escovedo, "Put You Down" ©

"All this I have tested with wisdom;
I thought I could become wise but it is beyond me."
Ecclesiastes, Chapter 7, Verse 23.

When I began writing this essay, there was a horrific series of coordinated terror bombings and shootings in Paris. As always, this resulted in an overwhelming amount of analysis, opinions and talk, little of it very useful or insightful. This mind-numbing violence seemed to dovetail with an ongoing series of random stabbings, mostly of Jewish people, in Israel. During such trying times, I try to remind myself that, as it says in the

Book of Ecclesiastes, (or "Kohelet" in Hebrew), *"There is nothing new beneath the sun. Sometimes there is something of which one says: 'Look, this is new'; but it has already existed for ages before us."* (Chapter 1, verses 9-10). After reading one or two random chapters of Ecclesiastes, I try to convince myself that in the long run, light prevails over darkness, truth triumphs over falsehood and good eradicates evil. During dark days, I often turn to Ecclesiastes in order to regain my psychological footing and perspective. It reminds me that the world is frequently a difficult and sad place but that nevertheless, man's mission is to appreciate the good and to endeavor to live a worthwhile life.

Our Jewish tradition attributes Kohelet to Solomon, the King of Israel who built the First Temple in Jerusalem some 900 years BCE and was renowned for his unparalleled wisdom. The book's twelve chapters painstakingly dissect the futility and transient nature of our mundane existence, in which our vision is inevitably obscured and distorted by a hapless veil of vanity and foolishness.

Ecclesiastes bemoans the universal dilemmas people encounter in the material world, whether they are wise or foolish, rich or poor; and it highlights the inescapability of the mortal trappings and failings of the human condition. However, Kohelet also emphasizes that in spite of our inability to comprehend the meaning of life and what awaits us afterwards, it behooves us to make the most of our brief time in this world, in both a physical and spiritual sense.

Kohelet goes to some extremely dark places. It says that the dead are better off than the living, because the dead have been freed from the agonies of social injustice. Better off still are those who have never been born because they will not suffer at all. (Chapter 4, verses 2-3).

Despite its seemingly unrelenting negativity, Kohelet contains many brief bursts of positive exhortations. It preaches that there is *"nothing better for (man) than to rejoice and do good in this life"* and that *"every man who eats, drinks and finds purpose in his work — that is a gift from   G-d"* (Chapter 3, verses 12-13). In fact, the recurring theme of Kohelet is the importance of wringing some amount of joy and wisdom from a world filled with sadness and insoluble mysteries.

While some view the book as an indictment of the futility of our earthly endeavors and concerns, a closer reading shows that Ecclesiastes, far from preaching an austere or cloistered existence, actually encourages people to rejoice and partake in the physical pleasures of this world. We are told that fruitless though our efforts may prove to be, we should continue to seek meaning and understanding. Kohelet preaches against the monastic life, strongly favoring *"life with the wife you love through all your fleeting days..."* We are advised to be mindful of history. And we are instructed that, *"Whatever your hand finds to do, do it with your might"* (Chapter 9, Verse 10). In other words: give it your all!

Fairly recently, I discovered that Kohelet is Bob Dylan's favorite Biblical book. I was not surprised in the least that the world's greatest songwriter and lyricist was inspired by the wisest of kings. After all, Dylan's oeuvre, which transcends any one particular musical genre or literary tradition, includes many songs about man's place in a hostile, chaotic world, and of uncertainty in the face of the approaching end times. The following verse, from one of Bob's masterworks, was inspired both by Kohelet and by the book of Deuteronomy, as it speaks of humankind's penchant for corrupting the gifts that G-d has bestowed or at least put within our grasp.

> *"Well, G-d is in His heaven,*
> *And we all want what's His,*
> *But power and greed and corruptible seed*
> *Seem to be all that there is."*
> Bob Dylan, "Blind Willie McTell" ©

Dylan is not the only contemporary writer or artist who was influenced by Ecclesiastes. In fact, the book served as inspiration for some of mankind's greatest literature (in addition to Pete Seeger's "Turn, Turn, Turn"). King Solomon's dissection of life's trials and tribulations, has inspired artists as diverse as Shakespeare, Van Gogh, Dostoevsky and Kafka. American novelist Tom Wolfe once wrote of Ecclesiastes: *"Of all I have ever seen or learned, that book seems to me the noblest, the wisest, and the most powerful expression of man's life upon this earth—and also the highest flower of poetry, eloquence, and truth. I am not given to dogmatic judgments in the matter of literary creation, but if I had to make one I could say that Ecclesiastes is the greatest single piece of writing I have ever known, and the wisdom expressed in it the most lasting and profound."* In the musical sphere, we can discern its world view within the dark and introspective music of Leonard Cohen, Richard Thompson and Patty Griffin, not to mention Lou Reed, Lucinda Williams, Neil Young, and countless other great blues and folk singers. Some might find the work of these artists depressing. In my opinion, all they are doing is telling the truth, and telling it in a way that we can handle and maybe even enjoy.

In modern times, vanity, greed and confusion continue to be dominant societal themes. Therefore, the continued relevance of Ecclesiastes can hardly be called into question. As Tom Wolfe suggested, its "lasting and profound" power lies in its preternatural and seemingly prescient rumination on issues that continue to resonate today. Wide-ranging in scope, it discusses an array of seemingly modern topics, such as the unscrupulous wielding of power, income disparity and the preciousness of one's reputation. I never tire of re-reading it because of how applicable it seems to the present-day injustices and crises that unfold before my eyes.

As we move ahead through the 21st Century, despite all the

scientific and technological innovation, the state of humanity appears to be stuck in neutral. Some of our modern-day issues, such as global warming and pollution, even seem to have shifted us into reverse. Attempts at a level-headed examination of the world all too often only produce a *"where do we even begin?!"* type of reaction. And if I narrow my focus to my own country, the U.S., the most powerful nation on earth, I am tempted to follow up with, *"And where are we going?"* We repeatedly elect politicians who blithely enact policies that serve to destroy the post-World World II middle class, in favor of a permanent super-wealthy ruling class. Poverty, homelessness, unemployment and low minimum wages still factor into the lives of way too many Americans. Kids are receiving an education at an ever-increasing cost but, in many ways, they are less educated than ever. We are continuing to destroy the environment and cannot even agree that we ought to stop doing that. It appears that we will be saddling our children with a national debt that they will never be able to pay back. With the approval of the judicial branch of our government, our legislative branch remains at the beckon of the highest bidders. On the rare occasion when legislation actually benefits the lives of the majority or the under-served, the party of the rich and powerful threatens to undo it almost as soon as it is enacted. And just as I am finishing my last, final edit of this book, the nation elected, a man I view as a hateful, ignorant demagogue. I could go on and on, but then I would just sound bitter—and really, I am not. Just disappointed. We could be doing so much better.

I am finally arriving at the end of this book. I began this project full of the proverbial vim and vigor but I am staggering towards its conclusion, ever so haltingly and indecisively. One thing that is crystal clear is that unfortunately the wisdom of King Solomon is in short supply these days. Thankfully, we still have the tangible fruits of Solomon's wisdom, beautifully transmitted to us in the books of Proverbs, The Song of Songs and of course, Ecclesiastes. Perhaps inevitably, the final chapter of Kohelet finds King Solomon's metaphorical and dramatic description of man's precipitous but inevitable decline due to the ravages of old age. Solomon then 'book-ends' his treatise by reiterating its main theme, *"futility of futilities, all is futile."* But this was not the only conclusion he came to.

Through the twelve chapters of Ecclesiastes, the wise King put the state of humanity under the microscope, dissected and inspected it, and issued a frank pathology report. Despite a series of troubling, near-critical diagnoses, he found no malignancy and his long-term prognosis was guardedly favorable. To that end, Solomon abruptly shifted subject and tone in the epilogue, which contains several weighty verses about the dissemination of wisdom, the importance of listening and of not getting bogged down by writing too many books *"without limit."*

Solomon clearly wanted to close on a positive note and in the book's poignant penultimate verse, he tried to give us a sense of what it all comes down to in the end, when all the cards have been played. The language of that verse is simple but loses a little something in the translation. I prefer one of the modern translations, which goes along the lines of: *"That's the whole story; so when all is said and done, here's the bottom line: Fear G-d and keep his commandments because that's the entire essence of man."* King Solomon reminds us, plainly, that in spite of the vicissitudes, suffering and uncertainty, our mission is to live a righteous life, because that is what we were put on earth to do. When Kohelet is read in public, such as on the holiday of Succoth, we drive home that point by repeating the penultimate verse after reading the more tempered and (literally) judgmental final verse: *"For G-d will bring every deed into judgment, including everything hidden, whether it is good or evil."*

The concept of tempering the negative by closing on a

positive note was not lost on modern-day songwriters, who often employ the same device either lyrically or, in a musically subliminal fashion. Dylan's haunting "Ain't Talkin'" from the Modern Times album is a powerful example of what I mean by a subliminal positive ending. The entire song is written and performed in a mournful minor key, befitting the end-days dissipation of its world-weary narrator. But right at the end, after the final lyric and just as the music fades, we hear a single, solid major chord, thrown in seemingly randomly. It is the sonic equivalent of an unexpected, beautiful beam of bright light on the horizon at the edge of a dark and stormy sky.

I couldn't help but think that this surprising twist hearkened back to Dylan's work from thirty years earlier. Bob distilled so much personal angst, drama and trauma into his brilliant "Blood on the Tracks" album; but, he tempered the negativity of this heavy record by closing it with the light-hearted "Buckets of Rain," in which he sings playfully about moonbeams, little red wagons and monkeys. But Dylan is Dylan and at the final verse, he pivots once again and throws us this little curveball:

> *"Life is sad, life is a bust.*
> *All ya can do, is do what ya must*
> *You do what you must do and ya do it well*
> *I'll do it for you, honey baby, can't you tell?"*
> Bob Dylan, "Buckets of Rain" ©

Years became decades as I struggled to understand precisely what Bob was aiming for when he sang, *"all ya can do is do what ya must."* I knew that there was a message buried deep within those few simple words. Perhaps Dylan was commenting upon or mocking our ability to reverse the fates of a sad and disappointing world. Maybe he meant that within the confines and limitations of this troublesome world, the best way to get by is to keep our heads down and do what is required of us, that is, fulfill our minimum daily requirements and nothing more: *All ya can do is do what ya must"*. As in a school kid *"must"* do his or her homework, or as in someone *"must"* walk the dog. To even attempt to exceed the bare minimum would be futile and fated to be of no lasting value. A truly sad perspective on life. I wondered if that was the message—but given the overall lightheartedness of the song, I found this interpretation unsatisfying and confusing.

Then, about ten years ago, I saw a documentary film entitled, "Secret Lives: Hidden Children and their Rescuers During World War II" (co-produced by our friend, Toby Appleton). Near the end of the film, a non-Jewish Belgian man, named Jean Paul Goyens, was asked why he had rescued and hid a Jewish child at great personal risk. Mr. Goyens responded as follows: *"People do things because, I think, they have to. They can't do anything else."* After the movie ended, the credits rolled and I kept hearing those words in my head over and over, *"They have to, they can't do anything else."* I heard the words but as I sat in the still-dark theater, I also heard the echo of the familiar Dylan lyrics, *"All ya can do, is do what ya must, you do what ya must do and ya do it well..."* Suddenly, I finally "got" the ending to "Buckets of Rain".

In our darkest hours, people cannot be satisfied by merely doing the minimum; in fact, the complete opposite is true. During times of crisis, logic takes a backseat and I believe a person's inner conscience, or soul, directs his or her actions. When pushed to the brink, the good person acts, compelled by an inner compass to go above and beyond the call of duty. There is no need for an internal cost/benefit analysis of what the consequences or aftermath will be. While sitting in the darkened theater, I realized that for nearly 30 years, I had (and not for the first or last time) misunderstood and misinterpreted the Great White Wonder.

Dylan was using his most simple of songs to tell us

something quite profound. In this sad world full of busted hopes and dreams, our sole chance for redemption is to trust and act upon our highest and noblest instincts. Much as Jean Paul Goyens did, we must do the things that are instinctively correct, without calculation or contrivance. We must never be satisfied with the bare minimum. We must follow our hearts and not our minds. We must do what we know is right without compromise or rationalization. We must join the silent minority of people who do the right thing while abandoning the loud majority who act out of expediency, self-interest or convenience. And when it is time to act, *"do it well,"* as Dylan advises — or in the words of King Solomon, *"Whatever your hand finds to do, do it with your might."* Go for it!

In composing the final verse of his masterpiece, "Blood on the Tracks," I believe Bob Dylan was referencing King Solomon's magnum opus. By placing this message at the very end of the album, Dylan ensured that despite his customary vagueness, this universal truth would not be obscured or diluted amid the many recriminations and bittersweet musings of the album. And so, in ending my book, I will channel two of my heroes: Israel's wisest King and America's most brilliant songwriter and Nobel Laureate. When all is said and done, it is up to each of us to take the high road, to work hard to distinguish right from wrong, to do the only thing we can do, and to do it well.

ACKNOWLEDGEMENTS & THANKS

Navigating the murky waters of the print licensing world proved to be a daunting task for a fledgling author. A few individuals made the sailing a bit smoother. First and foremost, the author wishes to thank Jeff Rosen and David Beal for their extraordinary generosity in granting him the rights to quote from a host of Bob Dylan's songs. Similarly, he wishes to express appreciation and thanks to the following individuals:

David Bromberg and Gary Haber for their kindness in granting him the rights to quote from David's "New Lee Highway Blues" and to David for his input with respect to the essay "Bob Dylan's Another Self Portrait" and for David's quote at the end of that essay. If any of you are unfamiliar with David's music and repertoire, the author strongly recommends virtually any and all of David's recordings and his virtuoso live performances.

Garland and Claire Jeffreys for permission to quote from Garland's "I Was Afraid of Malcolm". Too many years ago, the author first saw Garland dancing across the tables at NYC's Bottom Line, when he was a guest performer at a David Bromberg show and was immediately smitten. He continues to rock on. Check him out.

Thank you to Amanda Petrusich for allowing him to quote in "Sugar Blue Plays Rosa's Lounge" from her superb book, "Do Not Sell At Any Price". That book is a poignant and fascinating look at the world of rare 78 rpm blues and country recordings and its dedicated if eccentric inhabitants. Read it.

Thank you to Toby Perl for giving the author permission to quote from her exceptionally moving film "Secret Lives: Hidden Children and Their Rescuers During WWII."

The author also thanks the following folks for the thoughts and quotes that they contributed to some of the essays: Myron Baer, Efrem Nulman, Dov Kahane, Neil Stein, Aaron Stein, Stavros Sitinas, Steve Eidman, Elliott Landy, Gabriel Klausner, Benjamin Eidman and Sam Rosmarin.

Finally, much thanks and appreciation is owed to the "real" Alvin Charles Davidoff, for his good-natured manner in greenlighting that essay.

ABOUT THE AUTHOR

Michael K. Eidman is a trial lawyer in New York and New Jersey, representing seriously injured victims of careless conduct and medical negligence. He also promotes concerts in northern New Jersey.

Michael resides in Englewood, NJ with his wife Daphne and has three sons, one daughter-in-law and a grandson. In his spare time, Michael enjoys fishing, the outdoors, music, movies and retreating to the Catskill Mountains.

Zion National Park, UT, 2013

Made in the USA
Middletown, DE
29 November 2016